GENDERED
TRADEOFFS

GENDERED TRADEOFFS

Family, Social Policy, and Economic
Inequality in Twenty-One Countries

Becky Pettit and Jennifer L. Hook

Russell Sage Foundation • **New York**

The Russell Sage Foundation

Library of Congress Cataloging-in-Publication Data

Pettit, Becky, 1970–
  Gendered tradeoffs : family, social policy, and economic inequality in twenty-one countries / Becky Pettit and Jennifer L. Hook.
      p. cm.
  Includes bibliographical references and index.
  ISBN 978-0-87154-661-6 (alk. paper)
  1. Sex discrimination in employment—Case studies. 2. Sex role—Case studies.
  3. Families—Case studies. I. Hook, Jennifer Lynn. II. Title.
  HD6060.P48 2009
  306.3'615—dc22   2009034685

Text design by Suzanne Nichols.

RUSSELL SAGE FOUNDATION
112 East 64th Street, New York, New York 10065
10 9 8 7 6 5 4 3 2 1

To Our Parents
Tim and Sue
and
John and Joyce

CONTENTS

ABOUT THE AUTHORS

Becky Pettit is associate professor of sociology and faculty associate of the Center for Studies in Demography and Ecology at the University of Washington, Seattle.

Jennifer L. Hook is research scientist in the School of Social Work and research affiliate of the Center for Studies in Demography and Ecology at the University of Washington, Seattle.

PREFACE AND ACKNOWLEDGMENTS

This book is about gender inequality in the labor market. We approach this project as scholars of social inequality with a particular interest in how the processes that shape inequality also cloud its measurement. To gain a comprehensive understanding of cross-national variation in gender inequality and its measurement, we study four dimensions of labor market inequality that often generate different explanations for gender inequality across different countries.

We examine outcomes by gender across four realms or measures: involvement in paid work, hours worked, occupational sex segregation, and gender inequality in wages. We attempt to reconcile inconsistencies in the measurement of gender inequality across countries using these four indicators. We are particularly interested in both the micro- and macro-level mechanisms associated with gender inequality in each of these four realms and in how the factors that contribute to gender inequality in the economy relate to societal conceptions about gender and family obligations.

It has taken a long time to complete this project. We have had a lot to learn in the process, and a great many people and organizations have had a hand in the project's development and completion. This research builds on our substantive interests in families and gender and our theoretical interests in institutions and inequality.

Our work is undoubtedly influenced by our contacts with a number of tremendous mentors, colleagues, and friends. Bruce Western was an early and enduring supporter of this project. His wise counsel helped us clarify our purpose and the presentation of our ideas. Stewart Tolnay offered us un-reserved support and careful reading of our work. His insightful comments on the entire manuscript have helped us communicate our ideas more effec-tively, and his intellectual generosity has inspired us. Janet Gornick paved the way for us to use the Luxembourg Income Study (LIS) data. In no small way, her experience and support made this project possible. Tim Larson has been a champion of the project from its inception. His constant affirmation of its importance has strengthened our resolve to complete it, and his labor has sustained it.

Many others participated in seminars, read drafts, and provided the intel-lectual stimulation to help us keep this work moving along. We are deeply in-debted to Amy Bailey, Julie Brines, Sara Curran, Frank Dobbin, Raine Dozier, Eric Gleave, Kieran Healy, Elizabeth Hirsch, Se-Ook Jeong, Nika Kabiri, Erin Kelly, Meredith Kleykamp, Amy Kovak, Shelly Lundberg, Christopher Lyons, Sara McLanahan, Marcia Meyers, Bob Plotnick, Erin Powers, Barbara Reskin, Katherine Stovel, Ted Welser, and the Monday Writing Workshop at the University of Washington.

Parts of chapter 3 come from our paper "The Structure of Women's Em-ployment in Comparative Perspective," which appeared in 2005 in *Social Forces* (84(2): 779–801). Although the analyses presented here are new, the volume takes off from ideas presented in that paper.

This work has been supported by the Center for Statistics and the Social Sciences with funds from the University Initiatives Fund at the University of Washington, the Russell Sage Foundation, the National Institutes of Health K-01 Mentored Research Development Award (K01-HD049632-01A1), the Sloan Foundation Work-Family Career Development Award, and the College of Arts and Sciences of Pennsylvania State University. We are also grateful to Northwestern University and the American Bar Foundation for providing a productive and hospitable work environment that enabled the completion of this project.

We owe sincere thanks to Eric Wanner and Suzanne Nichols of the Russell Sage Foundation, who have supported this project from its inception through its completion. Our reviewers provided invaluable feedback on multiple drafts of our manuscript; we have been profoundly influenced by them and their comments, and we are deeply indebted for their generosity toward our work. We also have been fortunate to have the support of terrific department chairs while working on this project. Bob Crutchfield and Stewart Tolnay were especially beneficent and enabled us to get this work done by helping us manage our time and other responsibilities.

Although we have benefited from the sage advice and wise counsel of many friends and colleagues, all errors and shortcomings, of course, are our own.

CHAPTER 1

Gender Inequality in the Labor Market in Comparative Perspective

In February 1993, the U.S. Congress passed the Family and Medical Leave Act (FMLA). The bill was soon signed into law by President Bill Clinton. The passage of the FMLA was a watershed event for American families, and for American women. For the first time in the nation's history, the federal government required employers to provide twelve weeks of job-protected leave for new parents and other workers with family caregiving obligations.

The FMLA has been characterized as a pivotal moment in work-family policy in the United States. Its passage signified widespread government recognition of the competing demands of the workplace and family caregiving and an explicit endorsement of measures that promote flexibility for workers. At the same time, the FMLA positioned the federal government squarely between employers and families. The act received support from workers' rights organizations, women's rights organizations, and disability organizations (Sawyers and Meyer 1999). Yet passage of the bill mandating unpaid leave took nearly twelve years and endured significant objections from the business community (Marks 1997; Elison 1997).

Although the passage of the FMLA signaled a new era in American politics surrounding work and family, its use by workers is highly variable and its effects on workers and their families uncertain (Gerstel and McGonagle 1999).

Not all workers are covered, and not all employees can afford to take unpaid time off from work. Moreover, some employees, especially highly skilled professional workers, may either be exempt from the provisions of the FMLA or already have more generous employer-sponsored parental leave.

The central provisions of the FMLA—twelve weeks of unpaid, job-protected leave—are exceedingly meager viewed in cross-national comparison. For example, since 1979 Germany has offered federal paid maternity leave of at least fourteen weeks. In 1986 the leave and benefit policy was changed in several ways, including the introduction of parental leave of more than a year, thus creating a "powerful instrument for delaying mothers' return to work after childbirth" (Ondrich, Spiess, and Yang 1996, 247). By the time the United States passed the FMLA, German women had the option to take 162 weeks of leave, nearly two-thirds of which is paid (Gauthier and Bortnik 2001). Germany's generous leave policies are not without critics, and the German parliament has continued to revisit their length and configuration. Recently, in response to concerns about fertility and labor supply, the German parliament changed the parental leave policy to compensate middle- and high-earning families for the additional income loss associated with leave-taking and to encourage the participation of fathers in child-rearing (Spiess and Wrohlich 2008).

Germany's leave and benefit provisions are outmatched by those of the Czech Republic. After the fall of the Communist regime, the Czech Republic pursued work-family policies that encouraged women to stay at home with young children (Saxonberg and Szelewa 2007). Maternity leave, or leave reserved for mothers of newborns, continues at its pretransition level of twenty-eight weeks. In addition to maternity leave, parental leave gives parents time away from work to engage in caregiving responsibilities. Parental leave can be taken by either mothers or fathers. In the Czech Republic, parental leave has been extended from two and a half years to three and a half years. With declines in access to child care and increases in parental leave, mothers now often stay home with young children for three to four years (Saxonberg and Szelewa 2007).

Dramatic variation in parental leave policies across countries raises critical questions about how policy conditions like job-protected parental leaves influence gender inequality in economic outcomes. In this book, we consider the economic consequences for women, men, and families of job-protected leaves and other conditions purported to affect gender inequality in the home and the workplace. How do the configuration and length of leave influence gender inequalities in caregiving? How consequential are variations in the length of leaves—from three months to nearly four years—for the labor market fortunes of women and men? How does government-mandated or state-supported leave affect employment among women and men with different levels of skill and experience?

Although it is valuable to discern the effects of parental leave on inclusion into or exclusion from paid employment for women and men, and for mothers and fathers, we are also concerned with whether and how parental leave and other conditions influence other aspects of economic inequality between women and men once they are in the labor force. No single measure captures the essence of economic inequality between women and men, either within or across countries. For example, although there is growing evidence that job-protected parental leaves foster women's labor market attachment and return to work after childbirth (Ruhm 1998; Gornick and Meyers 2003), there is also concern that extended parental leaves—especially those lasting more than a year—promote gender specialization and exacerbate gender inequality on other dimensions.

Parental leave helps families reconcile tensions between home and work by relieving the demands of employment for a period of time and enabling parents—typically mothers—to care for children at home. In contrast to policies and conditions that are conceptualized as "work-facilitating," parental leave may be thought of as a "work-reducing" policy (see, for example, Jacobs and Gerson 2004). Parental leave may therefore affect hours worked, occupation, and wages through its influence on labor force participation, and these effects may last well beyond the child-rearing years by shaping household and societal expectations about gender roles and domestic responsibilities. The skills and competencies that women gain caring for children, managing a household, and supporting a partner in the paid labor force typically go unrewarded if and when they return to the labor market. In contrast, while women are at home caring for young children, men are concentrating their effort in the paid labor force and thus gaining valuable experience that pays dividends in salaries and long-term economic security. While women in places like Germany and the Czech Republic gain two, three, or even four precious years at home with their young children, they simultaneously lose value in the labor market.

A brief discussion of cross-national variability in parental leave helps to illustrate how the contours of gender inequality in economic outcomes may be shaped by policies and conditions that structure inequality within households and the marketplace. Yet parental leave is not the only policy available across advanced industrialized economies to help families manage the sometimes competing demands of paid work and caregiving. Countries intentionally and unintentionally influence the tensions between work and home through taxation structures, the regulation of working hours and school days, the provision of child allowances, and early childhood education and care, to name a few mechanisms (Gauthier 1993, 1996: Gustafsson 1992; Gornick and Meyers 2003). Throughout this book, we draw contrasts between the different mechanisms that influence gender inequality within both the household and the workplace. For example, some countries provide extensive public child care to support families—both materially and symbolically—in combining work in the paid labor force with the demands of caring for children. The United States is not among these countries, but a brief look at history reveals that it almost was.

Although a laggard in parental leave policy, the United States considered universal child care coverage almost forty years ago in an effort to facilitate the growing involvement of women in paid work. In 1971, after several years of debate, both the Senate and the House of Representatives passed the Comprehensive Child Development Act (CCDA). The CCDA promised universal child care for America's children, free to some though available to all on a sliding-scale fee basis; the act promised to provide federally funded child care for nearly one-third of America's preschool-age children.

Fierce political debate surrounded the CCDA. Feminists largely supported it, while conservatives called for private solutions to work-family problems. Yet even supporters of universal child care could not agree on the extent of coverage or on which level of government would administer the program, and opposition to various dimensions of the act ultimately diluted its provisions (Michel 1999). Conservative opposition to the CCDA was so intense, however, that even the compromise bill passed by Congress was vetoed by President Richard Nixon (Dinner 2004).

The federal government continues to provide support for public child care for low-income children through the Head Start program, but the targeted benefits of Head Start have not had the widespread impact that CCDA promised. Even at Head Start's peak in the mid-1990s, fewer than one in twenty American children under age three were being cared for in publicly supported child care—nowhere near the one in three the CCDA aimed to cover.

Although U.S. child care policy is meager in contrast to what is offered by some advanced industrialized nations, it is not unique in that distinction. Few countries have universal child care or child care coverage that meets the expectations outlined in the CCDA. There are, however, some particularly notable examples of countries that have invested significantly in early childhood education and care (ECEC).

Among European and English-speaking advanced industrialized nations, Denmark is the leader in the public provision of child care. Nearly half (48 percent) of children under age three in Denmark were in publicly funded child care facilities through the early 1990s. Sweden, Norway, and Finland all exhibit relatively high rates of young children in public care, though lower than Denmark's. France has long been a leader in public support for child care: in the mid-1990s, nearly one-quarter of children under age three in France were in public child care facilities (Morgan 2006).

Public child care reconciles the tension between employment and caregiving by moving some caregiving labor outside of the household and into the public domain. As suggested earlier, just as parental leave may be conceptualized as "work-reducing," the public provision of child care may be thought of as "work-facilitating" (Jacobs and Gerson 2004). Previous research has not adequately examined, however, how the labor market inclusion associated with the public provision of child care might influence other aspects of economic inequality in the prime childbearing years and over the life course.

In this book, we examine four measures of gender inequality—employment, hours worked, occupation, and pay—to provide a nuanced assessment of the factors that influence the contours of inequality across and within countries. Assessments of women's relative economic standing across countries depend not only on whether women are included in the labor market but on how they are included. Any employment—even part-time—gives some indication of women's access to economic rewards and public endorsement of the concept of working women, wives, and mothers (Blossfeld and Hakim 1997). Part-time and part-year work, however, decreases access to economic rewards and can generate inequality in other domains, including occupational sex segregation and the gender wage gap, and lead to the persistence of inequality over the life course (Bardasi and Gornick 2001). Occupational sex segregation is an important feature of gender inequality in the labor market because separate is seldom equal. Segregation generally reflects inequalities in other social domains, including education and family responsibilities, and it is often associated with inequalities in pay and promotion (Roos and Reskin 1992; Bridges 2003; Charles and Grusky 2004). Finally, the gender wage gap provides an important measure of women's relative economic standing, indicating how employed women are compensated for their work in comparison to men.

While employment rates, hours worked, occupational segregation, and wages all provide some indication of women's relative economic standing, no country ranks high on all these measures. Table 1.1 ranks twenty-one European and English-speaking countries on commonly used indicators of women's economic standing: employment, involvement in part-time work, occupational integration, and wage equality. Sweden, Finland, and Denmark post the highest levels of women's employment; the Czech Republic, Hungary, and the United States document the highest concentration of women in full-time work or the lowest concentration of women in part-time work; Belgium, the Netherlands, and Slovenia exhibit the highest levels of occupational sex integration or the lowest levels of occupational sex segregation; and Italy, Belgium, and France record the smallest gender wage gaps. No single country does better than average on all four indicators of gender inequality in the labor market.

How is it that Nordic women post such high employment rates but remain heavily concentrated in female-dominated jobs? How do the relatively few Belgian women working in the paid labor force succeed in making inroads into male-dominated occupations? How can we reconcile extremely low rates of women's employment in Italy with near-parity in their wages with men? These inconsistencies beg the question: is there a tradeoff between women's inclusion in the labor market and their equality within it? In other words, do high rates of women's employment come at the cost of gender wage equality? As women enter the labor market in greater numbers, will they inevitably work in different occupations and jobs than men? Are high wages among working women found only when few women work in the paid labor force?

This book asks these and related questions to develop the notion that there are tradeoffs between different aspects of gender inequality in the economy. Our central purpose is to explain how those tradeoffs are shaped by individuals, markets, and states. A comprehensive account of gender inequality demands attention to multiple dimensions of women's economic standing,

Table 1.1   Four Measures of Gender Equality, Country Rankings, Mid-1990s

	Employment (1 to 21)	Full-Time Work (1 to 15)	Occupational Integration (1 to 18)	Wage Equality (1 to 12)
Sweden	1	14	6	8
Finland	2	—	14	6
Denmark	3	—	13	—
United States	4	3	4	10
Norway	5	—	—	—
United Kingdom	6	13	15	12
Czech Republic	7	1	9	—
Canada	8	8	5	9
Australia	9	12	8	5
Austria	10	6	12	4
Russian Federation	11	4	18	—
France	12	7	16	3
Luxembourg	13	9	17	—
Netherlands	14	15	2	7
Germany	15	11	11	11
Slovenia	16	—	3	—
Hungary	17	2	7	—
Belgium	18	10	1	2
Poland	19	—	—	—
Italy	20	5	—	1
Spain	21	—	10	—

Source: Luxembourg Income Study (LIS 2003).
Notes: Data for rankings appear in table A.1. Employment is ranked 1 for highest employment rates. Full-time work is ranked 1 for highest percentage of employed women working full-time. Occupational integration is ranked 1 for most integrated. Wage equality is ranked 1 for the greatest equality in wages. Using the full sample in table A.1, the correlation between women's employment and full-time work is .03, between women's employment and occupational integration .12, between women's employment and wage equality –.25, between full-time work and occupational integration –.35 ($p < .05$), between full-time work and wage equality .19, and between occupational integration and wage equality .01.

since equality in one domain often conceals inequality in another. Only through considering how different economic outcomes reveal different aspects of the gendered character of work at home and within the marketplace can we identify how different policy conditions structure tradeoffs between labor market inclusion and labor market equality.

Throughout the book, we build our argument that conditions that foster labor market inclusion do not necessarily guarantee equality by other measures. Similarly, conditions that foster labor market exclusion do not necessarily guarantee inequality by other measures. We concern ourselves not only with whether women are included in the labor market, but with *how* they are included in the labor market. For example, publicly provided child care promotes labor market inclusion but does not necessarily ensure gender equality in hours worked, occupation, or wages. If publicly provided child care pulls women who would otherwise eschew employment into the labor market, we may observe that women appear to do less well on gender equality measures such as occupational segregation and wages. This is a simple selection argument. On the other hand, if publicly provided child care allows women to work similar hours to men, in similar occupations, and at similar pay, we may observe that such child care promotes both inclusion and equality.

In this book, we investigate economic inequality not only across countries but within them as well. For example, long parental leaves foster labor market exclusion, but their effect on women's labor market outcomes is likely to vary by parental status and educational level. Mothers who take time out of the paid labor force to care for their own children may see their economic fortunes deteriorate relative to women who either do not have children or do not leave the labor force to care for them. Women with high levels of education may be less likely to utilize long parental leaves because of the ramifications for career advancement or low levels of wage replacement. This highlights the need to specify not only which labor market outcome is of interest and which policy is under consideration, but also which women are most affected.

We investigate the labor market inclusion-equality tradeoff by examining how the work lives of women and men are organized over time across twenty-one countries. We take advantage of cross-national and over-time variation in economic outcomes and the conditions thought to produce them to investigate the underpinnings of gender inequality in the labor market. We examine how employment, hours worked, occupation, and pay are shaped by the domestic obligations associated with child-rearing and individual investments in education. We also consider how each of these outcomes is influenced by government policies and programs—like parental leave and public child care—that regulate, routinize, and reinforce gender differences in home production and market work. The contours of inequality across and within countries are shaped by specific aspects of social policy that variably relieve or concentrate the demands of caregiving within households, often in the hands of women, and at the same time structure workplace expectations and the allocation of workplace rewards. Government policies and conditions—like parental leave and public child care—affect gender inequalities in power within the household and the marketplace and have implications for women's economic standing on a number of fronts.

ENGENDERING INEQUALITY

There is little disagreement that women still lag behind men in many measures of economic well-being, and scholars from a range of disciplines agree that even though women have made progress in some domains, significant inequality in the labor market persists (Blau, Brinton, and Grusky 2006). Yet despite agreement about the existence of inequality, the causes of gender inequality in the labor market are contested, and there is little consensus about the best methodological approach for resolving the dispute. We argue that gender inequality in economic outcomes across countries and over time can be best understood by integrating the prevailing micro-economic and comparative explanations.

Micro-economic explanations for gender inequality rest on the assumption that women and men within households make collective decisions about how to allocate their labor to paid and unpaid work in an effort to maximize the well-being of the household (Mincer and Polachek 1974; Becker 1981). With few exceptions, however, micro-economic explanations for gender inequality in the workplace pay little attention to how social and economic conditions, including state policies and conditions, influence women's and men's investments in, and productive capacities for, paid labor and domestic work across countries (compare Del Boca and Locatelli 2007; Wetzels 2007; Boeri, Del Boca, and Pissarides 2005).

Comparative studies of economic inequality broadly defined, and gender inequality specifically, often examine economic well-being and inequality in relation to the level and configuration of welfare state provision. The term "welfare state" typically refers to how countries ensure the economic productivity and overall well-being of the population. While there are many ways to classify the nature and extent of welfare state provisions (Meulders and O'-Dorchai 2007), countries are commonly categorized by the level and configuration of such provisions and the extent to which citizens are protected against the instabilities and uncertainties of the labor market, particularly how well they are shielded from the poverty or economic instability associated with unemployment.

Gøsta Esping-Andersen (1990) classifies advanced industrial societies as social democratic, liberal, or conservative-corporatist. Social democratic countries are characterized by generous income transfers and support for full employment and high wages. Liberal welfare states take a hands-off approach to social policy, leaving the market relatively unrestricted. Corporatist countries also have generous income transfer systems, as well as labor market policies that encourage high wages. Their benefit systems, however, are family-centered rather than individual-centered, and they tend to reinforce traditional divisions of labor between women and men and between social classes. Many comparative accounts of women's economic standing have found that Esping-Andersen's (1990, 1999) welfare state typology accounts for variation in women's involvement in the paid labor force, but that the classifications are less instructive for explaining gender inequality in other economic outcomes and give short shrift to the full range of women's productive activity, both at home and at work (Sainsbury 1996; Orloff 1993; O'Connor, Orloff, and Shaver 1999).

Cross-national studies of women's employment typically find that welfare state institutions have a moderately consistent relationship with women's employment. High rates of women's employment are found in the social democratic countries of northern Europe, and low levels of women's employment are found in the conservative-corporatist countries of southern Europe. The liberal countries, including the United States, the United Kingdom, Canada, and Australia, demonstrate a more mixed pattern, with medium to high employment rates (Oppenheimer 1994; Gornick, Meyers, and Ross 1997).

Variability within welfare state regimes in the levels of women's employment and the shortcomings of welfare state theory for understanding other measures of gender inequality have led to the development of alternative classification schemes of contemporary welfare states (see, for example, Lewis and Ostner 1995; Pfau-Effinger 2004; Gornick, Meyers, and Ross 1997; Korpi 2000; for a review, see Meulders and O'Dorchai 2007). Feminist scholars have called attention to how the configuration of welfare state provisions reflects and reinforces existing productive activities within the home as well within the marketplace (Meulders and O'Dorchai 2007). One common theme is to highlight the effect of "family policy" on women's employment and economic security (Gornick, Meyers, and Ross 1997; Gornick and Meyers 2003).

Family policy is particularly consequential for women given their disproportionate involvement in family caregiving across countries (Gornick and Meyers 2003), and indices of family policy generosity have been shown to influence aggregate levels of women's employment and employment at the individual level (Gornick, Meyers, and Ross 1997, 1998; Mandel and Semyonov 2005; Stier, Lewin-Epstein, and Braun 2001). In our view, however, "family policy" conflates a variety of specific policies that may have countervailing effects on women's employment and other economic outcomes. Policies that foster women's inclusion in the labor market may lead to inequality among those employed, while other policies associated with women's exclusion from paid work may increase equality among those employed. Recent research indicates that particular policy features like the length of parental leave or the public provision of child care have different impacts on the work lives of women (see, for example, Pettit and Hook 2005; Stryker, Eliason, and Tranby 2007; Boeri, Del Boca, and Pissarides 2005). In our work, we try to distinguish the relationship between specific policy conditions and the economic fortunes of women from the generalized effects of overall welfare state classification or family policy generosity. By looking at multiple outcomes, we generate a more complete portrait of the factors that shape gender inequality.

Significant cross-national variability in the size of the part-time workforce and women's concentration within it illustrates some of the tensions between labor market inclusion and equality measured within the market, and it also suggests that states play an important role in structuring levels of employment and shaping working hours for women and men. Part-time work has been viewed as both a mechanism to incorporate women into the labor market and a means to marginalize them in the workplace (Blossfeld and Hakim 1997; Fagan and O'Reilly 1998; Pfau-Effinger 1998). The Netherlands claims the highest rate of part-time workers: well over one-third of Dutch workers are employed less than thirty hours per week, and a majority of women in the Netherlands are part-timers. A number of social democratic and liberal countries routinely classify between one-quarter and one-fifth of their workforce as part-time. Data from the Luxembourg Income Study (LIS) show that women are overrepresented in part-time work across all advanced industrialized countries, though part-time work is rare—even among women—in the former socialist nations of Hungary, the Russian Federation, and Slovenia and in the conservative countries of Luxembourg, Italy, and Spain.

Research seeking to explain cross-national differences in involvement in part-time or part-year employment has focused less on overall welfare state typologies or family policy generosity and more on macroeconomic conditions and the size of the public sector as determinants of women's concentration in part-time work. Periods of economic expansion and recession have generated growth in the part-time sector, though involvement in part-time work is not equally distributed across social and demographic groups. Men are more likely to be found in part-time work during recessionary periods, when unemployment and underemployment run high, than during periods of economic growth and full employment (Farber 1999). When the economy is strong, new workers, including women and the young, are often brought into the labor market through part-time jobs (Fagan and O'Reilly 1998; Hakim 1997). The size of the public sector is a key determinant of women's involvement in part-time work (Gornick and Jacobs 1998). Perhaps ironically, the size of the public sector may be driven by an ideology to provide services for working families and reduce work-family conflict, yet the disproportionate incorporation of women in part-time work may fuel occupational sex segregation and the gender wage gap.

Tradeoffs between women's labor market inclusion and equality within the labor market are also found when we consider cross-national accounts of occupational sex segregation. Again, we see evidence of the multifaceted individual and societal conditions undergirding gender inequality. Women entered the workplace in increasing numbers through the latter half of the twentieth century, yet women and men continue to be highly segregated in the workplace in most countries (Charles and Grusky 2004; Chang 2000). Moreover, high rates of occupational sex segregation are typically found in the countries with high rates of women's employment. The social democratic countries of northern Europe consistently post high levels of occupational sex segregation, and countries with the lowest levels of female employment post the lowest levels of occupational sex segregation (Charles 1992; Jacobs and Lim 1995; Semyonov and Jones 1999; Charles and Grusky 2004).

Although the comparative literature on occupational sex segregation has shadowed research on women's employment, it has generated startlingly different conclusions. Welfare state theory is less instructive for occupational segregation than for measures of employment. In fact, the conditions that enable high rates of women's employment and are linked with women's concentration in part-time employment contribute to the concentration of women in particular occupations and jobs. Large service sectors, large part-time workforces, and large public sectors all contribute to high levels of occupational sex segregation (see, for example, Charles and Grusky 2004; Charles 1992; Gornick and Jacobs 1998). Although women and men do different jobs in most countries, they are more likely to be doing roughly equivalent jobs with similar responsibilities and pay in countries that exhibit strong ideological support for gender equality. Where gender egalitarian ideologies are weaker, women and men are still likely to be working separately, but are also more likely to be found in occupations that are unequal in terms of pay, prospects for promotion, and prestige (Charles 1992; Charles and Grusky 2004).

Examining gender differences in wages across countries points, again, to the tensions between labor market inclusion and the measurement of equality among those in the paid labor force and illustrates how specific policy conditions structure wage inequality indirectly through labor supply and demand and directly through the allocation of wages within the market. Although the gender wage gap conflates differences in employment rates and wages, it is often used to gauge cross-national differences in the relative economic standing of women. According to data from the Luxembourg Income Study, women's wages are highest relative to men's in conservative-corporatist countries and lowest in social democratic countries. Additionally, family responsibilities are more salient determinants of wages in conservative-corporatist and liberal countries than in social democratic ones (Rosenfeld and Kalleberg 1990).

Like research on employment, hours worked, and occupational sex segregation, cross-national research on the gender wage gap has examined the structural determinants of women's relative wages. A strong correlation has been found between overall wage inequality in the job market and gender gaps in wages (Blau and Kahn 2002), and researchers contend that economic conditions and wage-setting mechanisms are important causes of cross-national variability in the gender gap in wages (Blau and Kahn 1996, 2002; Mandel and Semyonov 2005). Recent research has also focused increasingly on selection—both into the labor market and into particular occupations and jobs—as important to comparative assessments of gender inequality using the gender wage gap (Brainerd 2000; Wetzels 2007). Women's strong wage gains in eastern Europe in the 1990s have been traced to declining employment levels among low-skill women who would have otherwise commanded low wages in the transitional economy (Brainerd 2000; Hunt 2002). Although limited to only one country, research also demonstrates that the gender wage gap in the United States narrowed in the early 1990s largely because of wage losses among men and not because of wage gains among women (Bernhardt, Morris, and Handcock 1995).

Even a brief review of the existing literature makes clear that we should expect indicators of women's economic standing to vary across welfare state regimes, and within them, in relation to specific supports for parents and workers. Comparative explanations of gender inequality posit a key role for states in structuring inequality, though different indicators suggest different aspects of state policy. While family policy generosity promotes women's employment, the size of the public sector correlates with women's concentration in part-time work and occupational segregation. Moreover, centralized wage-setting mechanisms that affect the overall level of wage inequality also affect gender wage inequality. Our work builds on the insights of previous research to develop an overarching theory of how states institutionalize inequality—through policies and conditions that affect households and the market—in ways that influence a broad range of economic outcomes, including employment, hours worked, occupation, and wages.

We adopt an interdisciplinary approach that brings together insights from economics and sociology, paying attention to (1) how women and men within households decide to allocate their labor to paid and unpaid work, and (2) how these decisions are embedded within specific configurations of social policies like parental leave and public child care. We analyze for whom and how specific policies and conditions affect employment, hours worked, occupation, and wages. We argue that microeconomic explanations for gender inequality in economic outcomes must account for historical and cross-national variation in state policies and conditions. These policies and conditions influence the gender balance of power within households in ways that affect women's and men's allocation of time to domestic work and work in the paid labor force. Moreover, they influence employer norms and expectations in ways that shape the allocation of workplace rewards.

Yet the specific importance of state policies and conditions is likely to vary in relation to individual investments in education and children. The economic fortunes of highly educated workers—especially those who are strongly committed to the paid labor force and well rewarded within it—may be less responsive to state policy conditions than those of other workers. The economic fortunes of mothers—especially those with young children—may be particularly responsive to the state policy conditions that influence caregiving.

Recent economic and political changes across advanced industrialized nations provide motivation to examine the mechanisms undergirding gender inequalities in employment, hours worked, occupational sex segregation, and wages. Economic fluctuations through the late twentieth century across advanced industrialized economies accompanied women's grand entrance into the labor market. The fall of state socialism and widening inequality within countries may have served increasingly to differentiate the work lives of women from those of men, and the well-educated from those with less education. A conservative turn in some European countries in the late 1980s and early 1990s ushered in a new era of family policy conditions focused on providing for the well-being of families by enabling women to care for children at home (Morgan and Zippel 2003). Germany and the Czech Republic were not the only countries that expanded parental leave; even the Scandinavian countries increased parental leaves in the face of declines in public child care. These policy shifts may threaten the economic equality of women.

THE PLAN OF THE BOOK

In this book, we conduct a cross-national analysis to consider how individual and collective economic opportunities are shaped by education and the domestic obligations associated with child-rearing and how state policies and conditions shape those relationships. We rely largely on data from the Luxembourg Income Study to investigate gender inequality in the labor market.

The LIS database is a collection of over one hundred household income surveys that provide demographic, income, and employment information for twenty-nine member countries (Luxembourg Income Study 2003). We include surveys from European and English-speaking countries that contain the demographic and employment information necessary for the analyses outlined in the remainder of the book. We analyze data from women and men collected in sixty-three micro-level data sets from twenty-one countries, spanning the years 1969 to 2000: Australia, Austria, Belgium, Canada, the Czech Republic, Denmark, Finland, France, Germany, Hungary, Italy, Luxembourg, the Netherlands, Norway, Poland, the Russian Federation, Slovenia, Spain, Sweden, the United Kingdom, and the United States. Table A.1 includes a full list of the countries, the abbreviations used throughout the book, and information on data availability by country. A map of the countries is shown in Figure A.1.

We use these data to examine four indicators of economic gender inequality: employment, hours worked, occupation, and wages. We use all available LIS data to explore how individual characteristics and state conditions structure inequality between countries and within them. Peculiarities in data collection over time and across countries limit our analysis of employment to twenty-one countries, of hours worked to fifteen countries, of occupation to eighteen countries, and of wage inequality to only twelve countries. This is an unfortunate but unavoidable shortcoming of our methodological approach and available data.

Each chapter also includes an in-depth analysis of the United States and the former West Germany. We limit our country spotlights to the United States and the former West Germany because they are the only two LIS countries that have over-time data on all four outcomes of interest to us. A reliance on such a small number of cases is generally ill advised, but differences in country conditions across these two cases and over time within them provide sufficient variation to generate some striking contrasts. Comparisons between the United States and West Germany clearly illustrate how states shape the contours of economic inequality.

We do not aim to rehash commonly understood stylized facts about gender inequality, although there are plenty of them in the book. Instead, we seek to show how state policies and conditions affect who works in the paid labor force. Gender inequality in hours worked, occupational sex segregation, and pay are also acutely affected by state policies and conditions directly and indirectly through their influence on employment. In summary, our understanding of gender inequality both in the cross-section of nations and over the life course requires a careful consideration of the institutional conditions that generate gender differences in employment prospects and outcomes.

The second chapter reviews the prevailing explanations for gender inequalities in economic outcomes. We outline the conditions hypothesized to affect gender inequality in employment, hours worked, occupation, and wages. Our central question is whether a tradeoff exists between women's inclusion in the labor market and equality within the market. In chapter 2, we explain why we think certain country-level conditions—and state policies and conditions like parental leave and public child care—should influence both labor market inclusion and equality measured within the market. We argue that specific features of government policy and practice—including aspects of family policy like the length of parental leave and public support for child care but also employment conditions such as unionization and the size of the part-time workforce—both shape the gendered obligations associated with child-rearing and structure inequalities within the labor market.

The remainder of the book is devoted to the empirical investigation of gender inequality in economic outcomes. Chapter 3 carefully examines cross-national variability in women's and men's employment. Chapter 4 is devoted to the factors associated with involvement in full-time and part-time work. Chapter 5 examines cross-national variability in occupational sex segregation, paying close attention to the extent to which women and men are concentrated in particular occupational categories. Chapter 6 considers how measures of the gender wage gap across countries might be reconsidered in light of differential patterns of employment, involvement in part-time work, and occupational sex segregation. Although chapter 6 illustrates some of the problems associated with a compendium measure that conflates employment and wage outcomes, the chapter also indicates how state policies and conditions influence cross-national and over-time accounts of the gender wage gap. Chapter 7 focuses on women in the United States and Germany in its examination of all four indicators—employment, hours worked, occupational segregation, and wages. We are acutely aware of the limitations of a focus on only two countries, but the chapter helps reveal how the same policies and conditions that affect gender inequality may also influence our understanding of inequalities on the basis of class, race, ethnicity, and nationality.

The last chapter of the book returns to the question of a tradeoff between labor market inclusion and economic equality within the market. This work makes clear that state policies and conditions that foster women's employment in the paid labor force do not necessarily engender equality within the labor market as measured by hours worked, occupational sex segregation, and pay. Persistent gender inequalities in domestic obligations—especially those related to children—have great consequences for women's labor market prospects. Tensions between domestic inequality and workplace inequality are aggravated in some environments more than in others, and gender-neutral economic conditions often disadvantage women.

Although there is clear support for explanations that emphasize the importance of investments in education and work, a review of the economic progress of women in the United States and other advanced industrialized nations also reveals ways in which gender inequality is institutionalized by states. State policies and conditions affect gender divides in the home and the workplace, especially in relation to their provision of supports for women and men to care for children. State policies and conditions institutionalize gender inequality by endorsing behavioral patterns and setting expectations that shape and constrain future behavior. Our central concern is with how state conditions influence the behavioral patterns and expectations surrounding women's and men's allocation of time to home and work. State-level policies and conditions also affect gender inequalities directly and indirectly within the market by providing employment opportunities that shape workplace expectations about ideal workers and guarantee workplace protections for different classes—and genders—of workers.

CONCLUSION

The Treaty of Rome (1957), the Civil Rights Act of 1964, the Equal Employment Opportunity Act of 1972, and other legislation and executive orders were watershed events that led to the protection of the rights of women as workers throughout the advanced industrialized economies. Research shows that affirmative action and equal employment opportunity legislation has diminished explicit discrimination against women in the workplace in the United States (Darity and Mason 1998) and many other countries (Hakim 1996; Simonton 1998). Not surprisingly, the past several decades have witnessed women's significant gains on a number of indicators of economic well-being, and their employment experiences across advanced industrialized countries increasingly approximate men's.

Nevertheless, while many barriers to equality in the workplace have fallen, women continue to lag behind men in many measures of economic equality. This book details the contemporary mechanisms that, in contrast to the overt and legally sanctioned employment discrimination of the early and mid-twentieth century, generate gender inequality in the United States and other advanced industrialized nations in ways that are subtle yet deeply embedded in family policy, the organization of work, and the societal norms governing gender relations and the care of children.

Our research analyzes the impact of particular state policies and conditions on the work lives of different groups of women and men. We take advantage of cross-national and over-time variation in economic outcomes and the conditions thought to produce them to investigate the underpinnings of gender inequality in the labor market. The core argument of this book is that gender inequality in the workplace is routinized through policies and conditions that are generated and reinforced by states.

We attempt to avoid normative prescriptions for the organization of women's and men's work and family lives. Our research implicates particular aspects of government policy and practice for gender inequality across different outcomes, however, and shows that gender inequality in the labor market has deep institutional underpinnings.

We study gender inequality in the labor market because work in the paid labor force shapes the contours of inequality in many other domains. Work carries both economic and psychic rewards that are distributed unevenly between women and men. While much attention has been paid to the variable influence of labor force attachment on economic instability and inequality across countries (Esping-Andersen 1990, 1999), one of the key insights of feminist critiques of the welfare state literature is that women's long-term economic stability and well-being often are tied either to the economic independence associated with work in the paid labor force or to the economic security associated with marriage (Christopher et al. 2002; Sorensen and McLanahan 1987).

Not being in the labor force carries unique economic risks and psychic costs for women, although men are also at risk from specialization. For women out of the labor market who depend on a male breadwinner, there is a risk that the breadwinner will cease to provide through death, divorce, or unemployment. One cause of the "feminization of poverty" is the high number of women without much labor force experience suddenly finding themselves without a breadwinner upon whom to rely. In terms of psychic costs, women out of the labor market may have less power or control within relationships, and they may be more likely to experience the stress of economic insecurity. Although men may experience improved economic standing after divorce, they are also more likely to lose children and family in a divorce and thus may lose access to family care when ill or elderly (Goldscheider 2000).

Studies of occupational segregation also confirm that separate is not equal. "Women's" jobs generally receive lower pay, have less prestige, and provide fewer opportunities for advancement (Padavic and Reskin 2002), entailing both economic and psychic costs. Occupational sex segregation may create problems for men too. Some "men's" jobs carry disproportionate health risks, and men's concentration in manufacturing has made them especially vulnerable to deindustrialization.

The accumulated cost of lower labor force involvement, fewer hours worked, concentration in low-wage jobs, and low pay makes women more likely to live in poverty, more likely to raise a child in poverty, and less likely to be economically secure in retirement. Clearly, employment, hours worked, occupation, and earned wages have important implications for economic and social stability and security in both the short and long terms. Hence, our investigation into the causes of gender inequality in the workplace is not purely academic, but has broad relevance and application for policymakers and the public alike.

CHAPTER 2

The Institutional Underpinnings of Gender Inequality

Across advanced industrialized economies, women are entering the labor force in record numbers; they have made inroads into all types of occupations and jobs and achieved great advances in garnering equal pay for equal work. Women's gains in the labor market have been tied to several factors: legal changes that protect the rights of women as workers; worldwide increases in women's educational attainment; declines and delays in childbearing; and growing preferences for gender equality in work and family, articulated in attitudinal surveys. Historical trends suggest that women's labor market experiences now more closely approximate the experiences of men than at any other time since industrialization; nevertheless, women still have not reached parity with men on most economic indicators in most countries. These trends raise concerns that women's economic progress has stalled (Goldin 2006; Boeri, Del Boca, and Pissarides 2005). Research in the United States and other advanced industrialized countries consistently finds that women are less likely to be employed than men, continue to be underrepresented in the most highly paid occupations, and still earn between 50 and 90 percent of men's wages (van der Lippe and van Dijk 2001; Charles and Grusky 2004; Blau and Kahn 2002). This chapter addresses the question of why gender inequality in economic outcomes persists despite women's gains in other areas.

Women's uneven economic progress across measures of gender inequality and across countries exposes fundamental tensions between gender inequality in the domestic sphere and gender inequality in the labor market. We argue that gender inequality is institutionalized through households and within the labor market. There are two general types of institutional effects: those that foster women's labor market inclusion and those that influence inequality among workers. Previous work has observed that women's economic outcomes vary over the life course and across countries. For example, employment, occupational segregation, and wages correlate with individual investments in education and parenthood (Blau, Brinton, and Grusky 2006; Goldin 2006). Women's economic fortunes also vary over time in relation to the gender ideologies, economic growth, and policy conditions of states (Blau, Brinton, and Grusky 2006; Boeri, Del Boca, and Pissarides 2005). We argue that variation in economic inequality both within and across countries can also be attributed to the specific ways in which gender inequality is structured by states. States institutionalize inequality within households by influencing the norms and expectations surrounding the domestic division of labor and within the market by influencing the allocation of jobs and wages.

In this chapter, we review alternative explanations for women's economic standing. We begin with a review of the arguments that emphasize that women's economic opportunities are shaped by individual investments in education and that they vary over the life course in relation to the demands of child-rearing. Next, we turn to cross-national comparative research that investigates how state conditions structure inequality. We then develop our theoretical argument, which integrates life-course theories with comparative explanations for gender inequality. Finally, we discuss the measures we employ to examine empirically our theoretical argument, using data from twenty-one countries.

A LIFE-COURSE PERSPECTIVE ON GENDER, FAMILY, AND WORK

Existing micro-level explanations for women's relative economic standing emphasize human capital and domestic obligations. Education—one indicator of human capital—is positively and consistently associated with higher rates of employment, working in gender-integrated jobs (for example, managerial and professional jobs), and higher pay. Classic microeconomic arguments contend that education is rewarded in the workplace because it is an indicator of investment in work-related skills and competencies that enhance productivity (Mincer 1958). Growing inequalities within the labor market highlight the contemporary relevance of education for economic outcomes (Katz and Murphy 1992; Bernhardt et al. 2001; Kenworthy 2004).

Gender differences in domestic obligations—especially those associated with the bearing and rearing of children—are critical for understanding gender inequalities in economic outcomes. Mothers generally have poorer labor market outcomes than childless women, and inequalities associated with gender are commonly linked to the differential effects of parenthood on women and men (England 2005; Wetzels 2007; Del Boca et al. 2007). To the extent that the division of household labor is gendered—and becomes increasingly so with marriage and child-rearing—having children is associated with greater gender inequality in the workplace (Becker 1981). Married men and fathers should be more likely to be employed, to work longer hours, and to be concentrated in high-wage jobs or jobs that enable them to provide for their families. Married women and mothers should be less likely to be employed, more likely to work fewer hours if they do work, and more likely to be concentrated in low-wage jobs or jobs that enable them to balance work and family obligations. These life-course explanations may help us understand why, even in the face of growing educational equality between women and men across countries, gender inequality in the labor market persists in ways that relate to how states support women and men as workers and caregivers.

The next section reviews the available empirical evidence on the factors thought to affect gender inequality over the life course. We focus on gender differences in education and time spent in household labor across countries. Women have made great strides toward educational equality, yet gender differences in domestic work continue to be entrenched across countries.

Education

Skill differentials between women and men are commonly purported to explain gender differences in economic outcomes within and across countries. Microeconomic theories about gender inequality in the labor market contend that women do not do as well as men in the paid labor force because they have less education or fewer job-specific skills to allow them to compete in the marketplace. However, recent evidence that women's educational attainment has surpassed men's in most advanced industrialized nations (Bradley 2000) casts doubt on the relevance of skill-based arguments to explain women's economic standing.

Boys' and girls' preferences for work in the paid labor force are quite comparable, at least through the teenage years. In fact, some research indicates that in their teens girls have even higher educational and occupational aspirations than boys. Results from a recent Organization for Economic Cooperation and Development (OECD) study, shown in figure 2.1, indicate that when asked at age fifteen, girls show much higher expectations for their careers than boys of the same age (OECD 2004).

Attending college has become a normative experience among recent cohorts of both women and men. More than half of women (57 percent) and nearly half of men (45 percent) in LIS countries now attend some form of higher education after completing secondary school, although there is wide variability in college attendance between countries. For example, only 30 percent of women in the Czech Republic continue on after secondary school, compared to almost 92 percent of Swedish women in recent cohorts (OECD 2002). The gender divide in college attendance is low where attendance rates are low, and women are much more likely to attend college than men where attendance rates are high.

Not only are women more likely than men to attend college, but women also receive more than 50 percent of the tertiary degrees in nearly all the countries in our study. Women's rate of college completion now exceeds men's in all LIS countries except Austria, where women graduate from college at a rate just slightly behind that of men. The observation that women are more likely than men to attend and graduate from college should be associated with declines in gender inequality in work-related outcomes, including employment and earnings. Evidence partially supports this claim: among recent cohorts of labor market entrants, research finds little difference in the employment, occupation, and wage outcomes of well-educated women and men upon entry into the labor market, controlling for college major (see, for example, Xie and Shauman 2003).

Despite women's educational progress across countries, significant gender segregation persists in higher education. Consistent with findings from the United States (Xie and Shauman 2003), cross-national comparisons of gender and college major show a great deal of gender segregation in higher education (Bradley 2000). Figure 2.2 shows that in the countries for which data are available, women receive disproportionately few degrees in math and engineering and disproportionately many degrees in the health sciences and the humanities. The gap between women's concentration in engineering or math and health or humanities is not clearly correlated with educational or occu-

Figure 2.1   Gender Differences in Occupational Expectations at Age Fifteen, by Country, 2000

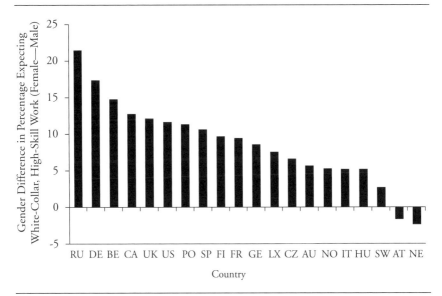

Source: Organization for Economic Cooperation and Development (OECD 2004).
Note: See country abbreviations in figure A.1.

pational aspirations and is strikingly consistent across all countries. In addition to large gender differences in college major, recent OECD (2004) data indicate that women generally receive well under half of advanced research degrees. (Italy is a perhaps notable exception to this trend.)

Domestic Obligations

Near-parity in some measures of educational and occupational expectations in the teenage years stands in contrast to empirical evidence of stark gender divides in domestic labor. Domestic labor—the work done within the household—includes cooking, cleaning, performing routine household tasks, and caring for children. The gender divide in domestic labor becomes increasingly apparent, at least in the United States, in adolescence. Teenage girls complete a greater share of household tasks than teenage boys, perhaps most notably with respect to taking care of younger siblings (Goldscheider and Waite 1991). Child care responsibilities also mark a key point of departure for women's and men's labor market outcomes. Figure 2.3 demonstrates the

Figure 2.2 Tertiary Degrees Awarded to Women, by Subject, by Country, 2002

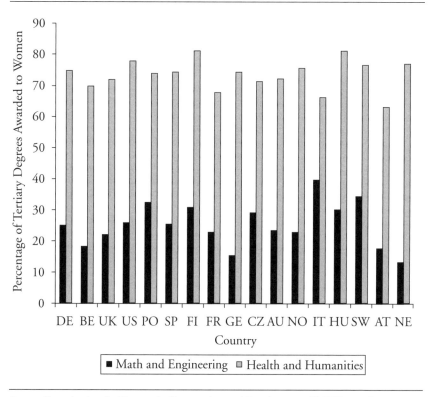

Source: Organization for Economic Cooperation and Development (OECD 2004).
Note: See country abbreviations in figure A.1.

ubiquity of the gender gap in domestic work among parents with children across advanced industrialized countries. On average, women spend almost twice as much time as men engaged in domestic tasks, though the gap is much wider in some countries than in others.

Explanations that attribute gender inequality in the labor market to the gender disparity in domestic work emphasize the importance of supply-and-demand effects (referencing individuals' supply of labor and employers' demand for it). At least since Jacob Mincer's (1962) work on married women's labor supply, economists have considered women's labor market involvement and pay in relation to the costs and benefits of wage labor relative to domestic work and

Figure 2.3   Hours of Domestic Work per Day, by Country and Sex, for Couples with Children Ages Zero to Six, Around 2000

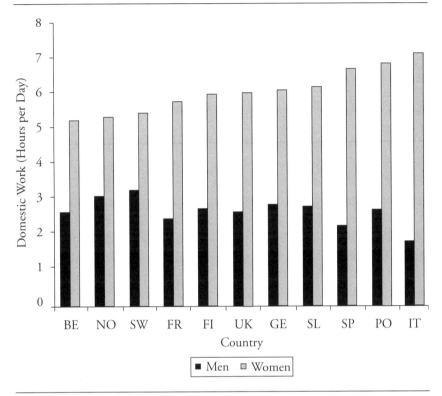

Source: Harmonized European Time Use Study (HETUS 2005–2007).
Note: See country abbreviations in figure A.1. Table produced June 24, 2008. Data subset by twenty to seventy-four years old, couples (married or cohabiting) with youngest child zero to six years old.

other pursuits (see also Becker 1981). In general, these supply-side explanations for gender inequality at work imply that women decrease and men intensify their paid work effort with increasing family responsibilities. Mothers (or potential mothers) may seek jobs that offer nonmonetary benefits, such as a lower penalty for discontinuous employment or flexibility (Filer 1985; Jacobs and Steinberg 1990). To the extent that the labor supply effects associated with family responsibilities vary by gender, additional family responsibilities slow advancement for mothers and accelerate advancement for fathers, contributing to occupational segregation and gender differences in pay.

Recent sociological research emphasizes that workers take account of the characteristics and demands of their work and home lives when ranking their preferences for work in paid employment or time at home to do domestic labor, including taking care of children (Blair-Loy 2003; Hakim 2000). Catherine Hakim's (2000) preference theory contends that variation in women's employment rates can be explained quite simply by women's desire (or preference) to work in the paid labor force in relation to their desire (or preference) to stay at home. Cross-national variation in women's employment, she argues, is largely attributable to cross-national differences in the degree to which women prefer to work in the paid labor force versus at home.

Although the simplicity of preference theory may be intuitively appealing, like earlier work on household economics, it does not adequately address the range of conditions and constraints that shape preferences over the life course and across countries. For example, the effects of having children on labor market outcomes may be particularly acute when children are young, but the consequences may also be long-lasting, particularly if opportunities are constrained by the availability of employment or the demands and expectations of employers. Preference theory also cannot explain why the gender divide in paid work that emerges with the arrival of a child increases with the arrival of a second child (Lundberg and Rose 2002). The intensity of household demands, not just preferences, may play a central role in gender inequalities in the workplace.

Just as employees choose how to allocate time to the labor market and domestic work, employers decide whom to hire and promote and what to pay. Demand-side explanations locate the cause of gender inequality in the decisions of employers. Employers make choices about whom to hire, promote, and fire on the basis of their preferences (both conscious and unconscious) for different types of workers. Employers may make decisions on the basis of expectations about productivity, in-group preferences, or implicit biases (Padavic and Reskin 2002). Regardless of the specifics, however, the argument implies that employer preferences may lead them to differentiate employees based on their parental status not only in relation to hiring and promotion generally but also in hiring for particular types of jobs (such as part-time) and in determining pay.

Employers may develop a preference for fathers and nonmothers if they interpret the parental status of job applicants as an indicator of potential productivity—a form of "statistical discrimination"—or if they privilege workers based on their membership in a particular group (Bielby and Baron 1986). Employers may think that men are most productive when they have a family to support and that women are most productive when they are not distracted by child-rearing obligations. If employers have a preference for the workers they believe will be the most productive—fathers and nonmothers—we would expect gender differences in employment, occupation, and pay to align closely with parenthood rather than gender.

A different demand-side mechanism for gender inequality is selective information processing, which may lead to biases in hiring and promotion decisions and performance evaluation (Heilman 1995). For example, to the extent that mothers are stereotyped as "uncommitted" workers, a supervisor may be more likely to notice the tardiness of a mother than a father when each exhibits the exact same behavior, and the supervisor may be more likely to remember the mother's tardiness and to interpret it as a signal of lack of commitment. There is growing evidence from experimental studies (in the United States) of employer discrimination on the basis of gender (Goldin and Rouse 2000) and articulated preferences for nonmothers and fathers as workers (Correll, Benard, and Paik 2007).

CROSS-NATIONAL VARIABILITY IN GENDER AND WORK

Existing accounts of gender inequality in the economy that rely on education and domestic obligations fail to explain the wide variation in women's economic standing across countries. Researchers of cross-national gender inequality have provided alternative macro-level accounts for women's economic standing, focusing on norms and ideology, national economic conditions, and policies.

Women's political gains in the twentieth century accompanied the fall of many barriers to female involvement in the paid labor force and may help explain cross-national differences in rates of female employment, occupational outcomes, and wages. Researchers have contended that overall indicators of gender equality—operationalized as women's representation in political office, domestic abuse rights, and reproductive rights—are also important determinants of gender equity in economic outcomes. National ideologies about gender equity may influence women's economic standing by influencing the acceptability of female employment and thus the attractiveness of employment to women (Crompton and Harris 1997; O'Connor, Orloff, and Shaver 1999). Cultural norms about gender role specialization and gender egalitarianism are reflected in rates of female employment (Crompton and Harris 1997; O'Connor, Orloff, and Shaver 1999) and occupational sex segregation (Charles 1992; Charles and Grusky 2004).

Attitudinal data on gender norms and expectations provide a useful, though limited, proxy for cross-national and over-time differences in gender attitudes, and recent studies show mixed results. Worldwide studies that include developing countries show some concordance between gender egalitarian attitudes and women's economic empowerment (Inglehart and Norris 2003), yet the relationship between attitudes and economic outcomes is less clear when the focus is limited to advanced industrialized nations (see, for example, Mandel and Semyonov 2006).

Rapid increases in women's economic standing in recent history have been traced to economic conditions, including expansions that incorporated women into the paid labor market. Early studies of the post–World War II rise in women's employment in the United States demonstrated that increased demand in female-dominated occupations helped drive married women into the paid labor force (Oppenheimer 1970; Goldin 1990). Sectoral shifts in the economy, including a movement away from agriculture and manufacturing, increased the share of employment in female-typed occupations, such as those in the service industries. Since these occupations were already dominated by women, employers sought to fill new positions with women as well.

Although economic and sectoral growth promote women's inclusion in the labor market, their effects on occupational sex segregation and gender wage inequality are less clear. For example, economic growth may fuel gender segregation in occupations and exacerbate wage inequality if new women workers are incorporated into traditionally female employment sectors with low pay. In fact, research demonstrates clear links between the growth of the public sector and women's concentration in female-dominated industries (see, for example, Gornick and Jacobs 1998), and economic growth—including growth in female-dominated sectors—is associated with the incorporation of women into highly gender-segregated occupations and jobs (Oppenheimer 1970; Goldin 1990; Boeri, Del Boca, and Pissarides 2005).

Comparativists have also understood women's economic standing in relation to policy configurations and welfare state development. Esping-Andersen's (1990, 1999) typology of welfare states has been invoked and extended to explain the high levels of women's labor force participation in social democratic states, the slightly lower levels of female employment in liberal welfare states, and the even lower levels of employment in conservative-corporatist welfare states (see, for example, Esping-Andersen 1999; Gornick 1999; Gornick, Meyers, and Ross 1997; Huber and Stephens 2000). Although the welfare state typology and its derivatives have been less instructive for explaining cross-national variability in occupational segregation, particular features of the welfare state, including wage protections and wage-setting institutions, have been used to explain gender wage inequality (see, for example, Blau and Kahn 2002; Mandel and Semyonov 2006). Recent research emphasizes the central importance of family policy generosity and wage-setting mechanisms for women's employment and for wage outcomes in particular (Mandel and Semyonov 2005, 2006; Gornick and Meyers 2003; Blau and Kahn 2002; Boeri, Del Boca, and Pissarides 2005; Wetzels 2007).

INSTITUTIONALIZING INEQUALITY

Existing theory and research have not comprehensively explained women's economic standing across various measures of inequality (wages, occupations, hours worked, and employment) across countries. Previous research has been limited by a focus on a single outcome, a reliance on a particular theoretical tradition, or data from a very small set of countries. To redress this, we build on research from both economics and comparative sociology to disentangle how and for whom social policies and employment conditions shape gender inequality in employment, hours worked, occupational segregation, and wages. Our argument calls for closer examination of how gender inequality—broadly defined—is institutionalized within households and labor markets and across countries. In our analysis, households are institutionally structured, relieving women in varying degree from child-rearing, thereby opening their access to the labor market. We argue that individual factors, such as education and having children (young children in particular), affect household responsibilities and have consequences for women's inclusion in the labor market and women's equality measured by hours worked, occupational integration, and wages.

For example, relative to their less-educated counterparts, highly educated women may be more likely to be relieved of the household obligations associated with child-rearing through their use of child care or their greater household bargaining power. In contrast, women with young children or more than one child may have greater household responsibilities because the demands of children on a household are exacerbated when children are young and with each additional child. To the extent that women with less education, young children, or more than one child disproportionately bear the costs of domestic production, we might expect them to participate less in the paid labor force, to be concentrated in part-time or female-dominated jobs, and to report lower wages.

States also influence the gendered division of labor within the household through policies and conditions that variably relieve women of the domestic obligations associated with caregiving, enable women to accommodate competing work and family demands, or concentrate the demands of caregiving in the hands of women. Cross-nationally, women are more likely than men to take time out of the paid labor force to care for children and attend to other family responsibilities. Factors at the national level—including social policies and employment conditions—affect the concentration of domestic responsibilities among women, thereby influencing women's labor market inclusion and indicators of gender equality within the market. For example, public support for child care relieves households, and especially women, of at least some of the domestic obligations associated with caring for young children. In countries with publicly provided child care, we might expect less divergence in the labor market fortunes of mothers—especially those with young children—from those of other women and less difference between women and men.

In our analysis, labor markets are also institutionally structured: by this we mean that there are discernible patterns in the allocation of jobs and wages. Both individuals and states influence the allocation of jobs and wages, though not necessarily in the same ways that they influence inequality within households. Contemporary labor markets are characterized by strong returns to skill and experience (see, for example, Katz and Murphy 1992; Blau and Kahn 2002; Charles and Grusky 2004; Kenworthy 2004). Accordingly, we might expect that women with high levels of education or fewer domestic obligations that deter their investment in paid employment are rewarded in the paid labor market. Inequality within the market is also driven, in our argument, by how states accommodate and compensate workers. For example, public child care is likely to reduce within-market inequalities, both by enabling women to maintain continuous attachment to the paid labor force while having young children and by signaling the social acceptance of working mothers.

We carefully examine how country-level conditions make the labor market more (or less) hospitable, depending on one's level of education and the number and ages of one's children, focusing on what we call mechanisms of labor market inclusion and exclusion. We refer to publicly provided child care and part-time work as mechanisms of labor market inclusion because they should help to incorporate women—even women with low levels of education or young children—into the labor market. In contrast, we refer to long parental leaves and high rates of unionization as mechanisms of labor market exclusion because they should exacerbate tensions between domestic responsibilities and work in the paid labor force. For example, long parental leaves may concentrate the demands of caregiving within the household, and extensive unionization may reinforce ideal-worker norms that preference full-time work (Gornick and Meyers 2003; O'Connor 1993). Mechanisms of labor market exclusion should also exacerbate inequality between women with more and less education and between women with young children and those without. Since women's labor is more elastic than men's, and because women are the dominant caregivers of children across countries, we suspect that the effects of mechanisms of labor market inclusion and exclusion should be felt more acutely by women than by men.

We argue that although the size of the part-time workforce and the level of unionization result from contested political processes, they signal government support—both material and symbolic—for workplace conditions that have implications for gender inequalities in the economy. There is wide variability across countries in the use of part-time work as a labor management device (see, for example, Fagan and O'Reilly 1998). Although the Netherlands consistently maintains a large part-time workforce, even countries where there is little part-time work, like Italy and Spain, use part-time employment to continue to employ workers when the economy is slow or the labor market is tight. Debates about the optimal size of the part-time workforce are less explicit than debates about the optimal length of parental leave or the allocation of funds for child care. Nonetheless, federal governments influence both the supply of and demand for part-time work through policies that regulate work hours, mandate benefits (including wage regulations), and otherwise influence the cost of additional workers (Montgomery 1988).

We are interested in unionization rates, not because governments explicitly debate the merits and sizes of labor unions, but because governments are implicated in the size and strength of labor unions across countries. Unionization rates vary dramatically, both across countries and over time, in ways that provide some indication of the strength of labor. Rates of unionization in the United States are low in comparative perspective, especially since the 1950s. One explanation for U.S. labor's relative weakness points to strong government support of employers and restrictions on union organization and activity (Clawson and Clawson 1999). Unlike many other countries, the United States has not historically prohibited the use of substitute employees during a strike. A declining U.S. labor movement was dealt a critical blow in 1981 when President Ronald Reagan replaced unionized air traffic controllers on strike with non-unionized employees. In contrast, union coverage has experienced a resurgence in some northern European countries as unions have received government support and expanded their presence in female-dominated industries, including public-sector work (Ebbinghaus and Visser 1999). A full examination of cross-national variability in the size and scope of labor unions is beyond the purview of this book, but a large body of research has examined cross-national variability in unionization and its implications for employment and wage inequality (see, for example, Western 1997; Golden, Lange, and Wallerstein 2002; Card, Lemieux, and Riddell 2003; Kenworthy 2004).

THE INCLUSION-EQUALITY TRADEOFF

The state policies and conditions that structure labor market inclusion and exclusion also have implications for gender inequality within the labor market measured by hours worked, occupation, and pay. The conditions that foster labor market inclusion do not necessarily guarantee equality by these other measures (Mandel 2008; Boeri, Del Boca, and Pissarides 2005). We expect to find a tradeoff between labor market inclusion and equality measured within the market if women are incorporated into the labor market through large part-time workforces—part-time work being an accommodation strategy that enables women to manage the competing demands of paid work and domestic work. High rates of part-time employment may fuel occupational sex segregation and exacerbate inequality in the labor market both between women and between women and men. Although the availability of more part-time jobs would ameliorate the negative effect of low education and having children on women's labor force participation, it would probably increase inequality within the labor market. Full-time jobs, gender-integrated jobs, and high-paying jobs would be reserved for highly educated women or women without children.

On the other hand, conditions that promote labor market exclusion—like high levels of unionization—may ensure greater equality for those who "get through." Although the effects of unionization vary across countries, one argument suggests that unions may provide a gatekeeping function to separate primary-sector workers with strong labor protections and benefits from unprotected workers (Reskin 1993). In this view, once women get into the labor market—and into primary-sector jobs—they are likely to be afforded the same jobs, wages, and benefits as men. Thus, we could expect greater equality between the women and men included in the labor market, but less equality between women in terms of access to full-time employment.

Contemporary accounts of gender inequality within the labor market fail to take account of the multiple dimensions of labor market inequality. Individual conditions (for example, parental status or education) and societal conditions (such as gender egalitarianism or service-sector growth) influence gender inequality and its measurement both indirectly through the supply of and demand for labor and directly within the labor market through the allocation of jobs and wages. Moreover, gender differences in labor supply and demand and involvement in segmented labor markets may perpetuate inequality over the life course by cleaving the work experiences of women from those of men, and mothers' work experiences from those of fathers and nonmothers.

Our tradeoff theory highlights the tension between women's labor market inclusion and their equality within that market, as measured by their hours worked, occupations, and wages. In this section and in table 2.1, we outline our expectations for specific tradeoffs, and throughout the book we question whether they are necessary and inevitable. We explain how specific policy conditions may differentially produce labor market inclusion and within-market equality for women.

Inclusion and Inequality: Part-Time Work

To illustrate the tradeoff argument we begin by considering how the availability of part-time work may foster women's inclusion in the labor market while at the same time engendering inequality across other economic outcomes. A growing body of work highlights how societal expectations about working arrangements, including time spent at work, can alleviate or exacerbate work-family tensions and fuel gender inequality in labor market outcomes (Hochschild 1997; Moen 2003). Large part-time workforces allow women to maintain a foothold in the labor market as they manage the potentially competing demands of domestic and paid work (Boeri, Del Boca, and Pissarides 2005; Fagan and O'Reilly 1998; Pfau-Effinger 1998; Blossfeld and Hakim 1997). Thus, we expect high rates of women's labor force participation in countries with large part-time workforces. At the same time, if women bear the brunt of child-related domestic obligations, we expect mothers to be concentrated in female-dominated sectors and poorly remunerated positions. Previous research has demonstrated that part-time work typically carries a wage penalty of between 8 and 15 percent (Bardasi and Gornick 2001). Recognizing the undesirable nature of much part-time work, in 1997 the European Union mandated that member states improve the pay and availability of part-time work (Europa 2006). Yet even when wage protections are in place for part-time workers, women's concentration in part-time work indirectly contributes to gender inequality in pay by decreasing women's work experience relative to that of men, who are concentrated in full-time jobs.

Inclusion and Equality: Public Child Care

In contrast to part-time work availability, we argue, publicly provided child care is likely to foster women's labor market inclusion and simultaneously afford greater equality in other economic outcomes. Public support for child care relieves households—and usually women—of child care responsibilities. Moreover, public child care provides symbolic support for the concept of working mothers and signals societal acceptance—if not approval—of the idea that children can be adequately cared for by persons other than their own mothers or fathers (Gauthier 1996; Michel 1999). It is likely that societies that endorse public child care also have weaker norms against women working in the paid labor force (Gauthier 1996; Morgan 2006; Morgan and Zippel 2003). Although there have been few empirical investigations of the specific effect of public child care on women's economic fortunes (see, for example, Boeri, Del Boca, and Pissarides 2005), we expect that public child care would foster gender equality in employment, hours worked, occupational integration, and pay. Public child care should relieve women of domestic responsibilities, enabling them to devote time to developing skills that would enhance their workplace performance and standing. Moreover, we suspect that employers are more willing to hire and promote women—and mothers—in countries that endorse parental employment and collective care of children.

Exclusion and Equality: Unionization

Unions may exclude some workers—particularly women—from the labor market, while fostering equality among those who remain. To the extent that unions have disproportionately male membership, are concentrated in male-dominated industries, and advocate for protections that reinforce traditional gendered divisions of labor, high levels of unionization may disadvantage women workers and promote specialization in home production and market work.

In some countries, high levels of unionization are associated with ideal-worker norms that are incompatible with managing family demands (O'-Connor 1993). Despite recent growth in women's involvement in labor unions, unions have long been critiqued for fostering labor market protections that preference full-time, career-oriented workers. Unions are also associated with a breadwinner-homemaker family model premised on the concentration of domestic work within the household and women's exclusion from the paid labor force (see, for example, Crain 1994; O'Connor 1993). To the extent that high levels of unionization concentrate domestic obligations in the hands of women, we suspect that they are negatively associated with women's economic fortunes, especially the employment fortunes of mothers.

At the same time, however, other labor market protections typically offered by unions—such as high wages and job security—are gender-neutral and therefore likely to foster equality within the labor market measured by hours worked, occupational segregation, and wages. High levels of unionization often signal broad worker-oriented protections and a well-developed welfare state (see, for example, Weste rn 1997). By negotiating wage agreements that raise the wage floor for employed workers, unions should decrease wage inequality, and union-negotiated wage agreements may have beneficial effects even for non-unionized workers working in unionized industries. In fact, significant research has demonstrated that levels of unionization and other measures of centralized bargaining systems are strongly and positively associated with lower levels of wage inequality (Western 1997; Blau and Kahn 2002; Kenworthy 2004). In short, although strong unions may be associated with low levels of women's employment, they may also foster greater gender equality among women and men in the paid labor force.

Exclusion and Inequality: Parental Leaves

Our analysis also considers how parental leave policies affect women's involvement in and equality within the labor market. Paid leaves following the birth of a child have been shown to increase women's attachment to the labor force (Waldfogel 1997; Ruhm 1998), yet there is growing concern that exceptionally long parental leaves may exacerbate inequalities between women and men by materially supporting and normatively endorsing a breadwinner-homemaker model (see, for example, Gornick and Meyers 2003; Kenworthy 2009). There is little doubt that lengthy paid parental leaves are associated with decreased representation of women in formal employment, since they are in effect paid to care for their own children at home (see, for example, Morgan and Zippel 2003; Gornick and Meyers 2003).

It is less clear how extended parental leaves affect gender inequality in pay and women's concentration in part-time and low-skill sectors. On the one hand, extended parental leaves are likely to exacerbate within-market inequalities by retarding the accumulation of work experience among mothers, thereby reducing their employability. If long parental leaves indicate societal expectations that children should be cared for by their own parents, and more particularly by their mothers, these leaves may be associated with weak employer demand for women—or mothers—as workers (Gauthier 1996; Morgan and Zippel 2003). On the other hand, it is possible that in countries where motherhood is closely aligned with caregiving and endorsed by extended parental leaves, women who eschew domestic responsibilities—either by not having children or by substituting nonmaternal care for them—fare particularly well in the paid labor market. If this is the case, lengthy parental leaves would be associated with the exclusion of women, especially mothers, from paid employment, but greater levels of equality would prevail among those who remain within the labor market.

MEASURING GENDER INEQUALITY

Table 2.1 outlines our theoretical framework and summarizes our empirical expectations concerning the tradeoffs between inclusion and equality. Our initial review of the available evidence in table 1.1 found that no country ranks uniformly high or low on all of the economic outcomes, suggesting that, in one way or another, women across countries experience tradeoffs. Yet there is reason to suspect that some groups of women fare quite well across in-

Table 2.1   The Theoretical Framework

	Inclusion	Exclusion
Equality	Conditions foster high levels of female employment by relieving women of the demands of child-rearing. Reduced domestic demands foster equality in hours worked, occupation, and pay among the employed.	Conditions foster low levels of female employment by establishing ideal-worker norms inconsistent with the demands of child-rearing. Gender-neutral employment protections, however, foster equality in hours worked, occupation, and pay among the employed.
Inequality	Conditions foster high levels of female employment by promoting flexible working arrangements that allow women to combine employment with disproportionate responsibility for child-rearing. Expectations of gender specialization at home and at work foster inequality in hours worked, occupation, and pay among the employed.	Conditions foster low levels of female employment by concentrating the demands of child-rearing within the home. Expectations of gender specialization at home and at work foster inequality in hours worked, occupation, and pay among the employed.

Source: Authors' compiliation.

dicators. Can highly educated women, for example, or those without children escape the inclusion-equality tradeoff?

The chapters that follow consider how individual characteristics and national conditions influence our four measures of economic standing differently across social and demographic groups. In chapter 3, we examine the self-reported employment of women and men. Chapter 4 analyzes the different factors that affect women's and men's involvement in full-time and part-time employment. In chapter 5, we focus on women's and men's employment in different broad occupational groups, including managerial, professional, and clerical, and in sales and service jobs. Finally, chapter 6 documents the impact of individual and national-level factors on gender differences in pay. We give special attention to how state policies and conditions structure differences in economic outcomes by education and domestic obligations.

Individual-Level Factors

Each chapter begins with a consideration of the implications of education and having children on labor market outcomes. First we document levels of employment, hours worked, occupation, and wages for women and men across countries. Then we examine how much those same outcomes vary for women and men with different levels of education and in relation to the number and ages of their children.

Throughout this book we examine women's and men's economic fortunes in relation to their level of education. We attempt to standardize educational attainment across countries by coding educational attainment into categories representing low, medium, and high education. Countries have diverse credentialing schemes (Sullivan and Smeeding 1997), but the categories approximate less than a secondary education, completion of secondary education, and more than a secondary education. Additional detail on the coding of education and all other variables is found in the methodological appendix.

Our theoretical argument implies that education is positively associated with employment, full-time work, involvement in gender-integrated jobs, and higher wages for women and for men. The specific effects of education, particularly for women, are likely to depend on the social policies and employment conditions associated with labor market inclusion or exclusion. While inclusionary mechanisms, by definition, should dampen the effects of education on employment, the empirical implications of inclusionary mechanisms for the relationship between education and gender equality within the market is a bit more complex. If women's inclusion in the labor market is not accompanied by commensurate declines in women's domestic obligations, we anticipate greater inequality in hours worked, occupational integration, and wages. Highly educated women working full-time in male-dominated industries may do quite well, but it is likely that significant inequality by both gender and education will persist. In contrast, when mechanisms of inclusion accompany greater gender equality in home production, we anticipate greater equality by gender and education as measured by hours worked, occupation, and wages.

We also consistently examine women's and men's economic fortunes in relation to their parental status indicated by the presence and ages of their children. We include information on the presence of a youngest child age three years or under, the presence of a child age four to six years, and the total number of children in the household under age eighteen. We use discrete categories to measure the age of the youngest child to ensure comparability across countries and to discern how mothers' and fathers' labor market outcomes are shaped by the intensity of the demands of child-rearing.

We expect to find that having young children and having more than one child are negatively associated with women's employment and their labor market equality, since women bear the burdens—both real and symbolic—of caring for children. The effects of child-rearing for men are more ambiguous, theoretically speaking, though previous empirical research leads us to believe that the labor market rewards men when they become fathers (Lundberg and Rose 2002; Correll, Benard, and Paik 2007).

The relationship between women's performance on economic indicators and having children depends on how state policies and conditions shape the relationship between parenthood and employment and on how those same policies and conditions structure inequality within the labor market. In chapter 1, we argued that working mothers are positively selected on characteristics such as high levels of education or employment in male-dominated jobs that are associated with strong labor market performance. If the norm is that mothers exit the labor force when they have children, then we are likely to find that mothers who remain in the labor market exhibit even more positive occupation and wage outcomes than women without children. In contrast, if it is normative for mothers to work in part-time or female-dominated jobs in order to accommodate their work and family obligations, then we are likely to find that mothers fare particularly poorly within the labor market. To disentangle the effects of motherhood from the caregiving duties associated with young children, we examine the direct effects on labor market outcomes of having young children in the household and of having more than one child in the household.

There is also reason to think that certain conditions, such as high levels of unionization, decrease levels of labor market inequality on the basis of gender or any other ascribed characteristic. If the labor market offers generalized protections for workers, there is reason to think that women and men benefit equally.

National-Level Factors

Existing cross-national research suggests that national-level conditions influence women's fate in the labor market. In this book, we make a special effort to disentangle the effects of specific policies, apart from welfare state classification, to gain a better understanding of the mechanisms behind cross-national variation in—and comparative accounts of—gender inequality. To address how welfare state provisions influence gender inequality, we include measures of state policies and conditions: the size of the part-time workforce, public support for child care, the level of unionization, and parental leave. Although these measures are most salient given our theoretical interest in the tension between inclusion and equality, we examine other factors purported to influence gender inequality: maternity leave, gender egalitarianism, economic conditions, and the size of the public sector. In this section, we detail our unique collection of indicators and clarify how we conceptualize these indicators.

We consider national levels of publicly provided child care, parental leave, part-time work, and unionization as determinants rather than products of gender inequality (see Huber and Stephens 2000; Morgan 2006). Established federal regulations regarding child care and parental leave have more than symbolic significance. Numerous studies have traced variability in the supply of and employer's demand for women's labor in response to shifts in child care policy and parental leave (see, for example, Waldfogel 1997; Gornick and Meyers 2003; Boeri, Del Boca, and Pissarides 2005; Ruhm 1998). The measure of child care we have adopted represents the percentage of children ages zero to two in publicly funded child care in the year prior to the survey. Parental leave represents the maximum number of weeks (paid or unpaid) of state-mandated, job-protected leave available to parents to care for a newly born or newly adopted child. We include a measure of the percentage of the workforce that is part-time and the percentage of unionized workers to examine how ostensibly gender-neutral employment conditions may have gendered effects, especially when they reinforce traditional divisions of domestic labor.

In addition to these measures of state-level factors, we also include an indicator of weeks of maternity leave. Maternity leave is distinct from parental leave and typically represents the number of weeks of job-protected leave after childbirth reserved for mothers. Parental leave, in theory, can be taken by either parent and is much longer in duration. The provision of maternity leave is nearly universal across our countries of study, though it is relatively short in duration—typically twelve to eighteen weeks. We include it in our analyses, but note that maternity leave has little effect on our economic outcomes, perhaps as a consequence of its universality and brief duration. Therefore, we focus on the effects of parental leave, which is highly variable and consequential for gender inequality.

To measure gender egalitarianism we include women's representation in lower parliament, since the propensity of the electorate to vote for women is a salient indicator of women's national standing (see Iversen and Rosenbluth 2006).

To capture the effects of economic conditions we include measures of service-sector growth, the size of the public sector, per capita GDP growth, and the unemployment rate. These measures tap different aspects of how economic expansion and growth incorporate and remunerate women and men.

We also examine the impact of the size of the public sector, which, perhaps surprisingly and in contradiction to some previous work, has little effect on our outcomes. We find that the size of the public sector is often correlated with the size of the part-time workforce and unionization, making it difficult to distinguish the independent effects of each. Because we assign causal priority to part-time work and unionization, and also because we value parsimony, we omit public-sector size from our analyses. All country-level characteristics, measured in the mid-1990s, are shown in table 2.2. Data for all years are shown in table A.2.

CONCLUSION

Existing research suggests that both individual- and national-level conditions shape labor market outcomes for women and men. It is also apparent that key gender divides in the economy hinge on women's disproportionate share of domestic responsibilities associated with caring for children. Our research explains how gender inequality in the labor market is institutionalized through households and markets. State policies and conditions variably relieve or concentrate caregiving within households and in the hands of women, influenc-

Table 2.2   Macro-Level Conditions, by Country, Mid-1990s

	Percentage of Part-Time Workers	Percentage of Children Age Zero to Two in Public Child Care	Union Density	Parental Leave Weeks
Australia	21%	2%	43%	0
Austria	13	3	37	112
Belgium	14	30	60	67
Canada	19	5	33	25
Czech Republic	6	1	30	214
Denmark	23	48	76	28
Finland	7	32	75	160
France	15	23	9	162
Germany	16	11	27	162
Hungary	5	9	20	160
Italy	6	6	32	48
Luxembourg	8	3	50	16
Netherlands	36	8	23	68
Norway	27	20	53	64
Poland	11	5	15	108
Russian Federation	4	15	69	166
Slovenia	8	14	41	56
Spain	5	5	9	162
Sweden	24	33	88	85
United Kingdom	22	2	34	18
United States	19	5	14	12

Source: See Methodological Appendix.

ing women's inclusion in or exclusion from employment in the paid labor force. How and when women—and especially mothers—are incorporated into the paid labor market has implications for gender inequality within the labor force. The tradeoffs that women face—between family and work and within the workplace itself—are the focus of the remainder of this book.

CHAPTER 3

Gender, Family, and Work in the Paid Labor Force

Women's labor force participation increased dramatically in most industrialized countries in the latter half of the twentieth century. Figure 3.1 shows the cross-national trends in women's involvement in the paid labor force from 1978 to 2001, with the mean level increasing from 50 to 65 percent. The figure further reveals that during the 1980s and 1990s women's labor force involvement rates converged across countries. In 1978 rates ranged from a low of 30 percent in Spain to a high of 70 percent in Sweden; by 2001 this forty-percentage-point gap had narrowed to twenty-five. Substantial variation remains, however, across countries and within welfare state regime types.

We begin this chapter by considering how rates of labor force participation vary across Esping-Andersen's (1990, 1999) welfare state regime types. The conservative-corporatist regime of continental and southern Europe—including Austria, Belgium, France, Germany, Italy, Luxembourg, the Netherlands, and Spain—posted the lowest levels of women's labor force participation for most of the 1978 to 2001 period. There are considerable differences in women's participation rates within this regime type, however, displayed in the sizable gap between the mean for these countries and the rates for Spain, which ranks lowest of our twenty-one countries on women's labor force participation.

The countries of eastern Europe, including the Czech Republic, the Rus-

Figure 3.1   Trends in Women's Labor Force Participation, 1978 to 2001

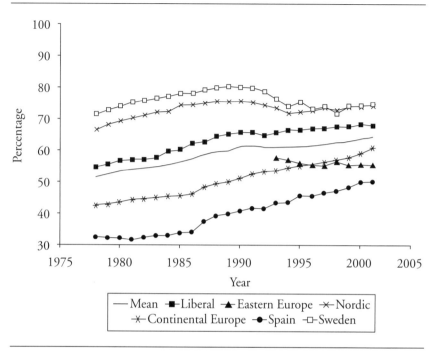

Source: Organization for Economic Cooperation and Development (OECD 2002).

sian Federation, Hungary, Poland, and Slovenia, enter the series in 1992. These countries witnessed a leveling-off, and even a decline, in women's labor force participation in the post-reconstruction era. Although the countries of eastern Europe entered the series at the twenty-one-country mean in 1992, they had fallen below the mean, and even slightly behind the conservative-corporatist countries, by 2001.

The liberal regime, including the United States, Australia, Canada, and the United Kingdom, posted rates of women's labor force participation above the twenty-one-country mean and displayed steady growth over the period. Countries of the liberal regime neither lead nor lag in the rate or the growth of women's labor force involvement.

Finally, the social democratic countries of northern Europe, including Denmark, Finland, Norway, and Sweden, exhibit the highest rates of women's labor force participation. Growth has been more modest in the Nordic countries, perhaps because they entered the series with high rates of female labor force participation. In 1978 approximately two-thirds of women in social democratic countries were involved in the paid labor force. Even with declines in women's involvement in the paid workforce in the 1990s, steady growth in women's employment in the 1980s led to the participation of nearly three-quarters of Nordic women in the paid labor force by 2000. Sweden posted the highest levels for most of the period but converged to the social democratic states' mean by the late 1990s.

In contrast to the generalized increases in women's involvement in paid work and the considerable variability in women's labor market participation both across countries and over time, there is greater stability and uniformity in men's involvement in paid work. Figure 3.2 shows a decrease of approximately five percentage points in the mean level of men's labor force participation from 1978 to 2001. The mean level of men's labor force participation across countries fell from about 85 to 80 percent over the period, with a great deal of clustering around the mean.

Men's participation rates in the conservative-corporatist countries are typically lower than the twenty-one-state mean. The regime average, however, obscures substantial variation across countries. Belgium, France, and Italy post the lowest male participation rates, while Germany, Luxembourg, and the Netherlands exhibit relatively high male participation levels. The Nordic and liberal countries, with participation rates over 80 percent throughout the 1980s and 1990s, have among the highest rates of men's labor force participation. Finally, the countries of eastern Europe show the lowest levels of participation. In Hungary, for example, only two-thirds of working-age men are employed or looking for work in the paid labor force.

Cross-national differences in levels and trends of female and male labor force participation underscore that gender differences in access to economic opportunities vary considerably across countries. The causes of those cross-national differences are the central concern of the remainder of this chapter. We examine variability in employment within and across countries to identify how social policies and employment conditions influence tradeoffs between home and work across different social and demographic groups.

First, guided by life-course explanations for economic inequalities, we examine how employment patterns shift in relation to educational attainment and child-rearing. Although we lack data both on employer demand for workers with different attributes and on individual preferences for spending

Figure 3.2   Trends in Men's Labor Force Participation, 1978 to 2001

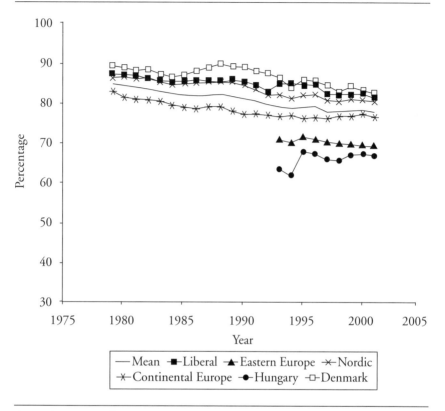

Source: Organization for Economic Cooperation and Development (OECD 2002).

time in the paid labor force, in domestic production, and in leisure activities, we are able to examine how education and having children systematically influence employment. Consistency in the effects of education on the employment fortunes of women and men confirm the enduring significance of human capital in the labor market. Gender differences in the effects of children on employment highlight the importance of child-rearing obligations for accounts of economic inequality.

Second, we examine how mean levels of employment are influenced by a host of national conditions hypothesized by comparative cross-national research to affect gender inequalities in work. Cross-national variation in levels of women's and men's employment correlates with state policies and conditions in revealing ways. Although women's employment is associated with economic conditions, mechanisms of inclusion such as large part-time sectors and publicly provided child care further affect rates of women's employment. Men's employment, in contrast, varies little in relation to mechanisms of inclusion and is more strongly associated with overall economic conditions like economic growth and unemployment.

Third, we consider how mechanisms of inclusion and exclusion affect individual determinants of employment. Variability in how education and child-rearing affect employment for women and men across countries underscores the centrality of state policies and conditions for gender inequalities in employment. Public support for child care—a policy of inclusion—is associated with higher levels of employment for women and for mothers in particular. Although there is some evidence that public provision of child care supports the employment of fathers of young children, men's employment is primarily affected by overall economic conditions like economic growth and unemployment.

Finally, we illustrate our findings with a focused comparison of the United States and West Germany. The United States and Germany exhibit important differences in social policies and employment conditions, both across countries and over time. We examine how those differences shape employment patterns in relation to education and child-rearing. Unless stated otherwise, all effects we discuss are statistically significant.

EMPLOYMENT OVER THE LIFE COURSE: THE EFFECTS OF EDUCATION AND CHILDREN

Table 3.1 shows the percentage of women and men age eighteen to sixty-four reporting employment for LIS countries observed in the 1990s. (Table A.3 reports all LIS years.) It displays men's and women's employment rates separately, both for all working-age respondents and for the following subgroups: those with a high level of education, those with a youngest child age six or younger, and those with a youngest child age six or older. The first thing to observe in the table is that in most countries the employment rate for all adult respondents under age sixty-five differs substantially from employment rates for specific subgroups. There is great variation in employment rates among subgroups within countries, as illustrated by data from Austria. Fifty-nine percent of Austrian women are employed, but among the one-third of the

Table 3.1 Employment of Women and Men, by Parental Status and Education, Mid-1990s

Country	Year	Women				Men			
		All	Highly Educated	Young Children Age Zero to Six	Older Children Age Seven to Seventeen	All	Highly Educated	Young Children Age Zero to Six	Older Children Age Seven to Seventeen
Austria	1994	59%	78%	57%	66%	80%	91%	91%	87%
Australia	1994	59	77	44	66	81	88	86	85
Belgium	1997	48	62	62	53	70	72	90	75
Canada	1994	63	72	57	68	74	79	83	78
Czech Republic	1996	63	75	37	80	80	88	92	86
Denmark	1992	72	86	76	82	79	90	91	87
Finland	1995	59	74	50	74	64	80	84	75
France	1994	56	60	57	64	73	71	88	80
Germany	1994	58	74	40	66	78	86	89	87
Hungary	1994	50	80	36	67	64	87	76	68
Italy	1995	41	74	48	44	68	80	88	76
Luxembourg	1994	48	57	43	46	87	90	100	96
Netherlands	1994	55	76	52	56	77	86	94	83
Norway	1995	66	80	66	71	81	87	94	82
Poland	1995	45	59	40	59	65	71	79	75
Russian Federation	1995	59	67	50	72	75	79	81	81
Slovenia	1997	55	83	72	68	66	83	82	76
Spain	1990	29	46	28	29	73	72	86	77
Sweden	1995	76	86	81	85	79	84	91	95
United Kingdom	1995	63	76	48	71	76	85	83	83
United States	1994	67	76	58	72	82	87	88	83
Mean		57	72	52	65	75	83	88	82

population with the highest level of education, women's employment rises to 78 percent. In contrast, among women with children age six or younger, employment is 57 percent, compared to 66 percent for women with children age seven or older.

There is considerable support—across a range of countries—for microeconomic models of employment that emphasize the costs and benefits of working relative to other pursuits. Both women and men with the greatest expected returns to participation in the paid labor force are more likely to work in the paid labor force. In all cases (except for men in France and Spain), respondents with high levels of education show a higher employment rate than all other respondents. In some cases, differences in employment across educational categories is dramatic. For example, whereas only 41 percent of Italian women report employment, 74 percent of highly educated Italian women report employment. Although the relationship between education and employment is consistent across countries, there appears to be important variation in the strength of this relationship across countries.

Family obligations associated with young children have an adverse impact on the employment of women (especially mothers) but are positively associated with men's employment in most countries. Male and female parents with older children have similar employment rates, since men's rates fall and women's rates rise over the life course. The Czech Republic is a particularly dramatic example of this pattern. Overall, 63 percent of women and 80 percent of men age eighteen to sixty-four are employed. Only 37 percent of mothers with young children work compared to 80 percent of mothers with older children. This contrasts starkly with employment rates for fathers, 92 percent of whom work when their children are young and 86 percent of whom work when their children are older. Again, these patterns generally hold across countries but show considerable variation.

Table 3.2 reports the mean effects of education and child-rearing on women's and men's employment from regression models of women's employment. The regression framework allows us to examine the specific effects of education and children while holding other relevant information, such as age, marital status, and access to other household income, constant. In the regression analysis, we disaggregate the effects of having very young children (ages zero to three) from the effects of having slightly older children (ages four to six) and the total number of children under age eighteen living in the household. We focus our attention on the effects of living with infants or toddlers

Table 3.2   Cross-National Variability in Logistic Regression Predicting Employment

	Women			Men		
	Highly Educated	Youngest Child Age Zero to Three	Number of Children	Highly Educated	Youngest Child Age Zero to Three	Number of Children
Mean	1.07	−0.64	−0.29	0.74	0.23	−0.04
Median	1.09 (RF00)	−0.56 (US94)	−0.28 (HU94)	0.73 (CA97)	0.24 (US74)	−0.04 (LX97)
Minimum	−0.35 (GE84)	−2.79 (CA96)	−0.61 (NE91)	−0.34 (FR89)	−0.59 (LX94)	−0.35 (BE88)
Maximum	2.45 (SL97)	0.78 (SW92)	−0.04 (DE92)	2.56 (HU94)	1.26 (NO95)	0.38 (AT97)

Source: Luxembourg Income Study (LIS 2003).
Note: Models also include age, age-squared, medium education, marriage, youngest child age four to six, and other household income. See country abbreviations in figure A.1.

(ages zero to three) and the number of children to illustrate the economic consequences related to the demands of child-rearing. The table shows observed median, minimum, and maximum effect sizes with country-year indicated in parentheses.

The results from the regression models are generally consistent with the unadjusted descriptive findings shown in table 3.1. Higher levels of education are consistently related to higher probabilities of employment for both women and men across countries; this is demonstrated by a positive mean effect of education on employment. The mean effect of education on the likelihood of women's employment is larger than the effect on men's, indicating that education plays a larger role in determining women's employment than men's.

There is a great deal of variation, however, in education effects across countries, suggesting that in some countries education is a stronger predictor of employment than in others. Among women, the largest positive effect of education on employment is in Slovenia (1997), where highly educated women are significantly more likely than women with lower levels of education to be employed in the paid labor force. This contrasts with Germany (1984), where highly educated women are less likely to be working than their less-educated counterparts. Among men, Hungary (1994) posts the largest positive education effects, and France (1989) posts the largest negative education effects.

The regression-adjusted effects of having children are also generally consistent with those found in the descriptive analyses, though we show only the employment effects of having infants and toddlers (ages zero to three) and number of children to illustrate how the demands of caregiving are concentrated at different points in the life course. On average, living with infants and toddlers decreases the likelihood of women's employment and increases the likelihood of men's employment across countries, although there is considerable cross-national variation. The magnitude of the effect is larger for women than for men, suggesting that the negative effect of having very young children on women's employment is not fully offset by the positive effect for men's. Having an infant or toddler in the home signals a key turning point in women's work lives and is commonly associated with wholesale exit from the paid labor force.

The presence of very young children in the household has wide-ranging effects on employment outcomes across countries. Among women, the largest negative effects on employment of living with a child age zero to three are found in Canada (1996), where mothers of young children are significantly less likely to be employed than mothers without young children. In contrast, in Sweden (1992) the effect of having very young children is moderately positive, indicating that mothers of children age zero to three are more likely to report working than other women. Among men, the effects of having infants or toddlers are generally positive; the high employment rate reported among Norwegian (1995) fathers of very young children is typical. The negative relationship between having young children and father's employment in Luxembourg (1994) is more unusual and may be an artifact of high labor mobility in Luxembourg (Bentivogli and Pagano 1999).

The average effect of each additional child in the household is also consistent with expectations derived from the descriptive analysis. Each additional child is negatively associated with women's employment—above and beyond the effects of having a very young child in the household—yet has no discernible effect on men's employment. Although the effects of each additional child are generally smaller than they are for having very young children, they are more consistently negative among women and exhibit less variability among men across countries. This indicates that how families reconcile women's employment and child-rearing is more variable across countries in the early stages of child-rearing than at other stages.

CROSS-NATIONAL VARIABILITY IN WOMEN'S AND MEN'S EMPLOYMENT

The considerable differences in levels of women's and men's employment across countries call for exploration of the sources of this variation. Table 3.3 displays the associations between employment rates and national-level conditions, separately for women and men. Controlling for all other national-level factors, the year of each data point shows a positive relationship with women's employment and a negative relationship with men's employment. Consistent with figure 3.1, this table indicates a general increase in women's employment over the last quarter of the twentieth century and a smaller, yet significant, decline in men's employment.

Our measure of gender egalitarianism—women's representation in lower parliament—is not significantly related to cross-national variability in women's and men's labor force involvement. Certain economic conditions, however, have effects. For example, as unemployment increases, men's and women's employment decreases, and vice versa. Women's employment is also negatively related to per capita GDP and positively related to service-sector growth.

Table 3.3   The Association Between National Conditions and Mean
                Employment Levels

	Women	Men
Intercept	33.856*	85.143*
Year	0.742*	–0.202+
Gender egalitarianism		
Women in parliament	–26.386	–3.330
Economic conditions		
Unemployment	–118.102*	–104.707*
Service-sector growth	153.032*	22.116
Per capita GDP growth	–100.848*	–1.807
Mechanisms of inclusion		
Maternity leave	31.239*	–2.379
and inequality		
Part-time employment	51.325*	21.998*
and equality		
Child care	22.563+	–6.912
Mechanisms of exclusion		
and equality		
Union density	2.842	8.019+
and inequality		
Parental leave	1.196	–0.383
Adjusted R-squared	0.483	0.558

Source: Luxembourg Income Study (LIS 2003).
Note: * T-ratio ≥ 2; + T-ratio ≥ 1.8

Several state policies and conditions are also related to women's employment. Both the availability of part-time employment and the extent of public provision of child care are associated with higher levels of women's employment. Where states and markets accommodate women's labor through part-time employment and publicly provided child care, women's employment is greater. We also find that the length of maternity leave is positively associated with women's employment. The level of men's employment is less responsive to the social policies that we measure. The availability of part-time employment and union density, however, are both positively associated with overall levels of men's employment.

In summary, our results indicate the relevance of labor market conditions and aspects of welfare state policy—especially mechanisms of inclusion—for the employment of women. They also highlight the central importance of national economic cycles and labor market conditions for men's employment.

INSTITUTIONALIZING GENDER INEQUALITY IN EMPLOYMENT

We argue that national policies and conditions not only affect the overall level of employment for women and men across countries and over time but also differentially affect the employment prospects of particular social and demographic groups. Our theoretical framework implies that mechanisms of inclusion and exclusion structure the division of labor within households and influence how women and men allocate time between domestic obligations and work in the paid labor force. Moreover, these same policies and conditions indicate societal norms about the acceptability of working women and working mothers (Morgan and Zippel 2003; Morgan 2006; O'Connor 1993).

Table 3.4 summarizes results from models that examine how the effects of individual-level social and demographic characteristics vary in relation to mechanisms of inclusion and exclusion. Specifically, our models test how the effects of education and the presence and age of children in the household depend on country differences in the percentage of the workforce that is part-time, the percentage of children age zero to two in publicly funded child care, union density, and the number of weeks of parental leave. We also control for the effects of the year and other national conditions, including gender egalitarianism, unemployment, service-sector growth, per capita GDP growth, and weeks of maternity leave.

The first column of results reported in table 3.4 shows how national-level factors condition the effects of education on women's employment. The intercept—which indicates the mean effect of education with all other variables set to zero—shows a positive, and statistically significant, relationship between having high levels of education and women's employment. The positive effect of the year in our model indicates that, over time, women with high levels of education are increasingly more likely to be employed than women with less education. In addition, we see that the effect of high levels of education is more positive when there is a greater availability of publicly

Table 3.4 The Association Between National Conditions and Factors Predicting Employment

	Women			Men		
	Highly Educated	Youngest Child Age Zero to Three	Number of Children	Highly Educated	Youngest Child Age Zero to Three	Number of Children
Intercept	1.089*	0.071	-0.543*	0.167	0.725*	-0.093
Year	0.049*	0.065*	-0.003	0.034*	0.007	0.000
Part-time employment	1.466	-0.962	-0.673*	-0.531	-0.597	-0.381
Child care	2.111*	4.493*	0.081	0.077	1.095*	-0.076
Union density	-0.487	-0.610	-0.032	0.211	-0.264	0.085
Parental leave	-0.183	-0.765*	-0.034	-0.253+	-0.083	-0.008

Source: Luxembourg Income Study (LIS 2003).

Note: Models also include age, age-squared, medium education, marriage, youngest child age four to six, and other household income at the individual level and women's employment, service-sector growth, per capita GDP, unemployment, maternity leave, women in parliament, and year at the country level.

*T-ratio ≥ 2; +T-ratio ≥ 1.8

funded child care, which indicates that a country is doing a better job of incorporating well-educated women into the labor market.

The effects of education and child-rearing on women's employment shown in the table are associated with mechanisms of inclusion and exclusion, but not quite in the manner suggested by our theoretical framework. The effect of attaining a high level of education or having very young children on women's employment does not vary with the availability of part-time work, but the effect of the *number* of children does. Countries that have large part-time workforces do a worse job of incorporating women with more children into the paid labor force. This is somewhat surprising because we expected that the availability of part-time work would help to incorporate women generally—and mothers in particular—into the paid labor force. However, table 3.4 suggests that large part-time workforces foster specialization over the life course. In countries with high levels of part-time work, mothers are more likely not to be in the paid labor force than mothers in otherwise similar countries.

Publicly provided child care, another policy of inclusion, fosters the labor market participation of women and mothers with very young children. This employment boost for highly educated women suggests that child care may facilitate the participation of women—and mothers in particular—who have the most to gain from employment.

Although their effects are not always statistically significant, mechanisms of exclusion consistently influence the effects of education and child-rearing on women's employment. Parental leave is negatively related to the effect of very young children in the household on employment: not surprisingly, long parental leaves are associated with mothers leaving the labor force, particularly when their children are very young.

We find some important similarities, illustrated in the table, in the relationship between country-context and women's and men's employment. Like women, men exhibit a widening gap in employment by level of education over the years for which we have LIS data. The social and demographic correlates of men's employment, however, are generally less sensitive to country-level conditions than are women's. Public child care is an exception, as it is positively associated with the employment of fathers of very young children. The education-employment relationship is less pronounced for men in countries that offer long parental leaves.

In summary, there is evidence that mechanisms of inclusion and exclusion structure the effects of social and demographic characteristics on the probability of women's employment. Inclusionary mechanisms, including the availability of part-time work and public supports for child care, help explain the effects of education and child-rearing on women's employment. Exclusionary mechanisms, including lengthy parental leave, are particularly salient for understanding low employment among mothers of very young children. In contrast, inclusionary and exclusionary mechanisms have less influence on the effects of education or family status on men's employment. Since these policies and conditions contribute little to explaining variation in the social and demographic characteristics associated with men's employment across countries, we must pay greater attention to national economic cycles.

SPOTLIGHT: TRENDS IN WOMEN'S EMPLOYMENT IN THE UNITED STATES AND WEST GERMANY

In this section, we explore whether we can observe the influence of institutional conditions on the social and demographic correlates of employment within countries over time. In each chapter of this book, we turn our attention to trends in the United States and West Germany as a way to further explore and illustrate our findings. We choose the United States and Germany for theoretical and practical reasons.

The United States and West Germany present useful comparative cases because they represent different welfare state regimes and exhibit different configurations of policies and conditions that affect women's labor force inclusion and exclusion. The United States is an exemplar of the liberal welfare state regime, and its social policies and employment conditions form a hybrid model of inclusion and exclusion. The U.S. government has, in many respects, adopted a laissez-faire approach to conflicts between work and home, leaving them to be resolved by families and employers. We conceptualize the United States as a country with limited inclusion policies and conditions and limited exclusion policies and conditions. Across LIS years, the United States falls in the middle of countries in terms of availability of part-time work, and it mandates comparatively little public child care. Throughout the time series, the United States has had low levels of unionization and been a laggard in parental leave policy. The United States is the only LIS country that offers no federally funded parental leave.

West Germany is an exemplar of the conservative-corporatist regime, and its social policies and employment conditions affecting inclusion and exclusion show a great deal of change over the LIS years. In the early LIS years, West German policies and conditions were characterized by low inclusion and low exclusion. Through the 1980s, it had relatively low levels of part-time work and very little publicly funded child care. These low-inclusion policies and conditions were coupled with high levels of unionization and relatively low, though increasing, parental leave. By the end of the 1990s, German state policies and employment conditions had become both more inclusive and more exclusive. Both the availability of part-time work and public support for child care rose through the 1990s, while union density fell. Perhaps most importantly, however, the length of parental leave was extended dramatically, making it normative for mothers to stay home with young children for extended periods of time. Although German political reunification has had significant implications for the employment situation in both West and East Germany—and among women in particular—we lack adequate data to examine the specific economic effects of reunification. We therefore limit our attention to women living in the former West Germany.

The United States and West Germany are the only two countries we observe over more than a seven-year span for all four of our economic outcomes—employment, hours worked, occupation, and wages. It is important to note that, with only a few data points from two countries, we cannot test causal explanations; however, we can see how well the trends in each country fit with results from the multilevel analysis. Although our analysis would certainly be richer if we could examine data from another country that represented a different welfare state regime type and had different conditions of inclusion and exclusion, data limitations prevent it.

Table 3.5, which displays the trends in German and U.S. women's employment rates, illustrates a large gulf between employment patterns in these two countries, primarily among women with young children (six and under). In the United States, there was a significant shift from 1986 to 2000: while all women increased their labor force employment by about twelve percentage points, women with young children increased their employment most, by fifteen points, moving from 54 to 69 percent.

In contrast, West Germany displays dramatically lower employment rates among women with young children. From 1984 to 2000, West German women closed the gap with American women by increasing their employment rates by eighteen percentage points. The increase was especially dramatic for women with older children: their employment increased by twenty-

Table 3.5   Trends in Women's Employment Rates in the United
             States and West Germany

	All	Highly Educated	Young Children Age Zero to Six	Older Children Age Seven to Seventeen
United States				
1986	63%	74%	54%	66%
1991	71	81	62	76
1994	67	76	58	72
1997	69	77	62	73
2000	75	81	69	78
West Germany				
1984	49	68	38	50
1989	54	69	39	57
1994	58	67	37	62
2000	67	76	45	77

Source: Luxembourg Income Study (LIS 2003).

seven points, from 50 to 77 percent. Women with young children, however, increased their labor force employment by only seven percentage points, and in 2000 they were more likely to be out of the labor force than in. Only 45 percent of women with children age six or younger were employed in 2000 in West Germany.

Table 3.6 shows trends in the individual correlates of women's employment in the United States from 1986 to 2000. The first column shows the effect of high education levels on the likelihood of women's employment, and the next two columns show the confidence interval around the estimate. The influence of high education on employment remained relatively stable over the period.

The fourth column shows the effect on the likelihood of women's employment of having a child age zero to three. Examining the confidence intervals shown in the adjacent rows, we can see whether the estimates have changed over time (by looking for non-overlapping intervals). The estimate and the confidence interval for 1991 stand out from other years as the only data point in which the United States was in a recession. Recall that we find that higher

Table 3.6   Logistic Regression Predicting Women's Employment in the United States and West Germany

	High Education			Youngest Child Age Zero to Three			Number of Children		
	Estimate	95 Percent Confidence Interval		Estimate	95 Percent Confidence Interval		Estimate	95 Percent Confidence Interval	
United States									
1986	1.35*	1.20	1.49	-0.52*	-0.68	-0.36	-0.24*	-0.30	-0.19
1991	1.37*	1.30	1.44	-0.69*	-0.77	-0.62	-0.22*	-0.24	-0.19
1994	1.22*	1.15	1.29	-0.56*	-0.63	-0.48	-0.21*	-0.24	-0.18
1997	1.18*	1.11	1.26	-0.50*	-0.58	-0.42	-0.18*	-0.21	-0.15
2000	1.25*	1.18	1.33	-0.47*	-0.56	-0.39	-0.15*	-0.17	-0.12
West Germany									
1984	0.89*	0.56	1.21	-0.78*	-1.09	-0.47	-0.49*	-0.60	-0.27
1989	0.81*	0.47	1.15	-1.02*	-1.39	-0.65	-0.40*	-0.54	-0.26
1994	0.89*	0.52	1.26	-1.35*	-1.77	-0.94	-0.51*	-0.63	-0.38
2000	0.45*	0.23	0.67	-1.72*	-2.01	-1.44	-0.29*	-0.41	-0.18

Source: Luxembourg Income Study (LIS 2003).

Note: Models also include age, age-squared, medium education, marriage, youngest child age four to six, and other household income.

*p < .05

unemployment rates are associated with lower rates of women's employment in the aggregate. The trends in the effect of very young children on women's employment appear to reflect this. Women with children age three or younger were less likely to work during the recession year of 1991, suggesting that economic conditions are important to understanding women's employment in the United States.

The results also show that the number of children was a weaker predictor of women's employment in 2000 than in 1986. The effect of the number of children indicates the influence of having children, controlling for the specific, and often more substantial, influence of having very young children. These results gauge the effects of having children over the life course. U.S. data show a decline of about one-third in the effects of number of children on women's employment from 1986 to 2000.

The bottom panel of table 3.6 shows trends in the individual correlates of women's employment in West Germany from 1984 to 2000. The clearest pattern is that the effect of having a very young child was increasingly negative, more than doubling over the sixteen-year period. The shift in the effect on women's employment of having children age three or younger reflects changes in Germany's parental leave policy over this period. In 1984 Germany offered fourteen weeks of maternity leave. In 1986 parental leave was introduced to provide an extended leave after maternity leave was over. By our next observation in 1989, women were eligible to take seventy-nine weeks of total leave. In 1992 this was raised to 162 weeks, and leave remained at this level for the last two observations in 1994 and 2000 (Gauthier and Bortnick 2001).

Recall the finding from analyses with all LIS countries that longer parental leaves predict a more negative effect of very young children on women's employment. Germany is an interesting illustration of this trend because there is evidence that having older children becomes less negatively associated with women's employment. This signals that the majority of women with infants or toddlers exit the labor force and then return when their children are older. In the later chapters, we see how these women fare relative to men after returning to employment. The trends in West Germany suggest that women's employment is responsive to shifts in family policy and that low rates of employment among mothers may exacerbate inequality between women and men over the life course on other measures like hours worked, occupational segregation, and pay.

CONCLUSION

Although some scholars claim that women's employment is increasingly determined by personal preferences for paid employment or domestic production (Hakim 2000), our research demonstrates that women's and men's employment must be considered in relation to highly variable country-level conditions that institutionalize gender differences in domestic work and work in the paid labor force. The contradictory effects of mechanisms of inclusion and exclusion on the employment of mothers of very young children in particular highlight how states variously institutionalize gender inequality or promote equity in employment by variably concentrating or relieving the demands of caregiving within households and in the hands of women.

Although previous research has drawn similar conclusions (Gornick, Meyers, and Ross 1997, 1998; Gornick and Meyers 2003; Stier, Lewin-Epstein, and Braun 2001), it has not examined the relationship between specific policies and the employment of particular groups of women and men. Our findings suggest that disentangling specific policies is critical to understanding how states influence employment inequalities. While public child care provision and parental leave are generally seen as constituent parts of overall family policy packages, they have starkly contrasting implications for employment outcomes. Measures of overall family policy generosity do not allow researchers to disentangle the effects of specific policies from the cultural norms and expectations about gender roles and employment embodied in overall policy generosity.

Mechanisms of inclusion and exclusion affect the employment of mothers and may have important implications for economic inequality by other measures like hours worked, occupational segregation, and pay. Publicly provided child care socializes the "costs" of children by shifting some of the burden of finding and funding child care from individual families to all workers. Because public provision of child care enables women and men to maintain attachments to the paid labor force, it should not increase gender inequality by other measures, as does extended parental leave.

Even when funded by the public purse, policies of exclusion like lengthy parental leave privatize the costs of children by locating employment inequality within families and between women and men. In states that provide parental leave with wage replacement, the costs of leave-taking are shared across social and demographic groups yet concentrated among caregivers, who are typically women. At the same time, the costs of children are highly individualized in countries *without* parental leave provisions. The costs of children are borne by families, though some families may be better equipped to cope with those costs than others. In this setting, childbearing may not only fuel inequality between women and men but also increase inequality between women.

For example, the United States provides no paid parental leave at the national level. Federal law requires certain employers to provide time off and guarantee job security for their employees, and some employers privately provide paid leave. Women working in professional occupations are much more likely than women working in service industries not only to be able to afford to take unpaid time off from work but also to have employers that fund their time off, through either paid parental leave or the accrual of sick leave or vacation time. American women who work in professional jobs therefore may be able to take parental leave with the expectation of job security and without significant loss of income. However, American women who work in service industries are much less likely to receive parental leave benefits, and even if their employers offer job security during leave, these women may not be able to afford the time off from work. The absence of paid parental leave therefore may increase inequality between professional workers and service workers.

In contrast, Germany's lengthy federally supported parental leave is associated with dramatic labor force withdrawals by women with young children across the economic spectrum. The provision of parental leave may decrease inequality between families, effectively socializing the cost of child-rearing by providing public support for families to care for their own children. However, extended periods of parental leave increase inequality between women and men by concentrating the demands of caregiving within households and on women. It is not surprising then that extended periods of parental leave are negatively related to the employment prospects of mothers of very young children. If and when mothers in Germany return to the paid labor force, they have a deficit of work experience compared with men and are likely to fare poorly on occupational and wage outcomes. Extensive parental leaves therefore exacerbate inequality between women and men, largely because of their effects on mothers' employment.

In summary, inequality is institutionalized through households and within markets. Comparative accounts of employment can be better understood by conducting analyses that situate individuals in the political and economic contexts in which they live. While the laissez-faire context of the United States may locate inequality in class terms, the exclusionary policies and conditions of Germany may exacerbate gender inequality, especially in relation to child-rearing. In the next three chapters, we explore how the employment prospects of women and men influence our understanding of contemporary patterns of, and future prospects for, gender equality within the labor market.

CHAPTER 4

Gender, Family, and Part-Time Work

Employment rates indicate a general level of access to economic opportunities, yet overall employment levels mask important differences in work hours (Buddelmeyer, Mourre, and Ward 2008). There is significant cross-national variability in levels of part-time work among women across countries, as well as scholarly agreement that women are more likely to work part-time than men (see, for example, Blossfeld and Hakim 1997; Fagan and O'Reilly 1998). However, explanations for overall levels of part-time work and gender differences in involvement in part-time work are routinely debated. Part-time work is sometimes viewed as a mechanism that employers use to regulate labor, particularly to accommodate underemployed workers during economic downturns (Buddelmeyer, Mourre, and Ward 2008). Alternatively, part-time work is seen as a means to incorporate women and mothers into the labor market in a way that enables them to manage their disproportionate domestic obligations (Fagan and O'Reilly 1998; Pfau-Effinger 1998).

The implications of differing levels of part-time work, both across countries and between women and men, are also debated (O'Reilly and Bothfeld 2002; Blossfeld 1997). On the one hand, the availability of part-time work may provide a foothold for women or other marginalized workers in the paid labor force (Blossfeld and Hakim 1997). On the other hand, involvement in part-time work may reinforce gendered divisions of labor, particularly when rates of part-time employment differ dramatically between women and men (Fagan and O'Reilly 1998). In any case, it is increasingly clear that cross-national variability in women's and men's involvement in part-time work has potentially important implications for cross-national accounts of gender inequality in the labor market.

HISTORICAL TRENDS IN PART-TIME WORK

Figure 4.1 shows the trends in women's part-time employment in LIS countries from 1983 to 2001. Part-time employment is defined as working thirty or fewer hours per week. The top panel of the figure demonstrates general stability in the level of part-time work among women, with a mean that hovers between 25 and 30 percent over the entire period.

This average conceals important variability in both the level and trend of women's involvement in part-time work across countries. In 2001 fewer than 10 percent of employed women worked part-time in the Czech Republic, whereas almost 60 percent of employed women worked part-time in the Netherlands. Moreover, while there has been a fairly steady increase in part-time work in conservative-corporatist countries like the Netherlands, part-time work has declined in other countries, including most of the social democratic countries and the United States.

The conservative-corporatist countries of continental and southern Europe had the highest average rates of part-time work among women as of 2000, but also exhibited a great deal of variability. The average level of part-time work among women in conservative-corporatist countries was over 30 percent in 2001. Although all the conservative-corporatist countries experienced growth in part-time employment among women, the overall increase masks considerable differences among countries. The Netherlands stands out for its particularly high and increasing rates of women's part-time employment, which rose from approximately 45 percent in 1983 to almost 60 percent in 2001. The Dutch economy has been called a "part-time" economy; by contrast, part-time employment is much less common in the southern European countries. In Spain, for example, only 17 percent of employed women were working part-time in 2001, even though part-time employment grew through the 1980s and 1990s.

Very few women were working part-time in the eastern European economies during our short window of observation. There is variability across countries and a small downward trend, but low absolute levels. Rates range

Figure 4.1   Trends in the Percentage of Working Women Employed
Part-Time, Thirty Hours per Week or Less, 1983 to 2001

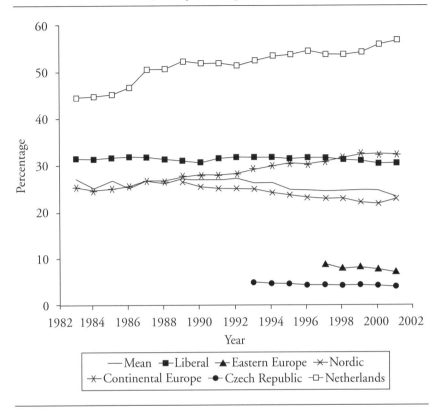

Source: Organization for Economic Cooperation and Development (OECD 2002).

from a low of 4 to 6 percent of employed women in the Czech Republic and Hungary to a high of 17 to 19 percent in Poland, with Slovenia and Russia in the middle.

Overall, liberal countries show a steady level of part-time work, hovering just above 30 percent, but as with conservative-corporatist countries, the average masks significant heterogeneity. After reaching a peak of almost 23 percent in the early 1980s, by 2000 just under one-fifth of American women workers were employed part-time. The level of part-time employment among women in the United Kingdom held steady around 40 percent through the last two decades of the twentieth century. In Australia the level of part-time work had grown to over 40 percent by 2000. There was also a slight increase

Figure 4.2   Trends in the Percentage of Working Men Employed
Part-Time, Thirty Hours per Week or Less, 1983 to 2001

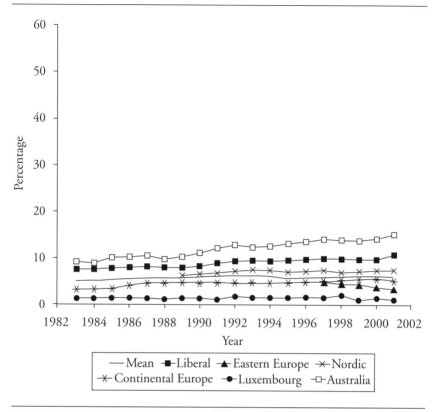

Source: Organization for Economic Cooperation and Development (OECD 2002).

in the percentage of Canadian women working part-time through the 1980s and 1990s; by 2000, nearly one-third of employed women in Canada were working thirty hours a week or less.

The incidence of part-time work among women has exhibited a slow decline in the social democratic countries of northern Europe. In 1990 the average level of part-time work was over 25 percent in the Nordic countries, but by 2000 it had fallen below 25 percent. The biggest declines were in Denmark, followed by somewhat smaller declines in Norway and Sweden. Finland, with much lower levels of part-time employment among women, exhibited small increases in women's involvement in part-time work in the late 1990s.

Men's rates of part-time employment, shown in figure 4.2, are drastically lower than women's and exhibit considerably less variation across countries. Although most countries experienced growth in men's involvement in part-time work through the 1990s in percentage terms, the absolute level of men's part-time employment continued to be exceptionally low.

The conservative-corporatist countries of continental and southern Europe have witnessed growth in men's involvement in part-time labor, although the overall level averaged only 6 percent in 2001. There are very few men working part-time in the eastern European economies—on average only 4 percent. The level of part-time employment among men in the United States has fluctuated but remains under 10 percent. Other liberal countries have shown greater increases in rates of part-time work among men, on average increasing from 8 to 11 percent. The level of part-time work among men has grown most in Australia, which posted the highest levels in 2001 at 16 percent. The incidence of part-time work among men has increased slowly in the social democratic countries of northern Europe—from 6 to 8 percent, on average, through the 1990s.

To get a better understanding of the variation in part-time work relative to full-time work at the country level, we display in figures 4.3 and 4.4 the percentage of all working adults, broken down by gender, and report employment by part-time and full-time status for LIS countries in the mid-1990s. These rates are different from those presented in figures 4.1 and 4.2, which showed the percentage of workers who were employed part-time.

There are three things to notice about figures 4.3 and 4.4. First, there is little clustering by regime type. In fact, the three countries posting the highest rates of women's part-time employment are the Netherlands, Sweden, and the United Kingdom, representing three different welfare state regimes. Second, countries with similar rates of part-time employment do not share full-time employment rates. For example, the United States and Australia show the same level of part-time employment in 1994, about 20 percent of working-age women, but very different levels of full-time employment. About 33 percent of working-age women were employed full-time in Australia, compared to 55 percent in the United States. Third, there is little correspondence between women's and men's part-time employment rates. In many countries in which women's part-time employment is higher than average, we see that men's part-time employment is lower than average.

Cross-national differences in levels and trends of women's and men's work

Figure 4.3   Percentage of Women Working Full- and Part-Time, Mid-1990s

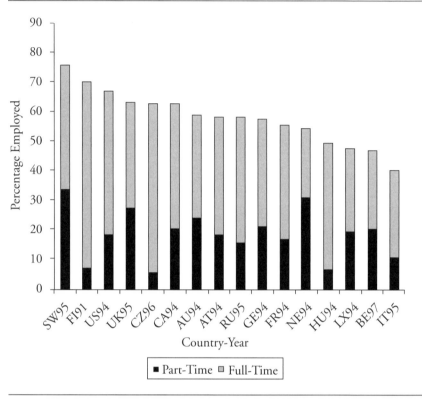

Source: Luxembourg Income Study (LIS 2003).
Note: See country abbreviations in figure A.1.

hours underscore that gender differences in access to economic opportunities vary considerably across countries. Although we do not have information on variability in the quality of part-time work across countries, the number of working hours is more tightly coupled with the quality of employment (for example, benefits, provisions for unemployment, guarantees of returning to full-time work when desired) in some countries than in others. Cross-national differences in the quality of employment—in addition to the number of hours worked—may have important effects on who becomes involved in part-time work and its consequences for other economic outcomes, including occupational segregation and wages. The causes of cross-national differences in part-time work are the central concern of the remainder of this

Figure 4.4   Percentage of Men Working Full- and Part-Time, Mid-1990s

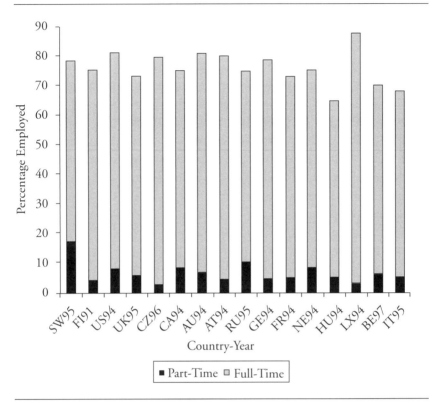

Source: Luxembourg Income Study (LIS 2003).
Note: See country abbreviations in figure A.1.

chapter. Our findings provide important clues about how social policy and employment conditions structure tradeoffs between labor market inclusion and equality.

THE LIFE COURSE AND HOURS WORKED

Similar to the effects of employment on labor supply generally, we expect educational attainment to be positively associated with working in both full- and part-time jobs. In general, we expect that highly educated individuals are more likely to be working—in either full- or part-time jobs—than their less-educated counterparts. Highly educated individuals may also be more likely to opt for full-time than part-time employment.

Existing theories of employers' demand for labor and women's and men's supply of labor lead us to expect that child-rearing will have different implications for the employment of women and men in full- and part-time jobs and will exhibit much more variability across countries. As pointed out in chapter 3, existing research suggests that child-rearing is associated with lower employment rates among women and higher employment rates among men, though effects vary across countries and in relation to mechanisms of inclusion and exclusion. We expect that women with children, particularly young children, will be less likely to work, either part- or full-time, than women without children, and vice versa for men. We further expect that the effects of child-rearing will be especially acute for women's involvement in full-time jobs, since the demands of such work may be inconsistent with those of child-rearing. Part-time work is a strategy used by both workers and employers to manage the competing demands of employment and child-rearing (see, for example, Fagan and O'Reilly 1998; Pfau-Effinger 1998).

Table 4.1 shows the percentage of women in the LIS countries who reported full-time or part-time employment in the 1990s. (Table A.4A reports all LIS years.) It displays employment rates for all working-age respondents, respondents with a high level of education, respondents with a youngest child age six or younger, and respondents with a youngest child age seven to seventeen. Table 4.2 shows analogous figures for men. (Table A.4B reports all LIS years.)

In most countries the part-time employment rate for all respondents is substantially different from the rates of specific subgroups, which vary significantly within countries. In the Netherlands, for example, 24 percent of women age eighteen to sixty-four are employed full-time. The corresponding rate of full-time employment for highly educated women is 42 percent. For women with children age six or younger and those with a youngest child age seven to seventeen, the rates of full-time employment are 10 and 12 percent, respectively. In contrast, the percentage of women working part-time varies from 34 percent of highly educated women to 43 percent of women with young children to 45 percent of women with older children.

Across a range of countries, there is evidence that both educational investments and child-rearing obligations structure the hours worked by women and men. Women and men with high levels of education are generally more likely to work full-time. In all cases (except for men in Belgium and France), respondents with high levels of education show a higher full-time employment rate than all respondents.

Table 4.1 Full- and Part-Time Employment of Women, by Parental Status and Education, Mid-1990s

Country	Year	Full-Time				Part-Time			
		All	Highly Educated	Young Children Age Zero to Six	Older Children Age Seven to Seventeen	All	Highly Educated	Young Children Age Zero to Six	Older Children Age Seven to Seventeen
Austria	1994	42%	52%	37%	44%	18%	26%	23%	24%
Australia	1994	33	49	15	29	20	21	21	30
Belgium	1997	31	42	37	30	16	21	26	23
Canada	1994	43	50	36	44	20	22	22	25
Czech Republic	1996	62	72	33	82	5	6	5	7
Finland	1991	70	78	64	82	8	9	10	9
France	1994	39	44	40	42	16	15	17	19
Germany	1994	38	51	17	36	20	23	22	30
Hungary	1994	41	57	31	57	5	19	4	7
Italy	1995	30	33	32	31	12	67	16	14
Luxembourg	1994	32	41	23	23	15	15	21	22
Netherlands	1994	24	42	10	12	31	34	43	45
Russian Federation	1995	40	43	32	50	14	19	12	16
Sweden	1995	36	49	33	39	28	25	33	30
United Kingdom	1995	32	45	16	25	23	21	24	34
United States	1994	55	62	47	55	19	21	21	24
Mean		41	51	31	43	17	23	20	22

Source: Luxembourg Income Study (LIS 2003).

Table 4.2   Full- and Part-Time Employment of Men, by Parental Status and Education, Mid-1990s

Country	Year	Full-Time				Part-Time			
		All	Highly Educated	Young Children Age Zero to Six	Older Children Age Seven to Seventeen	All	Highly Educated	Young Children Age Zero to Six	Older Children Age Seven to Seventeen
Austria	1994	77%	80%	89%	85%	3%	11%	2%	2%
Australia	1994	64	74	69	66	5	5	3	6
Belgium	1997	64	62	81	70	4	8	6	3
Canada	1994	67	72	80	71	8	8	4	8
Czech Republic	1996	84	89	92	91	2	2	1	2
Finland	1991	79	85	92	89	4	4	3	3
France	1994	62	59	78	66	4	5	3	4
Germany	1994	76	80	85	82	3	7	3	4
Hungary	1994	71	72	87	55	2	7	2	1
Italy	1995	51	61	61	72	5	28	6	5
Luxembourg	1994	81	86	96	90	2	3	1	1
Netherlands	1994	70	78	89	76	8	8	5	7
Russian Federation	1995	57	59	61	62	9	11	8	9
Sweden	1995	52	61	74	69	13	11	9	5
United Kingdom	1995	55	66	60	61	3	3	2	4
United States	1994	80	85	88	82	9	8	5	9
Mean		68	73	80	74	5	8	4	5

Source: Luxembourg Income Study (LIS 2003).

The relationship between education and part-time employment, however, is more complex. In most countries, part-time employment is more common among the highly educated than among all respondents. Italy presents the most extreme, if not uncommon, example. Whereas only 12 and 5 percent of Italian women and men, respectively, are employed part-time, 67 percent of highly educated women and 28 percent of highly educated men work part-time hours. The relationship between education and part-time employment suggests that highly educated workers who are unable to work full-time, for whatever reason, are more likely to be employed part-time than not employed. Alternatively, highly educated workers may demand employer accommodations for part-time work, may seek work in industries where part-time work is more readily available, or may successfully support families on a part-time income. In any case, more highly educated workers are generally more likely to be working—in either full- or part-time jobs—than those with less education.

As we expected, child-rearing has different implications for the full- and part-time employment outcomes of women and men. Having young children age zero to six in the household is associated with lower levels of women's full-time employment, but with higher levels of women's part-time employment. In most countries, women's full-time employment rebounds with older children (notable exceptions are the Netherlands and Luxembourg), while part-time employment rates are static. In the Czech Republic—a particularly dramatic example of this pattern—62 percent of all women are full-time workers, but 33 percent of mothers with young children versus 82 percent of mothers with older children are employed full-time. In contrast, men in most countries are more likely to work full-time and less likely to work part-time when they live with young children. Men living with older children are less likely to work full-time and more likely to work part-time.

In summary, while education shows consistent relationships with women's and men's involvement in full- and part-time work, young children are associated with substantial cleavages in the work hours of women and men. Mothers of young children are consistently more likely to work part-time than other women, but fathers of young children exhibit higher rates of full-time employment.

Table 4.3 reports the mean effects of education and child-rearing on women's and men's full-time and part-time employment in comparison to non-employment. The table also shows median, minimum, and maximum effect sizes, with country-years indicated in parentheses. The regression frame-

Table 4.3 Cross-National Variability in Multinomial Logistic Regression Predicting Full- and Part-Time Employment

	Women			Men		
	Highly Educated	Youngest Child Age Zero to Three	Number of Children	Highly Educated	Youngest Child Age Zero to Three	Number of Children
Full-time						
Mean	1.11	−0.85	−0.47	0.74	0.15	−0.06
Median	1.15	−0.64	−0.42	0.76	0.16	−0.07
	(AU85/IT91)	(CN87/US91)	(CN87/IT91)	(CN97/CZ96)	(FI91/NE94)	(US74/LX97)
Minimum	−0.24	−3.39	−0.94	−0.16	−0.68	−0.36
	(GE84)	(CZ96)	(NE94)	(FR94)	(UK86)	(BE88)
Maximum	2.10	0.81	−0.14	2.07	1.19	0.39
	(BE92)	(BE97)	(HU91)	(HU94)	(BE88)	(AT97)
Part-time						
Mean	0.95	−0.56	−0.07	1.60	0.02	−0.04
Median	0.85	−0.56	−0.03	1.04	0.02	−0.02
	(RF95/CA97)	(GE89/US86)	(HU84/UK96)	(US94/US00)	(RF95/US74)	(CA94/US91)
Minimum	0.00	−3.37	−0.30	−0.31	−1.86	−0.58
	(LX00)	(CZ96)	(GE84)	(UK95)	(AT94)	(BE97)
Maximum	3.33	0.95	0.23	21.04	1.46	0.43
	(HU94)	(BE88)	(HU91)	(LX94)	(BE88)	(LX00)

Source: Luxembourg Income Study (LIS 2003).

Note: Models also include age, age-squared, medium education, marriage, youngest child age four to six, and other household income. See country abbrevi-

work allows us to examine the specific effects of education and children on full- and part-time work while holding other relevant information (such as age, marital status, and access to other household income) constant.

Higher levels of education are consistently related to higher probabilities of full-time and part-time employment for both women and men. The mean effect of education on involvement in full-time work is larger, on average, for women than for men, suggesting that women who work full-time are more strongly selected on the basis of education than men. In contrast, the mean effect of education on *part-time* work is larger for men than for women, suggesting that part-time work is more inclusive of women with lower levels of education.

There is a great deal of variation, however, in the relationship between education and full- and part-time employment for women and men, indicating that in some countries workers are more strongly selected on education than in others. Variability in the individual-level determinants of hours worked may stem from cross-national differences in the availability and relative quality of full- and part-time jobs. Although we lack sufficient data to investigate that conjecture directly, the available evidence is consistent with such a claim. For example, while highly educated women were disproportionately concentrated in full-time work in Belgium in 1992, high levels of education showed a negative relationship with women's full-time work in Germany in 1984. The strongest positive association between education and part-time employment was found in Hungary in 1994, though the relationship is positive across all countries. Among men, the strongest positive effects of education on full-time employment were found in Hungary in 1994, and in Luxembourg in 1994 for part-time employment. In only a few cases is the education-employment relationship negative for either full- or part-time work: education was negatively associated with men's full-time employment in France in 1994 and with men's part-time employment in the United Kingdom in 1995.

On average, across the fifteen countries we study, having very young children (age zero to three) decreases the likelihood of women's full- and part-time employment in comparison to non-employment. That is, women with an infant or toddler are more likely to exit the labor force than to work—either full- or part-time—compared to similar women who do not have very young children. In contrast, there is, on average, a small positive effect of living with very young children on men's full-time and part-time employment.

The magnitude of and variability in the effect of having very young children on full- and part-time employment is larger for women than for men. Although living with an infant or toddler is generally negative for women's employment in both full- and part-time work, and those effects are large and significant in some cases (for example, the Czech Republic in 1996), in other cases the effects are more muted or even positive (Belgium in 1988 and 1997). Among men, the effects of living with very young children are generally positive and sometimes large (Belgium in 1988), but sometimes having very young children in the household is negatively associated with men's full-time employment (United Kingdom in 1986) or part-time employment (Austria in 1994). In general, these results confirm those in chapter 3: having an infant or toddler in the home signals a key turning point in women's work lives and is associated not only with wholesale exits from the paid labor force but also with women's concentration in part-time work.

The effect of the number of children on full-time employment is negative for women, and there is little relationship for men. Across countries, however, the effects of the number of children show less variability than the effects of having very young children. The effects of children, generally, on women's and men's part-time employment converge over time, and there is little evidence that older children have an effect on part-time employment across the fifteen countries we study. These results indicate that the cross-national variation in the effects of having children is particularly salient in the early stages of child-rearing and less so at later stages.

CROSS-NATIONAL VARIABILITY IN WOMEN'S AND MEN'S WORK HOURS

There is wide variation across countries in the levels of women's and men's full- and part-time employment. Table 4.4 displays the relationship between mean levels of full- and part-time employment and national-level conditions, separately for women and men. Controlling for all other national-level factors, the year is significant for women only. Thus, we see a significant increase across countries in women's employment in full- and part-time work over the period, though no discernible trend for men.

As shown in chapter 3, we find no significant correlations between women's political empowerment and overall rates of full- or part-time employment for women or men. In general, the level of women's involvement in full-time work is negatively associated with overall levels of unemployment and per capita GDP, while service-sector growth fosters the employment of women in

Table 4.4   The Association Between National Conditions and Mean Full-Time and Part-Time Employment Levels

	Full-Time		Part-Time	
	Women	Men	Women	Men
Intercept	34.734*	97.291*	–1.520	1.615
Year	0.855*	–0.251	0.164*	0.018
Gender egalitarianism				
Women in parliament	–27.987	28.080	15.288	4.891
Economic conditions				
Unemployment	–126.804*	–197.815*	19.653	4.970
Service-sector growth	138.178⁺	–36.890	15.561	53.688⁺
Per capita GDP				
Growth	–120.800*	46.533	0.879	–26.025
Mechanisms of inclusion				
Maternity leave	26.792	–23.826⁺	–4.280	3.286
and inequality				
Part-time employment	–23.817	–21.007	64.989*	4.242
and equality				
Child care	23.842	–1.323	–10.930	1.002
Mechanisms of exclusion				
and equality				
Union density	–18.228	–10.661	9.482*	1.361
and inequality				
Parental leave	1.589	2.293	–1.398	–0.889
Adjusted R-squared	0.201	0.561	0.756	0.057

Source: Luxembourg Income Study (LIS 2003).
*T-ratio ≥ 2; ⁺T-ratio ≥ 1.8

full-time jobs. Among men, there is a negative association between unemployment and full-time employment, though growth in the service sector is positively associated with men's involvement in part-time work.

Table 4.4 offers some evidence that state policies and conditions affect overall levels of part-time work among women. Not surprisingly, women's involvement in part-time work is associated with the overall level of part-time work.

The overall level of men's involvement in part-time work, however, is not associated with the availability of part-time work. In short, where the part-time labor force is larger, greater numbers of women, but not men, are employed part-time. In addition, union density is positively associated, in the aggregate, with the level of part-time work among women. Where union density is higher, greater numbers of women, but not men, are employed part-time.

In summary, these findings emphasize the extent to which part-time work is performed by women across countries. Large part-time workforces are associated with the entrenchment of women in part-time work. Moreover, countries with high levels of unionization foster the specialization of women in part-time work. Furthermore, these results are robust to the inclusion of other national political and economic conditions purported to affect gender differences in work hours. Although we cannot distinguish between labor supply and employer demand effects, our findings suggest that macro-level conditions help to explain women's concentration in part-time jobs.

INSTITUTIONALIZING GENDER INEQUALITY
IN HOURS WORKED

Mechanisms of inclusion and exclusion should affect the level of women's part- and full-time employment across countries and over time through their effects on the employment prospects of women, especially mothers, in different social and demographic groups. Table 4.5 summarizes results from models that examine how the effects of social and demographic characteristics at the individual level vary with national institutional context. Specifically, we test how the effects of education and the presence and age of children in the household vary in relation to mechanisms of inclusion and exclusion.

The first column of results in Table 4.5 shows the relationship between national-level context and the effects of higher levels of education on women's full-time employment in the top panel and part-time employment in the bottom panel. The intercept shows a positive and statistically significant relationship between higher levels of education and women's full- and part-time employment, in comparison to not being employed. The positive effect of year indicates that the relationship between education and employment in both full- and part-time jobs becomes more significant over time. Reading down the column, we see that where the part-time sector is larger, the effect of education is more positive for women's full-time employment and less positive for their part-time employment. The effect of education on women's overall employment is more positive where publicly funded child care is more

Table 4.5   The Association Between National Conditions and Factors Predicting Full- and Part-Time Employment

	Women			Men		
	Highly Educated	Youngest Child Age Zero to Three	Number of Children	Highly Educated	Youngest Child Age Zero to Three	Number of Children
Full-time						
Intercept	1.016*	−1.711+	−0.649*	0.519	0.990*	−0.024
Year	0.045*	0.093*	−0.002	0.019	0.011	−0.001
Part-time employment	2.428*	−3.335	−1.663*	−0.386	−2.577*	−0.376
Child care	2.850*	5.710*	0.354	−0.829	2.969*	−0.548*
Union density	−0.941*	0.312	−0.177	−0.422	−0.073+	0.000
Parental leave	−0.224	−0.981*	−0.058	−0.109	−0.266+	0.025
Part-time						
Intercept	2.125*	−0.331	−0.358*	2.923*	1.338*	0.170
Year	0.043+	0.052*	−0.004	0.018	0.007	0.005
Part-time employment	−3.225+	−1.906	0.216	−2.042	−1.827	0.122
Child care	2.877+	3.243*	−0.228	0.600	3.444*	−0.764+
Union density	−1.991*	0.760	−0.025	0.419	−0.073	−0.188
Parental leave	−0.404	−0.730*	−0.011	−0.104	−0.100	−0.043

Source: Luxembourg Income Study (LIS 2003).

Note: Models also include age, age-squared, medium education, marriage, youngest child age four to six, and other household income at the individual level and women's employment, service-sector growth, per capita GDP, unemployment, maternity leave, women in parliament, and year at the country level.

*T-ratio $\geq$ 2; +T-ratio $\geq$ 1.8

widely available, and it is less positive (and becoming negative) where union density is higher.

As in chapter 3, mechanisms of inclusion and exclusion are associated with the effects of education and child-rearing on women's full- and part-time employment—but again, not exactly as our theoretical framework would predict. Where part-time employment is greater, the positive effect of having more education on full-time employment increases, but the positive effect of having more education on part-time employment decreases. This means that countries with large part-time workforces do a worse job of incorporating women with low levels of education into full-time jobs and do a better job of incorporating women with low levels of education into part-time jobs. Moreover, where part-time employment is high, highly educated women are more likely to be found in full-time jobs and less likely to be found in part-time ones.

It is somewhat striking that the availability of part-time employment is negatively and significantly associated with the effects of the number of children on women's full-time employment. Countries with large part-time workforces do a worse job of incorporating mothers with children into full-time jobs. It is quite likely in this instance that women, even those with older children, maintain part-time jobs and continue to shoulder disproportionate domestic responsibilities. Alternatively, employers may be reluctant to hire women with children in full-time jobs when they can hire them into part-time work instead, leaving full-time jobs open for workers who have no family commitments and the associated domestic obligations.

Publicly provided child care, another mechanism of inclusion, shows a consistent and positive association with the effects of education on both full- and part-time employment. In other words, highly educated women are more likely to be employed full- or part-time where child care provision is high, suggesting that child care may facilitate the participation of highly educated mothers in the paid labor force. As expected, publicly provided child care is associated with a decrease in the negative effect of very young children on working full- and part-time. Differences in the likelihood of employment— in both full- and part-time jobs—between women with very young children and those without very young children tend to shrink with higher levels of publicly funded child care.

Mechanisms of exclusion are significantly associated with the effects of education and child-rearing on full- and part-time employment. Union density, associated with exclusion, correlates with less educational specialization among women in both full- and part-time work. Higher levels of union density are associated with more negative effects of education on both full- and part-time employment. Parental leave, in contrast, has significant and negative associations with the effect of having very young children on women's involvement in both full- and part-time employment. Differences in the likelihood of employment—in both full- and part-time jobs—between mothers and nonmothers tend to be larger in countries with longer parental leaves. Long parental leaves are associated with a greater likelihood of mothers' unemployment, even in comparison to working part-time.

Table 4.5 illustrates that the social and demographic correlates of men's full- and part-time employment are generally less sensitive to country context. Country-level conditions do not appear to influence the effects of education on men's full- or part-time employment, although a variety of factors, including mechanisms of inclusion and exclusion, change the effects of children—especially very young children. Specifically, part-time employment is associated with lower concentrations of fathers of very young children in full-time work, the availability of child care is associated with higher full- and part-time employment among fathers with very young children, and union density and parental leave have somewhat unanticipated and negative associations with the employment of fathers with very young children in full-time jobs.

In summary, there is consistent evidence that mechanisms of inclusion and exclusion condition the effects of education and child-rearing on women's full- and part-time employment. The availability of part-time employment fosters the inclusion of women in the workforce, yet for women it commonly signifies a two-tiered labor market in which full-time employment is performed by well-educated women and those with few domestic obligations. Public child care is associated with higher levels of women's employment; it enables mothers with very young children to take on full-time work. Finally, long parental leaves are associated with the wholesale exclusion of mothers of very young children from paid work—both full- and part-time. In contrast, men's employment prospects—and hours worked—are less clearly structured by these same mechanisms of inclusion and exclusion.

SPOTLIGHT: TRENDS IN WOMEN'S WORK HOURS IN THE UNITED STATES AND WEST GERMANY

Again we turn to time-series data from the United States (1986 to 2000) and West Germany (1984 to 2000) to observe in greater detail how country context shapes economic outcomes. In this section, we explore whether we can observe the influence of institutional conditions on the social and demographic correlates of full- and part-time employment within countries over time.

Table 4.6 displays the trends in women's full-time and part-time employment rates, illustrating a large gulf between employment patterns in the United States and West Germany, particularly among women with young children. In the United States, women age eighteen to sixty-four increased their full-time participation by sixteen percentage points, moving from 44 to 60 percent from 1986 to 2000. Although there is variation in the level of full-time employment between subgroups, all groups experienced a similar increase during these fourteen years. During this period, there was almost no change in part-time employment rates among U.S. women.

In contrast, in West Germany, there was almost no change in *full-time* employment rates from 1984 to 2000, and full-time rates were very low in comparison to the United States. Whereas 52 percent of mothers with young children were employed full-time in the United States, only 10 percent of West German mothers were. West Germany does show a significant increase in part-time employment rates: all women increased their part-time participation by nine percentage points, moving from 18 to 27 percent. The increase in part-time employment was especially dramatic for women with older children: rising by seventeen points, their rate moved from 23 to 40 percent. West German women with young children, however, increased their involvement by only seven percentage points and in 2000 were more likely to be out of the labor force than working in either a full- or part-time job.

Overall, the trends show that American women's increases in employment have been driven by full-time employment, whereas West German women's increases have been driven by part-time employment. Furthermore, the presence of children—especially young children—affects the hours worked by women in West Germany to a greater extent than in the United States.

Table 4.7 shows the trends in the individual-level correlates of women's full-time and part-time employment in the United States and West Germany in the years in which we have data. In the United States, the effect of education is relatively stable across the time period, but the effects of having children vary over time.

Turning our attention to the effects of very young children on women's full- and part-time employment, we see that the estimate and the confidence interval for 1991 stand out from the other years. In chapter 3, we found that

Table 4.6 Trends in Women's Full- and Part-Time Employment Rates in the United States and West Germany

		Full-Time				Part-Time		
	All	Highly Educated	Young Children Age Zero to Six	Older Children Age Seven to Seventeen	All	Highly Educated	Young Children Age Zero to Six	Older Children Age Seven to Seventeen
United States								
1986	44%	52%	34%	45%	16%	18%	17%	18%
1991	55	63	45	55	19	21	20	23
1994	55	62	47	55	19	21	21	24
1997	57	63	50	58	19	20	20	21
2000	60	65	52	60	17	18	19	20
West Germany								
1984	33	46	14	29	18	24	23	23
1989	36	47	14	31	19	23	26	28
1994	35	43	12	27	23	29	25	34
2000	36	47	10	32	27	26	32	40

Source: Luxembourg Income Study (LIS 2003).

Table 4.7 Multinomial Logistic Regression Predicting Women's Full- and Part-Time Employment in the United States and West Germany

	High Education			Youngest Child Age Zero to Three			Number of Children		
	Estimate	95 Percent Confidence Interval		Estimate	95 Percent Confidence Interval		Estimate	95 Percent Confidence Interval	
Full-time compared to not employed									
United States									
1986	1.37*	1.21	1.54	-0.58*	-0.76	-0.41	-0.34*	-0.40	-0.28
1991	1.50*	1.42	1.58	-0.66*	-0.74	-0.58	-0.34*	-0.37	-0.31
1994	1.46*	1.38	1.54	-0.45*	-0.53	-0.36	-0.35*	-0.28	-0.32
1997	1.42*	1.34	1.50	-0.38*	-0.47	-0.29	-0.28*	-0.31	-0.25
2000	1.32*	1.24	1.40	-0.44*	-0.53	-0.35	-0.23*	-0.26	-0.19
West Germany									
1984	1.01*	0.62	1.39	-1.39*	-1.80	-0.99	-0.59*	-0.73	-0.45
1989	0.91*	0.47	1.34	-1.73*	-2.26	-1.21	-0.75*	-0.92	-0.57
1994	0.91*	0.50	1.32	-1.53*	-2.14	-0.92	-0.85*	-1.02	-0.68
2000	0.69*	0.43	0.95	-2.27*	-2.68	-1.85	-0.66*	-0.83	-0.49

Part-time compared to
not employed

United States									
1986	0.98*	0.78	1.19	-0.57*	-0.78	-0.36	-0.02	-0.09	0.05
1991	1.18*	1.08	1.27	-0.89*	-0.99	-0.79	0.01	-0.02	0.04
1994	1.19*	1.10	1.29	-0.70*	-0.80	-0.60	0.00	-0.03	0.03
1997	1.09*	0.99	1.19	-0.62*	-0.73	-0.52	0.02	-0.02	0.05
2000	1.13*	1.03	1.24	-0.65*	-0.76	-0.53	0.05*	0.01	0.08
West Germany									
1984	0.83*	0.44	1.23	-0.50*	-0.87	-0.13	-0.29*	-0.43	-0.15
1989	0.66*	0.22	1.10	-0.70*	-1.12	-0.28	-0.14	-0.31	0.02
1994	0.84*	0.38	1.30	-0.97*	-1.45	-0.49	-0.20*	-0.35	-0.05
2000	0.22	-0.03	0.46	-1.26*	-1.57	-0.94	-0.08	-0.20	0.04

Source: Luxembourg Income Study (LIS 2003).

Note: Models also include age, age-squared, medium education, marriage, youngest child age four to six, and other household income.

*p < .05

higher unemployment rates are associated with lower rates of women's employment. Although we do not find evidence of this in the cross-national analyses of full- or part-time employment, in the United States the effects of very young children on women's part-time employment covary with (or trend in the same direction as) rates of unemployment. Women with infants or toddlers were less likely to work during the recession year of 1991, particularly on a part-time basis, suggesting that economic conditions are especially salient for women's employment in the United States.

The results also show that, controlling for having very young children in the household, women with children were more likely to be in the labor force—and particularly in full-time employment—in 2000 than in 1986. The negative effect of the number of children on full-time employment shows a decline of about one-third over time.

Now we turn to trends in the effects, shown in table 4.7, of individual correlates of women's full-time and part-time employment in West Germany from 1984 to 2000. Beginning with education, there is evidence that having more education is becoming a less important determinant of hours worked over time. The positive effect of education on both full-time and part-time employment decreased from 1984 to 2000.

The decreasing salience of education, however, coexists with the increasing significance of family responsibilities. The effect of having a very young child was increasingly negative, on both full-time and part-time employment, over the sixteen-year period. The shift in the effect of living with an infant or toddler on women's employment correlates well with changes in Germany's parental leave policy over this period. Expansions of parental leave through the 1980s and 1990s in Germany correlate with increased effects of very young children on women's labor market opportunities. Recall that in the multilevel analyses we find that longer parental leaves predict a more negative effect of very young children on women's part-time employment. The trends in West Germany suggest that family policies—especially parental leave—help explain mothers' retreat from both full- and part-time employment.

CONCLUSION

A focus on the determinants of full- and part-time employment further illuminates how mechanisms of inclusion and exclusion structure gender inequality. While part-time work fosters the involvement of women—and mothers—in the paid labor market, it also typically signals a bifurcated labor market. In economies with large part-time workforces, highly educated women are increasingly concentrated in full-time work, while less-educated women are disproportionately found in part-time jobs. Moreover, when the part-time workforce is large, mothers are increasingly concentrated in part-time work. The concentration of mothers in part-time work is heightened in large families and persists over the life course. In contrast, publicly provided child care fosters the labor force involvement of women, especially those with very young children, in both full- and part-time jobs.

Long parental leaves are associated with lower levels of both women's employment and women's representation in full-time employment, and these effects are particularly acute among mothers. What is particularly striking is that the effects of extended parental leaves appear to be long-lasting, influencing even the employment prospects of women with older children and leading to an increased concentration of mothers in part-time employment.

Although these results are generally consistent with the findings about women's labor force participation presented in chapter 3, they reveal how state policies and conditions structure the inequalities associated with domestic obligations, which in turn foster gender inequalities in the labor market on another dimension. In countries that support women's efforts to work but do not necessarily alleviate the domestic demands associated with child-rearing (for example, by offering part-time work), mothers are disproportionately concentrated in part-time work. Perhaps more importantly, mothers' disproportionate concentration in part-time work, rather than being confined to the few years when their children are young, endures over the life course.

Large part-time workforces incorporate women into the paid labor market, but they simultaneously foster gender inequality within the labor market. The maintenance of a large part-time workforce disadvantages women, initially by cleaving their economic opportunities from men's when they have children, and more enduringly by entrenching them in part-time work even after the most intensive demands of child-rearing subside. Part-time work is a strategy that individuals use to balance the demands of work and family obligations; it also appears to be a strategy that employers use to accommodate and differentiate employees.

The quality and pay of part-time work vary across countries. Some of the negative effects of part-time work might be alleviated by policies that ensure equal pay, the provision of benefits, and fluid transfers between full- and part-time work. Nonetheless, our evidence suggests that women's disproportionate concentration in part-time work—across countries—is intimately tied to gender differences in the domestic obligations associated with child-rearing. Unfortunately, the evidence suggests that even short stints of part-time work have long-term implications, and we suspect that large part-time workforces fuel gender inequality in occupation and pay—not just among mothers of young children but among mothers of older children and women more generally.

In contrast, lengthy parental leaves exclude women—and women with very young children in particular—from the labor market and reinforce gender inequality within the home. In countries where parental leaves are long, mothers, but not fathers, are increasingly likely to leave the labor market altogether, eschewing both full- and part-time work. Women's disproportionate attention to the domestic sphere when children are young may have important implications for economic inequality not only between mothers and fathers when their children are young but also at other points in the life course. High rates of labor force withdrawal among mothers may exist alongside strong economic performance of women on other measures. Because women and mothers who remain in the labor market when it is normative to leave may be especially skilled, or perceived as exceptionally productive, they may be more likely to be disproportionately rewarded for their work.

In summary, like gender differences in employment, gender differences in hours worked are institutionalized by state policies and conditions that structure the division of labor within households and markets. Policies and conditions that relieve households from the burdens of caregiving foster women's involvement not only in paid work but in full-time jobs. Those that concentrate the demands of caregiving within households are associated with lower rates of female involvement in both full- and part-time jobs. Finally, policies and conditions that accommodate the dual demands of caregiving and work are associated with high levels of women's employment, but also their disproportionate concentration in part-time work.

The focus in this chapter on gender differences in hours worked begins to illustrate some of the tradeoffs between employment and other measures of economic well-being. Women's overrepresentation in part-time work is likely to be associated with increased occupational sex segregation and lower wages. Conversely, low rates of women's employment—in both full- and part-time work—are likely to be associated with strong economic performance among women without children, but also with enduring economic disadvantage for women with children. In the next two chapters, we consider these tradeoffs as we examine the individual- and national-level factors that influence gender inequality in occupation and pay.

CHAPTER 5

Gender, Family, and Occupational Sex Segregation

Despite women's inroads into the labor market through the late twentieth century, there is ample evidence across countries that women and men are segregated within the labor market (Charles and Grusky 2004; Chang 2000). By a host of measures, and across countries, women and men are located in different occupations and are not equally represented in managerial jobs (Grusky and Charles 1998; Charles and Grusky 2004; Jacobs 1993; Jacobs and Lim 1995; Bridges 2003; Reskin 1993; Chang 2000). The segregation of women and men into different jobs—horizontal segregation—has been framed in relation to norms about gender and cultural beliefs about appropriate work for women and men (Charles and Grusky 2004). Accounts of gender segregation into high-paying and managerial jobs—vertical segregation—emphasize the role of skills and experience (see, for example, Breen and García-Peñalosa 2002) and the structure of the labor market, including women's concentration in part-time and public-sector work (Hansen 1997; Melkas and Anker 1997; Charles and Grusky 2004).

The implications of gender segregation in occupations and jobs are debated. Exactly what jobs men and women do seems to have little consequence for research or policy unless those jobs confer different levels of status or pay. Therefore, scholarly attention is commonly directed at the measurement and consequences of vertical segregation (see Bridges 2003). Although the inequality-generating effects of vertical segregation may be mitigated by wage protections for workers (Rosenfeld and Kalleberg 1990; Blau and Ferber 1992), evidence suggests that a sizable component of gender wage inequality is attributable to gender segregation in occupations (Treiman and Roos 1983; Padavic and Reskin 2002; England 2005).

There is significant variability across countries in the extent to which women and men are segregated within labor markets. This variation highlights one of the key puzzles of cross-national studies of gender inequality: although gender-egalitarian social policies and programs tend to enhance the labor market involvement of women, they are often associated with higher rates of occupational sex segregation (Charles 1992; Charles and Grusky 2004). High levels of gender segregation in occupations are commonly found in countries with high levels of women's labor market involvement, especially where women are concentrated in part-time or public-sector work (see, for example, Gornick and Jacobs 1998).

HISTORICAL TRENDS IN OCCUPATIONAL SEX SEGREGATION

Figure 5.1 shows the overall level of occupational sex segregation measured by the index of dissimilarity (D) in LIS countries. The index represents the percentage of women who would have to change occupations in order to have an even distribution across occupations, given their overall employment levels. Higher dissimilarity scores represent higher levels of segregation, and a score of zero would mean that women are evenly distributed across occupations. The figure indicates a generalized decline in occupational sex segregation between 1970 and 1990. Yet the mean level of dissimilarity conceals important variability in the level of occupational sex segregation within welfare state regime types. Not all countries have witnessed gains in women's occupational integration. For example, the index of dissimilarity indicates growing occupational segregation among women in some continental countries, especially in Austria. In reality, the conservative-corporatist countries as a whole exhibit a wide range of occupational sex segregation. According to OECD data, Austria posts the highest levels of occupational sex segregation, while the Netherlands and Belgium post low levels of occupational sex segregation. Other conservative countries—Germany, France, and Spain—fall very close to median levels of occupational sex segregation. Survey data from LIS show exceptionally high rates of occupational sex seg-

Figure 5.1   Trends in Occupational Segregation

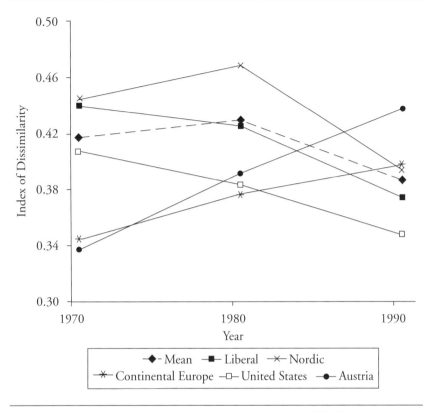

Source: Organization for Economic Cooperation and Development (OECD 2002).

regation in Luxembourg, an extremely small country with a relatively large male migrant labor force.

Liberal countries exhibit relatively low levels of occupational sex segregation using the dissimilarity index. The United States and Canada are consistently well below the eighteen-country mean level of dissimilarity, and both show evidence of declines in occupational sex segregation since the 1970s. The United States and Canada both had dissimilarity indices close to 40 percent in the mid-1980s, but by the late 1990s both had dipped below 35 percent. Australia's index of dissimilarity is slightly higher and has not declined dramatically over the period. In 1990 the United Kingdom posted the highest dissimilarity index among liberal countries, at almost 45 percent.

Although there was a slight uptick in sex segregation in the Nordic countries in 1980, the index of dissimilarity has fallen since. By the 1990s, Finland, Denmark, and Sweden all had posted levels of occupational sex segregation that would require approximately 40 percent of women to change jobs to achieve an equal distribution of women across occupations. In recent years there has been less evidence of declines in occupational sex segregation across social democratic countries than there is in some other welfare state regimes. According to LIS data, the index of dissimilarity in Finland dipped in the mid-1990s, only to rise again by 2000. In Denmark, the index grew from just under 40 percent in the late 1980s to just over 40 percent in the early 1990s. In Sweden, however, the index fell from the early 1990s to the mid-1990s.

The OECD data shown in figure 5.1 do not include eastern European countries, but LIS data demonstrate highly variable levels of occupational sex segregation in those countries as measured by the index of dissimilarity. Although a clear majority of women in the Russian Federation would have had to change occupations to achieve equal representation across occupations in the mid-1990s, fewer than one-third of women in Slovenia would have needed to change occupations for an equal distribution across occupations. The index of dissimilarity fell from over 45 percent in Hungary in the early 1990s to under 40 percent by the middle of the decade. In the Czech Republic, the index hovered just under 40 percent through the 1990s.

The index of dissimilarity, like any other single measure, has limitations. The index is an important indicator of the overall level of gender segregation in occupations and enables us to compare gender segregation in occupations across countries or over time. However, it does not enable us to make a careful examination of how women's and men's occupational locations relate to individual or state policies and the conditions that influence gender inequalities in domestic or paid work.

We focus the remainder of this chapter on measures of gender segregation in broad occupational categories that allow us to examine both the individual and country characteristics associated with employment in gender-segregated occupations. Specifically, we examine women's and men's involvement in professional, managerial, and clerical, sales, and service occupations. We separate professional occupations from clerical, sales, and service jobs because even though professional occupations are feminized in many countries at many points in time, this is not always the case. Additionally, there is a large difference in the quality of professional versus clerical, sales, and service occupa-

Figure 5.2   Percentage of Women Working in Five Occupational
Categories, Mid-1990s

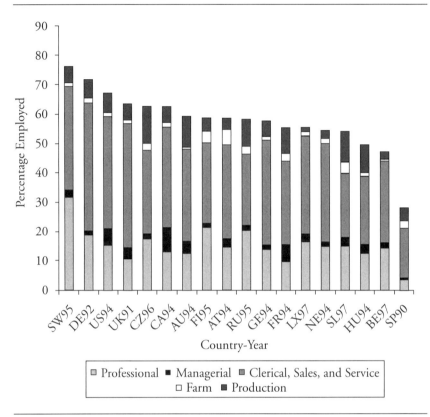

Source: Luxembourg Income Study (LIS 2003).
Note: See country abbreviations in figure A.1.

tions; grouping these occupations together obscures important variation in
the pay and prestige of these jobs or aspects of vertical segregation.

Figure 5.2 shows the occupational distribution of all working-age women
(age eighteen to sixty-four) using available LIS data in the mid-1990s. In addition to professional, managerial, and clerical, sales, and service occupations,
the figure includes farm and production occupations. The height of each bar
totals to the percentage of women employed. Figure 5.3 shows results for
men.

A comparison of women's and men's occupational distributions provides
evidence in support of three empirical claims: across countries, women and

Figure 5.3   Percentage of Men Working in Five Occupational
Categories, Mid-1990s

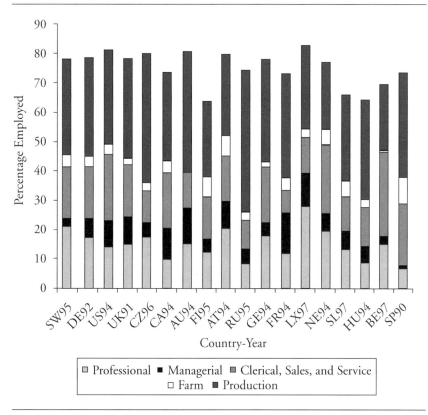

Source: Luxembourg Income Study (LIS 2003).
Note: See country abbreviations in figure A.1.

men are consistently employed in different occupations; women are consistently overrepresented in clerical, sales, and service jobs; and men are overrepresented in managerial and production jobs. Overall, 31 percent of all working-age women are employed in clerical, sales, and service jobs, and 33 percent of all working-age men are employed in production. In contrast, only 17 percent of men are employed in clerical, sales, and service jobs, and only 7 percent of women are employed in production work. Second, in all countries men outnumber women in managerial occupations: 6.5 percent of men are employed in managerial occupations compared to 2.5 percent of women. Third, there is great variation in women's and men's involvement in professional occupations. In some countries men outnumber women (for example, Austria and Luxembourg), in some there is parity (the United States), and in others women outnumber men (Russia and Sweden). On average, 16 percent of both women and men are employed in professional occupations.

There are considerable differences in the extent of occupational sex segregation and women's and men's concentration within particular occupations and jobs across countries. As already mentioned, there are large differences in women's and men's representation in professional occupations: women are overrepresented in professional occupations in some countries and underrepresented in others. Similarly, women exhibit a significant presence in managerial occupations in some countries, while women are extremely unlikely to work in managerial jobs in others. Finally, production work is largely reserved for men in some countries and not in others. Wide variability in the level of occupational sex segregation across countries, along with inconsistency within welfare state regime types, calls for further investigation of the factors that influence sex segregation in the workplace.

OCCUPATIONAL SEGREGATION OVER THE LIFE COURSE

At the individual level, microeconomic and sociological theories both lead us to expect that highly educated women and men will be concentrated in managerial and professional occupations, while those with less education will be concentrated in clerical, sales, and service jobs and production work. We also suspect that those with significant domestic obligations—especially women with very young children—will be underrepresented in managerial positions and overrepresented in clerical, sales, and service jobs. Depending on the character of professional occupations, they may be more or less accommodating of women or men with varying levels of education and domestic obligations.

Our data do not allow us to differentiate the effects of the supply-side processes that emphasize the influence of education and child-rearing on women's and men's occupational choice from demand-side explanations that occupational segregation is structured by employer decisions. Hiring, promotion, and pay may be influenced by employer preferences and beliefs about the productivity and suitability of workers. For example, employers may have stronger preferences for well-educated workers, fathers, and nonmothers because they anticipate that these workers will be more productive in the workplace and more suitable for full-time, career-oriented work if they do not have

Table 5.1   The Occupational Location of Women, by Parental Status and
            Education, Mid-1990s

Country	Year	Professional				Managerial			
		All	Highly Educated	Young Children Age Zero to Six	Older Children Age Seven to Seventeen	All	Highly Educated	Young Children Age Zero to Six	Older Children Age Seven to Seventeen
Austria	1994	26%	82%	24%	28%	4%	5%	6%	4%
Australia	1994	22	62	27	21	6	5	8	6
Belgium	1997	34	63	36	37	1	1	2	2
Canada	1994	22	32	21	22	13	15	12	11
Czech Republic	1996	28	56	28	29	2	4	2	3
Denmark	1992	26	82	32	28	2	3	1	2
Finland	1995	37	54	40	39	2	5	2	2
France	1994	19	43	19	19	10	18	9	9
Germany	1994	25	60	36	24	2	3	2	2
Hungary	1994	27	75	27	27	5	13	3	4
Luxembourg	1997	31	44	31	21	3	3	1	3
Netherlands	1994	29	64	38	27	2	4	1	2
Russian Federation	1995	36	68	37	33	2	5	1	3
Slovenia	1997	29	77	29	29	5	13	3	4
Spain	1990	16	43	18	12	0	0	0	0
Sweden	1995	42	80	44	47	3	4	2	3
United Kingdom	1991	18	35	19	17	5	7	3	4
United States	1994	24	37	24	23	7	10	6	6
Mean		27	59	29	27	4	7	3	4

Source: Luxembourg Income Study (LIS 2003).

competing demands on their time or energy. In either case, however, gender
differences in occupation—particularly in relation to having children—help
clarify the central role that domestic obligations play in gender inequality in
the economy.

Tables 5.1 and 5.2 show the percentage of employed women and men in
each occupation for LIS countries observed in the 1990s. (Tables A.5A and

Clerical, Sales, and Service				Production			
All	Highly Educated	Young Children Age Zero to Six	Older Children Age Seven to Seventeen	All	Highly Educated	Young Children Age Zero to Six	Older Children Age Seven to Seventeen
55%	12%	56%	52%	7%	1%	6%	6%
54	28	50	52	18	5	15	21
59	35	57	55	6	1	5	6
55	47	56	56	9	4	9	9
46	36	45	47	20	3	22	19
61	13	57	61	9	1	9	9
47	38	46	44	8	1	6	8
52	34	54	53	16	3	16	17
63	31	53	63	10	6	9	10
47	10	41	48	20	2	26	20
61	48	66	71	3	3	1	3
62	30	54	63	5	0	4	6
42	23	42	42	16	4	16	18
41	9	39	41	19	0	23	20
60	50	58	63	16	5	17	16
47	14	45	44	7	1	8	5
68	55	68	70	9	3	10	9
57	48	58	59	10	4	11	11
54	31	52	55	12	3	12	12

A.5B report all LIS years.) It displays the occupational distribution of employed respondents age eighteen to sixty-four, employed respondents with a high level of education, employed respondents with a youngest child age six or younger, and employed respondents with a youngest child older than six.

The first thing to observe is that the occupational distribution, at the mean, varies greatly by educational level for both women and men. For ex-

Table 5.2   The Occupational Location of Men, by Parental Status and Education, Mid-1990s

Country	Year	Professional				Managerial			
		All	Highly Educated	Young Children Age Zero to Six	Older Children Age Seven to Seventeen	All	Highly Educated	Young Children Age Zero to Six	Older Children Age Seven to Seventeen
Austria	1994	26%	68%	26%	24%	11%	22%	10%	12%
Australia	1994	20	54	21	21	14	16	17	16
Belgium	1997	22	50	23	22	4	6	6	4
Canada	1994	14	22	15	12	14	19	15	14
Czech Republic	1996	23	53	22	23	6	13	6	7
Denmark	1992	22	66	28	26	8	13	7	9
Finland	1995	20	51	22	19	6	16	6	9
France	1994	17	35	17	18	18	40	19	19
Germany	1994	24	61	26	24	5	8	7	5
Hungary	1994	14	53	8	12	8	28	7	10
Luxembourg	1997	34	44	30	31	14	15	12	18
Netherlands	1994	26	65	29	25	7	13	8	9
Russian Federation	1995	13	40	12	11	5	14	4	6
Slovenia	1997	21	63	17	21	9	24	10	9
Spain	1990	9	33	10	7	1	3	1	1
Sweden	1995	28	67	30	33	3	7	3	5
United Kingdom	1991	20	39	20	18	11	20	13	12
United States	1994	18	30	17	17	10	15	10	12
Mean		20	50	21	20	9	16	9	10

Source: Luxembourg Income Study (LIS 2003).

ample, 27 percent of employed women work in professional occupations, whereas 59 percent of highly educated, employed women work in professional occupations. Twenty percent of employed men work in professional occupations, in comparison with 50 percent of highly educated employed men.

The occupational distribution, at the mean, does not vary greatly by family obligations. The stability in the mean, however, conceals substantial het-

Clerical, Sales, and Service				Production			
All	Highly Educated	Young Children Age Zero to Six	Older Children Age Seven to Seventeen	All	Highly Educated	Young Children Age Zero to Six	Older Children Age Seven to Seventeen
20%	5%	21%	18%	34%	3%	34%	37%
16	14	11	15	51	16	50	48
42	39	37	39	32	5	33	35
26	23	21	25	41	33	44	43
14	15	14	13	55	17	55	53
22	14	22	20	42	6	39	39
23	24	22	21	41	7	40	40
10	8	10	9	49	14	49	49
25	18	22	22	45	12	44	47
21	13	22	19	53	6	58	55
15	13	13	11	35	25	43	38
30	16	27	26	30	3	30	34
14	23	18	11	65	22	64	67
18	6	16	19	44	5	49	45
29	34	30	28	49	28	51	52
22	18	21	22	42	7	42	36
23	25	20	22	43	15	45	45
28	30	26	27	40	23	43	41
22	19	21	20	44	14	45	45

erogeneity in the relationship between family obligations and occupation across countries. For example, in Germany, 25 percent of all employed women are in a professional occupation, compared to 36 percent of employed women with young children. At the same time, in the United States, 24 percent of all employed women are in a professional occupation—the same percentage of professionals among employed women with young children.

Both women and men with higher levels of education are more likely to be employed in professional and managerial occupations and generally less likely to be employed in clerical, sales, and service and production occupations. Women and men with high educational levels, however, are not equally likely to be in particular occupations. Across countries, 59 percent of highly educated employed women are employed in professional occupations compared to 50 percent of men. In contrast, 16 percent of highly educated employed men are employed in managerial occupations compared to 7 percent of women. This pattern is especially pronounced in some countries. For example, in Austria, 82 percent of highly educated employed women work in professional occupations, compared to 68 percent of men, and 22 percent of highly educated employed men work in managerial occupations, compared to only 5 percent of women. While cross-national variability in what constitutes higher education may explain some of the variability in the effects of education across occupations, the consistency with which higher education is associated with women's and men's concentration in professional and managerial jobs, and not in clerical, sales, and service jobs, is striking.

Overall, the relationship between family obligations and occupation appears weak in tables 5.1 and 5.2. There is often little difference in the concentration of employed mothers or fathers with young children in occupations relative to that among all workers, though gender differences in occupational segregation are quite large. Twenty-nine percent of mothers of young children are employed in professional occupations, compared to 20 percent of fathers. At the same time, 3 percent of mothers of young children are in managerial jobs, compared to 9 percent of fathers. Again, Austria is illustrative of the overall pattern of similarity in occupational segregation between all workers and parents of young children: 24 percent of mothers and 26 percent of fathers work in professional occupations, while 10 percent of fathers and 6 percent of mothers work in managerial jobs.

These results are somewhat surprising, especially in the extent to which gender- and family-based stratification in occupations is absent in some countries. The focus on broad occupational categories may generate conservative estimates of gender inequalities in occupations; prior research has shown higher levels of gender segregation in the labor force with more disaggregated measures of occupations and jobs (Bielby and Baron 1986). The overall pattern, however, conceals important differences in the relationship between child-rearing and occupational segregation across countries. In Germany and the Netherlands, employed women's representation in professional occupations increases by about ten percentage points with the presence of a young child, and then decreases about ten percentage points with the presence of an older child. This is coupled with decreases of about ten percentage points in employment in clerical, sales, and service occupations with a young child, and then a ten-percentage-point increase in representation in those occupations among women with an older child.

It is necessary to consider occupational segregation over the life course in relation to the patterns of employment documented in chapters 3 and 4. Very few women in Germany and the Netherlands are employed when they have young children: only 17 percent of mothers in Germany and 10 percent of mothers in the Netherlands are employed full-time. Thus, the women who remain in the labor force are a particularly select group and more likely to be found in professional than clerical, sales, or service jobs. Later, when women's labor market involvement increases, working women are a less select group and are more likely to be found in clerical, sales, and service occupations.

In summary, there is clear evidence of gender segregation even into broad occupational categories across countries. Education is a key mechanism undergirding occupational segregation for both women and men. Cross-national variability in the employment of mothers may help reconcile the somewhat counterintuitive positive association between child-rearing and women's concentration in professional and managerial jobs in some countries. Evidence suggests that when employment rates are low, mothers who remain in the paid labor force are likely to be a highly select group with particularly rosy labor market prospects.

Regression models confirm descriptive accounts of the concentration of highly educated women and men in professional and managerial occupations. Recall that the regression framework allows us to examine the specific effects of education and children on occupational location while holding other relevant information (such as age and marital status) constant. Table 5.3 reports the mean effects of education and child-rearing on women's and men's employment in professional, managerial, and clerical, sales, and service occupations. The top two panels of the table indicate that higher levels of education are consistently related to higher probabilities of employment in professional and managerial occupations for both women and men. The bottom panel of the table shows that higher levels of education are consistently related to lower probabilities of employment in clerical, sales, and service occupations for both women and men.

Some key gender differences emerge when we examine the effects of child-

Table 5.3   Cross-National Variability in Logistic Regression Predicting Occupational Location

	Women			Men		
	Highly Educated	Youngest Child Age Zero to Three	Number of Children	Highly Educated	Youngest Child Age Zero to Three	Number of Children
Professional						
Mean	3.12	0.11	0.01	3.08	0.09	-0.07
Median	3.03 (RF92)	0.07 (SW92)	0.00 (GE89)	3.07 (US97)	0.09 (FI91)	-0.04 (CZ96)
Minimum	1.62 (FI05)	-0.48 (BE97)	-0.24 (LX00)	1.74 (RF00)	-0.22 (RF00)	-0.37 (HU94)
Maximum	5.71 (SL97)	0.96 (GE94)	0.23 (BE97)	4.94 (HU91)	0.55 (AT97)	0.16 (HU91)
Managerial						
Mean	2.24	0.06	-0.22	2.39	0.11	-0.01
Median	1.37 (CA94/LX00)	0.14 (CA94/US00)	-0.23 (SL99)	1.69 (US94)	0.15 (UK91)	0.00 (US97)
Minimum	-2.79 (DE87)	-1.62 (LX97)	-0.72 (NE91)	-0.02 (AU94)	-1.36 (HU91)	-0.22 (SW95)
Maximum	16.96 (HU94)	1.41 (BE97)	0.23 (GE84)	18.21 (HU91)	0.72 (SL97)	0.35 (LX85)
Clerical, sales, and service						
Mean	-1.49	-0.14	0.01	-0.23	-0.02	-0.05
Median	-1.43 (HU91)	-0.17 (US00)	0.01 (GE00)	-0.16 (CA91)	-0.04 (FI95)	-0.04 (AT97)
Minimum	-2.88 (DE92)	-0.58 (GE94)	-0.21 (DE87)	-1.51 (AT94)	-0.43 (SL97)	-0.21 (GE00)
Maximum	-0.55 (AU85)	0.38 (BE97)	0.47 (LX00)	1.07 (RF95)	0.47 (RF92)	0.06 (SW95)

Source: Luxembourg Income Study (LIS 2003).

Note: Models also include age, age-squared, medium education, marriage, and youngest child age four to six. See country abbreviations in figure A.1.

rearing on the occupational location of women and men. On average, across countries, having very young children increases the likelihood of women's and men's employment in professional and managerial occupations and decreases the likelihood of their employment in clerical, sales, and service occupations. Yet for all three occupational categories, there is much more variability among women than men in the effect of living with an infant or toddler. For women, living with an infant or toddler has a sizable positive association with their employment in professional occupations in places like Germany (1994) and with their involvement in management in Belgium (1997). Among men, the effects of having very young children on working in professional and managerial jobs are close to zero and smaller in magnitude than those for women.

The effects of the number of children for women's and men's occupational location are generally smaller than those for living with very young children. The mean effects of the number of children on occupation for both men and women are close to zero. There is one exception: the number of children is negatively associated with women's likelihood of being in a managerial occupation in most countries. We suspect that the negative relationship between the number of children and women's involvement in managerial jobs is related to women's time out of the labor market with young children. The effect is particularly pronounced in countries where women are more likely to exit the labor force when their children are young (for example, the Netherlands in 1991).

It is important to consider how these results reflect the mechanisms that influence differences in women's and men's employment and hours worked. Patterns of labor force participation help reconcile inconsistencies in the measurement of gender inequality in employment and occupational location. Estimates of the individual determinants of involvement in occupations may be biased if participants in the labor market—from whom these estimates are generated—do not accurately represent the population as a whole. For example, it is puzzling to find that women with children are not more likely to be concentrated in clerical, sales, and service occupations in Germany than women without children. It is likely that relatively low labor force participation rates among German women with children at least partially accounts for this finding.

To the extent that women in the labor market differ in systematic ways from those women who are out of the labor market, any analysis of gender inequality generated only from women in the labor market might either overestimate or underestimate the underlying level of gender inequality. Moreover, we may also be misrepresenting the effects of particular individual-level characteristics on gendered occupational sorting. Whether estimates of inequality or estimates of individual-level determinants of employment in particular occupations are biased depends on: (1) who is included in different measures, and (2) how the processes that influence who is included relate to occupational segregation by gender. We suspect that our estimates of gender segregation in the labor market and the relationship between certain individual characteristics—especially concerning the presence of children—suffer from exactly this type of bias. Substantial evidence in chapters 3 and 4 shows that women who are not counted—that is, who are not employed—are selected on the basis of the same characteristics, such as having children in the household, that might engender higher rates of occupational sex segregation.

CROSS-NATIONAL VARIABILITY IN OCCUPATIONAL SEGREGATION

Table 5.4 displays the relationship between national-level conditions and the mean level of women's and men's representation in occupations. Controlling for all other national-level factors, the year shows a positive association with women's employment in professional occupations and a negative association with women's employment in clerical, sales, or service occupations. Over time, women have increased their representation in professional jobs and decreased their representation in clerical, sales, and service jobs. Results for men also show a positive over-time trend for involvement in professional jobs and a negative time-trend for involvement in clerical, sales, and service jobs.

Higher levels of gender egalitarianism—indicated by women's political representation—show a negative relationship with women's representation in managerial occupations. Although this finding may be counterintuitive, it does highlight the loose coupling of women's political empowerment with at least some measures of gender inequality in the economy. At the same time, women's political empowerment is positively associated with men's involvement in clerical positions. It may be possible that those countries protect traditionally feminized jobs in ways that make them attractive to men.

Economic conditions also correlate with occupational segregation at the aggregate level. The level of unemployment is negatively related to both women's and men's concentration in the professions. This suggests that when the labor market is tight, women and men are both less likely to be found in professional jobs relative to their overall representation in the labor market. At the same time, per capita GDP is negatively associated with women's con-

Table 5.4 The Association Between National Conditions and Mean Level of Representation in Occupations

	Professional		Managerial		Clerical, Sales, and Service	
	Women	Men	Women	Men	Women	Men
Intercept	0.433	7.689+	0.478	5.569	38.936*	14.208*
Year	0.847*	0.399*	0.181	0.234	-0.718*	-0.345*
Gender egalitarianism						
Women in parliament	-2.402	10.953	-17.306+	-21.432+	8.383	31.571*
Economic conditions						
Unemployment	-42.848+	-97.430*	14.073	5.923	12.288	5.817
Service-sector growth	61.194+	1.639	18.228	11.908	-36.214	-46.481
Per capita GDP growth	-42.181+	40.618+	-8.029	8.355	26.386	38.534+
Mechanisms of inclusion						
Maternity leave and inequality	6.915	2.615	8.237	4.398	-27.778*	-23.510*
Part-time employment and equality	-13.360	23.907*	22.036*	8.403	31.394*	-1.087
Child care	14.777*	-7.212	-1.147	-0.255	2.978	6.331
Mechanisms of exclusion and equality						
Union density and inequality	14.197*	6.348	-4.534	-2.037	2.410	0.390
Parental leave	1.670	1.943	-1.047	-1.193	1.540	0.175
Adjusted R-squared	0.747	0.574	0.260	0.176	0.479	0.108

Source: Luxembourg Income Study (LIS 2003).

*T-ratio ≥ 2; +T-ratio ≥ 1.8

centration in professional occupations, but it is positively associated with men's involvement in professional and clerical occupations. In countries with strong GDP growth, men are more likely to be found in sectors typically reserved for women.

State-level employment conditions exhibit several significant effects on gender segregation in occupations. Perhaps surprisingly, women in countries with large part-time workforces are disproportionately employed in managerial jobs. Part-time work also is associated with women's overrepresentation in clerical, sales, and service jobs. Consistent with findings from chapter 4, these results suggest that large part-time workforces are associated with a bifurcated labor market. While women are increasingly likely to be found in both high- and low-status occupations in part-time economies, men populate the middle tiers. Results indicate that the size of the part-time workforce is positively associated with men's representation in professional occupations.

In addition to the effects of the size of the part-time workforce, we find a few other significant relationships between social policies, employment conditions, and gender concentration within occupations. The provision of publicly funded child care and union density are positively associated with women's representation in professional occupations. While parental leave has no discernible effect in our analyses of women's and men's concentration in different occupations, maternity leave is associated with lower levels of concentration—among both women and men—in clerical, sales, and service jobs. Although rates of unionization are generally lower among women than among men and some argue that unions and the labor market protections they afford often reinforce traditional family ideologies and a gendered division of labor (O'Connor 1993; Crain 1994), strong positive effects of unionization on women's involvement in professional jobs may signal the importance of public-sector employment and women's unionization within it for gender integration in some countries. Although publicly funded child care may foster the inclusion of women in the labor market—and in professional jobs—high levels of unionization may signal the protection of women workers within the market.

INSTITUTIONALIZING GENDER INEQUALITY IN OCCUPATIONS

For a slightly more nuanced understanding of the mechanisms behind gender segregation in occupations across countries, we examine the relationship between national conditions and the individual-level characteristics associated with women's and men's involvement in particular occupations. Mechanisms of inclusion and exclusion structure the allocation of labor within the household and the marketplace in ways that affect occupational segregation in the aggregate and help make sense of individual-level correlates of employment in professional, managerial, and clerical, sales, or service jobs.

Table 5.5 summarizes results from models that examine how the effects of individual-level characteristics on occupational location vary with national institutional context. Beginning with the year, we see that, over time, highly educated, employed women are more likely to be working in professional occupations and less likely to be employed in clerical, sales, or service occupations. In contrast, highly educated, employed men are increasingly concentrated in managerial occupations over time. These results are consistent with characterizations of shifts in the labor market that increasingly reward women and men with higher levels of education.

The effects of education on occupational location also vary with policies of inclusion and exclusion. In countries where the part-time workforce is large, the effects of higher education on managerial employment among women are dampened. In other words, countries that have large part-time workforces do a better job of incorporating women with lower levels of education into managerial jobs. Whether they are incorporated into high-paying management jobs is unclear.

Publicly funded child care is positively associated with the employment of highly educated women in professional jobs and negatively associated with their employment in clerical, sales, and service jobs. In countries that offer more generous child care for very young children, highly educated women are able to eschew clerical, sales, and service occupations for employment in professional occupations.

The effect of higher levels of education on women's involvement in managerial jobs is dampened in countries where unionization is high. We observe the same relationship for men. This finding speaks to our central concern about the tradeoffs between patterns of employment and the measurement of inequality within the market. Although high levels of unionization are associated with women's exclusion from employment, they appear to foster more equal access to managerial jobs for women of varying education levels.

We now turn to the relationship between mechanisms of inclusion and the effects of children on women's and men's occupational location. Differences in the effects of part-time work and public child care illustrate that the con-

Table 5.5 The Association Between National Conditions and the Factors Predicting Employment in Occupations

	Women			Men		
	Highly Educated	Youngest Child Age Zero to Three	Number of Children	Highly Educated	Youngest Child Age Zero to Three	Number of Children
Professional						
Intercept	5.867*	0.278	0.088	5.067*	0.564+	-0.127
Year	0.075*	-0.007	0.001	0.009	-0.005	-0.001
Part-time employment	-0.571	0.276	0.096	-0.557	-1.044+	0.049*
Child care	3.617*	-0.524	0.429*	0.368	-0.178	0.174
Union density	-1.413	0.463+	-0.183+	0.054	-0.289	0.077
Parental leave	-0.507	0.055	-0.020	-0.029	-0.095	0.014
Managerial						
Intercept	8.084*	1.661	-1.651*	3.827*	0.602	-0.115
Year	0.044	0.008	-0.002	0.059*	0.008	-0.003

Part-time employment	−14.007*	−1.473	1.657*	−5.712*	0.260
Child care	1.220	0.318	−0.271	1.642*	−0.518
Union density	−7.028*	−0.734	1.170*	−3.140*	−0.073
Parental leave	−1.106	−0.195	0.291*	−0.475*	−0.023
Clerical, sales, and service					
Intercept	−2.258*	−0.053	−0.088	−0.686	0.000
Year	−0.078*	−0.007	−0.006	−0.027	0.002
Part-time employment	−2.427	−0.423	−0.322	−1.502	−0.148
Child care	−2.584*	0.207	−0.399*	−0.724	0.447
Union density	−0.040	0.188	−0.073	−0.127	0.021
Parental leave	0.166	−0.022	−0.027	0.118	0.127

Source: Luxembourg Income Study (LIS 2003).

Note: Models also include age, age-squared, medium education, marriage, and youngest child age four to six at the individual level and women's employment, service-sector growth, per capita GDP, unemployment, maternity leave, women in parliament, and year at the country level.

T-ratio ≥ 2; +*T*-ratio ≥ 1.8

ditions associated with high rates of women's employment—and the employment of mothers—are also associated with greater levels of gender segregation—especially among mothers. Large part-time workforces are positively associated with the likelihood that mothers—though not those with children age zero to three—will be in managerial occupations. Publicly funded child care is associated with a higher likelihood that employed mothers will be in professional occupations and a lower likelihood that they will be in clerical, sales, and service occupations.

The somewhat contradictory effects of mechanisms of exclusion—such as unionization and parental leave—again point to the tradeoffs between employment and other measures of labor market performance. Countries with high levels of unionization do a better job of incorporating mothers of very young children into the professional ranks, and unionization is positively associated with the employment of all mothers in managerial jobs. Long parental leaves are also positively associated with the likelihood that women with children will be in managerial occupations.

These findings suggest that there is positive selection of highly educated mothers in the labor force in heavily unionized countries and those that offer extensive leave. That is, only mothers who expect high returns to employment are in the labor market, and thus working mothers in these countries are a more select group than working mothers in other countries. Although exclusionary mechanisms may be implicated in gender inequalities in labor market participation, they are also associated with greater integration of those who "get through." Whether this is due to positive selection or enhanced labor market protections is unclear.

SPOTLIGHT: TRENDS IN WOMEN'S OCCUPATIONAL LOCATION IN THE UNITED STATES AND WEST GERMANY

Figure 5.4 shows trends in women's occupational location from the mid-1980s to 2000. The height of each bar totals to the percentage of women employed. The figure highlights four important points. First, compared to their U.S. counterparts, West German women have lower employment rates. Second, there has been growth in women's employment in both West Germany and the United States, with a small spike in employment in the United States in 1991. Third, in both countries growth in employment has included growth in professional and managerial occupations. And fourth, despite these increases, most women remain employed in clerical, sales, and service occupations.

Figure 5.4   Trends in Women's Occupational Location in the United States and West Germany

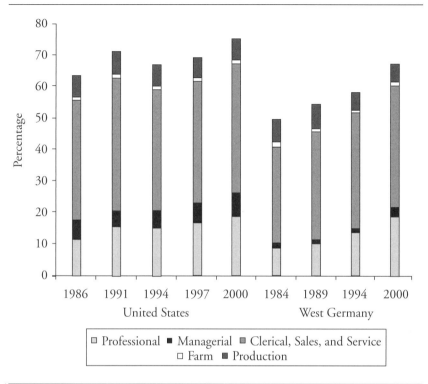

Source: Luxembourg Income Study (LIS 2003).

Table 5.6 displays the occupational distribution of all employed women, employed women with a high level of education, employed women with a youngest child age six or younger, and employed women with a youngest child older than six. In both the United States and Germany, we observe a shift from clerical, sales, and service work to professional occupations over time. In the United States, the percentage of employed women in professional occupations increased by seven percentage points, and their representation in clerical, sales, and service jobs declined by six percentage points. In West Germany, women's representation in professional occupations increased by ten percentage points, and their representation in clerical, sales, and service jobs declined by five percentage points. In both countries, general shifts

Table 5.6   Trends in Women's Occupational Location in the United States and West Germany

	United States					West Germany			
	1986	1991	1994	1997	2000	1984	1989	1994	2000
Professional									
All workers	19%	22%	24%	25%	26%	19%	19%	24%	29%
Highly educated	36	37	37	38	39	64	61	64	62
Young children (zero to six)	18	21	24	23	24	26	26	35	29
Older children (seven to seventeen)	18	21	23	24	24	17	17	21	28
Managerial									
All workers	9	6	7	8	9	1	1	1	3
Highly educated	12	9	10	11	12	1	5	1	4
Young children (zero to six)	7	5	6	7	8	0	1	0	1
Older children (seven to seventeen)	7	6	6	7	8	0	1	2	1
Clerical, sales, and service									
All workers	61	60	57	56	55	63	64	64	58
Highly educated	48	50	48	47	45	27	29	26	29
Young children (zero to six)	61	61	58	57	57	57	60	55	59
Older children (seven to seventeen)	62	61	59	58	57	67	61	66	58
Production									
All workers	11	10	10	10	9	14	14	10	9
Highly educated	3	4	4	4	4	6	5	8	5
Young children (zero to six)	12	11	11	12	10	17	11	9	8
Older children (seven to seventeen)	12	11	11	10	10	14	21	10	11

Source: Luxembourg Income Study (LIS 2003).

into professional occupations and away from clerical, sales, and service jobs are less pronounced for highly educated women, who began the period with much higher levels of professional employment and lower levels of clerical, sales, and service employment (relative to the mean).

In the United States, the shift from clerical, sales, and service occupations to professional occupations occurred at approximately the same rate among mothers, whether their children were younger or older. In West Germany, however, the shift into professional occupations was driven primarily by increases among mothers with older children. Women with children age six or younger increased their representation in professional occupations by three percentage points, compared to a gain of eleven points for women whose youngest child was older than age six (the associated declines in clerical, sales, and service jobs were two and nine points, respectively). In essence, women with older children had "caught up" to the more favorable occupational distribution of women with young children by 2000.

It is difficult to assess trends in management because relatively few women are employed in management occupations. There does appear to be one modest pattern in the United States: in 1991 employed women lost ground in management occupations and would not reestablish their 1986 level of representation level until 2000.

Table 5.7 shows the trends in the individual-level correlates of women's occupational location in the United States from 1986 to 2000. Having more education is positively associated with employment in professional and managerial occupations, although education has decreased in importance for professional occupations while it has increased for managerial occupations. Highly educated women are increasingly unlikely to be found in clerical, sales, and service occupations.

Regarding family obligations, although there is overlap in the confidence intervals, it appears that having a very young child is becoming less positively associated with employment in professional occupations over time. This is consistent with studies that document the growing labor force involvement of women with young children (Cohen and Bianchi 1999) and may signify that women in the labor force with young children are becoming a less select group. It also appears that the number of children is becoming less negatively associated with employment in managerial occupations. Overall, the United States shows a clear pattern of positive associations between having very young children and employment in professional and managerial occupations, and a negative association between living with an

Table 5.7 Logistic Regression Predicting Women's Employment in Professional, Managerial, and Clerical, Sales, and Service Occupations in the United States and West Germany

	High Education		Youngest Child Age Zero to Three		Number of Children	
	Estimate	95 Percent Confidence Interval	Estimate	95 Percent Confidence Interval	Estimate	95 Percent Confidence Interval
Professional						
United States						
1986	4.05*	3.38 4.72	0.23	−0.02 0.48	−0.12*	−0.20 −0.03
1991	2.86*	2.65 3.07	0.22*	0.12 0.32	−0.11*	−0.15 −0.08
1994	2.86*	2.63 3.09	0.15*	0.05 0.26	−0.07*	−0.10 −0.03
1997	2.98*	2.74 3.23	0.14*	0.03 0.24	−0.07*	−0.11 −0.03
2000	2.94*	2.68 3.19	0.12*	0.01 0.23	−0.10*	−0.13 −0.06
West Germany						
1984	3.38*	2.86 3.90	−0.22	−1.03 0.59	0.09	−0.17 0.35
1989	2.83*	2.27 3.39	0.39	−0.34 1.12	0.00	−0.26 0.26
1994	3.09*	2.63 3.55	1.05*	0.42 1.68	−0.03	−0.27 0.20
2000	2.74*	2.43 3.06	0.13	−0.36 0.61	0.03	−0.14 0.20

Managerial

United States									
1986	1.66*	1.15	2.17	0.25	−0.08	0.59	−0.24*	−0.37	−0.11
1991	1.56*	1.27	1.86	0.13	−0.05	0.30	−0.21*	−0.27	−0.14
1994	1.62*	1.32	1.91	0.14	−0.04	0.31	−0.30*	−0.36	−0.23
1997	1.65*	1.35	1.95	0.27*	0.11	0.43	−0.17*	−0.23	−0.11
2000	2.04*	1.70	2.38	0.15	−0.02	0.32	−0.15*	−0.21	−0.10
West Germany	—	—	—	—	—	—	—	—	—
Clerical, sales, and service									
United States									
1986	−0.72*	−0.91	−0.54	−0.30*	−0.49	−0.11	0.07*	0.01	0.14
1991	−0.64*	−0.73	−0.55	−0.18*	−0.27	−0.10	0.08*	0.05	0.11
1994	−0.61*	−0.70	−0.52	−0.19*	−0.28	−0.11	0.11*	0.08	0.14
1997	−0.82*	−0.92	−0.73	−0.29*	−0.38	−0.20	0.08*	0.05	0.11
2000	−0.98*	−1.07	−0.88	−0.17*	−0.27	−0.08	0.10*	0.07	0.13
West Germany									
1984	−1.79*	−2.26	−1.32	−0.17	−0.77	0.43	−0.03	−0.21	0.15
1989	−1.63*	−2.11	−1.16	−0.06	−0.69	0.56	−0.14	−0.33	0.04
1994	−2.07*	−2.46	−1.68	−0.11*	−1.27	−0.09	0.06	−0.12	0.24
2000	−1.80*	−2.08	−1.54	−0.18	−0.64	0.29	0.05	−0.10	0.19

Source: Luxembourg Income Study (LIS 2003).

Note: Models also include age, age-squared, medium education, marriage, and youngest child age four to six.

p < .05

infant or toddler and clerical, sales, and service employment. The opposite pattern is found for children more generally, as indicated by the effects of the number of children.

As a group, mothers of very young children appear to have made significant inroads into the labor market and into occupations typically reserved for men. But the reversal in effects for mothers more generally exposes an invidious tension: even though mothers of very young children have increased their overall labor force participation rates over the last few decades, many women leave the labor market when their children are very young. The good economic fortunes of the mothers who remain in the labor market may be as much a reflection of their strong commitment to the labor market as a marker of an economy that integrates mothers. Perhaps a better indication of how women—and mothers—are integrated into the labor market is by observing what happens when children are older and women return to work in the paid labor force in even greater numbers. Unfortunately, the effects of the number of children suggest that mothers—especially those of older children—are more likely to be segregated in female-dominated occupations.

Table 5.7 also shows the trends in the individual correlates of women's occupational location in West Germany from 1984 to 2000. There is no clear trend for the effects of education on occupational location. Trends in the effects of family obligations on occupational location are difficult to measure in West Germany because so few mothers with young children are in the labor force. Recall from chapter 4 that in 2000 only 10 percent of German women with young children were working full-time, with another 32 percent working part-time (compared to 52 percent full-time and 19 percent part-time in the United States). With only 42 percent of women with a child age six or younger (32 percent of women with infants or toddlers) in the labor market, it is difficult to obtain precise estimates of the effects of motherhood on employment in specific occupations. This problem is compounded when we examine occupations in which few women work, such as managerial ones. As a consequence, we are unable to estimate the trends in placement into managerial occupations because there are so few women in management in West Germany. In 1984, of 1,759 employed women in the sample, only 13, or 0.7 percent, were managers, compared to 4.6 percent of employed men. By 2000, of 3,777 employed women in the sample, 86, or 2.3 percent, were managers, compared to 5.2 percent of employed men.

CONCLUSION

An analysis of occupational sex segregation begins to reveal the complex relationship between gender inequality in full- and part-time labor market involvement and inequality related to the kind of work that women and men do. It is quite clear that the inclusion of women in the paid labor market, while an important indicator of women's access to economic opportunities, does not correspond with a more even distribution of women and men across occupations. In fact, some of the countries with the highest levels of women's labor force involvement continually post high levels of occupational sex segregation.

Results from this chapter illustrate the tradeoffs between high levels of women's employment and inequality in the labor market as measured by occupational segregation. The processes that influence employment are central to understanding inequality in the labor market by this and possibly other measures. Our analyses first established that inclusion in the labor market varies across countries in relation to gender, education, and family obligations. This variation is crucial for understanding the mixed evidence on the relationship between national-level conditions and both aggregate measures of occupational segregation and individual-level correlates of involvement in particular occupational categories.

Inclusionary mechanisms—like part-time work and public support for child care—foster the employment of women and mothers. Different mechanisms of inclusion, however, have different effects on inequality measured within the market. Large part-time workforces are associated with access to paid work, but they are also most likely to be found in bifurcated labor markets. Although some women appear to make inroads into male-dominated and managerial jobs, many more women—and especially mothers—manage their domestic obligations by remaining in sectors of the economy that are disproportionately part-time. We suspect that public supports for child care enable women—and mothers—greater access to more diverse jobs by relieving them from the domestic demands associated with caregiving and reducing employer perceptions that they cannot devote adequate time or attention to their jobs.

Mechanisms of exclusion—like union density and parental leave—may not foster high levels of labor force involvement among women or mothers.

But by filtering the most successful women into the labor market or providing protections for them within the labor market, these mechanisms generate greater levels of gender integration across occupations.

Gender inequality in occupations is ubiquitous and rooted in the domestic inequalities associated with raising children. Yet evidence is mounting that having children does not necessarily have a negative impact on women's occupational integration and that women need not forgo having children to be in managerial and professional jobs. States have a vital role to play in the production and maintenance of gender inequality in occupations. Country-level conditions influence how families resolve domestic inequalities, have implications for who is in the labor market, and structure inequality among workers. Moreover, those same mechanisms are likely to shape employer perceptions of workers, set expectations about appropriate work for women and men (and mothers and fathers), and provide (or not provide) protections for mothers and fathers who work.

Unfortunately, the consequences of the gender inequalities in employment, hours worked, and occupational location associated with having young children have enduring effects over the life course and for other aspects of gender inequality. Mothers who devote their time to caregiving are likely to have difficulty reentering the labor market and are likely to be excluded from male-dominated and managerial jobs. Although part-time work may be a useful accommodation strategy for mothers to manage the competing demands of caregiving and paid work, part-time work entrenches gender inequality in certain occupations and relegates women to separate—and largely unequal—domains of the economy. The lack of any state-level supports for managing competing work and family demands is no solution either; with no such support, the cost of child-rearing is privatized and the poorest families— and the poorest women—are consigned to segments of the labor market with little mobility. The next chapter considers how all of these factors influence gender inequality in pay.

CHAPTER 6

The Gender Wage Gap

Public policy initiatives have helped to mitigate explicit gender discrimination in pay, and the expansion of higher education and training programs has advanced the employment fortunes of women in many countries. Given the massive growth in women's education and their movement into sectors of the economy typically reserved for men, we might expect a narrowing of the gender wage gap, both over time and across countries. There is clear evidence of an improvement in the relative wages of women over the last two decades of the twentieth century, yet the gender gap in wages persists (Blau and Kahn 1996, 2002). Countries that post the highest levels of women's employment also demonstrate the highest levels of disparity between women's and men's wages. Striking inconsistencies between gender inequality in employment and wages highlight the tensions between women's labor market inclusion and their equality within the labor market.

Although evidence suggests that women have reached near-parity in wages with men when they first enter the labor force, earnings inequality widens over the life course, especially after childbearing. Social protections for citizens and workers vary across nations and shape women's labor market involvement when children are young and the demands of child-rearing are acute. Exactly how women balance the demands of paid work and caregiving has important implications for aggregate levels of gender inequality over the life course.

HISTORICAL TRENDS IN THE GENDER WAGE GAP

Figure 6.1 shows trends in women's weekly wages relative to men's among full-time workers by welfare state regime type from 1979 to 1998. A simple time trend indicates a strong increase in the relative wages of women and a decline in the male wage advantage since the 1980s. By the late 1990s, the median weekly wages of full-time women workers ranged from 90 percent of men's in France to approximately 70 percent of men's in Canada. On average, across countries, women's median weekly wages grew from just over 70 percent of men's in 1980 to close to 80 percent by the end of the 1990s.

The mean level of the gender gap in weekly wages conceals important variability and clustering in the level of women's relative wages within welfare state regimes: there is clear variation across countries in both the level and pace of change in women's relative economic standing. And evidence suggests that strong growth in women's employment is not always coupled with women's relative wage growth. In fact, relatively low levels of women's labor force participation often are coupled with high relative wages or low gender wage gaps.

The conservative-corporatist countries show a mixed pattern in the gender wage gap. Although all of the observed countries show steady improvements in women's relative wages, there are considerable differences in women's relative wages within continental countries. According to figure 6.1, women in France post the highest relative wages in observed countries; by the end of the time series, women in France earn approximately 90 percent of men's wages. Other conservative-corporatist countries post larger gender wage gaps; the overall average gender wage gap among continental European countries is close to the average of the LIS countries for which we have data to investigate gender differences in wages.

Although women's relative wages improved significantly in the last two decades of the twentieth century, the liberal countries exhibit significant variability in the size of the gender wage gap. All liberal countries exhibit relatively large median wage gaps, with Canada's being the largest. By the late 1990s, women in liberal countries earned just over 75 percent of men's weekly wages.

The social democratic countries of northern Europe consistently post

Figure 6.1   Trends in Women's Weekly Wages Relative to Men's for Full-Time Workers, 1979 to 1998

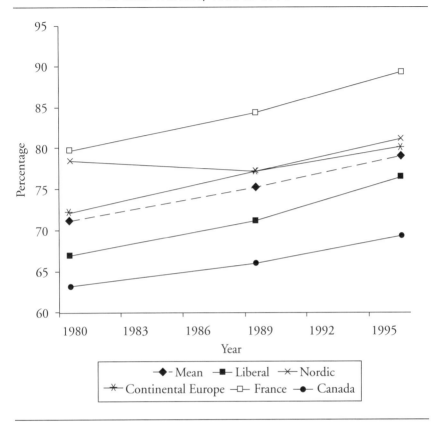

Source: Blau and Kahn (2002).

among the highest female employment rates of all LIS countries, but the relative wages of women in the Nordic countries fall somewhere in the middle of the observed countries. According to weekly wage data presented in figure 6.1, women in Sweden, Finland, and Norway earned just under 80 percent of men's wages in the early 1980s and just over that figure by the late 1990s. The data indicate that women in the Nordic countries lost ground in the 1980s, though they regained it later in the 1990s.

Unfortunately, our data do not enable us to investigate the relative wages of women in eastern Europe. Data from other sources, however, indicate strong and consistent improvements in the relative wages of women in these countries. Recent research shows that the gender wage gap in much of eastern Europe fell dramatically through the 1990s (Brainerd 2000; Hunt 2002). There are concerns, however, that the narrowing of the gender wage gap in eastern Europe, and the former East Germany in particular, was strongly influenced not by real improvements in the wage offers for women but by increasing levels of unemployment and the exclusion of low-wage women from the paid labor force (Hunt 2002).

The gender gap in weekly wages among full-time workers is an important indicator of the relative economic well-being of women. As a compendium measure, however, it not only reflects women's and men's differential earning capacities but is sensitive to gender differences in the level of labor market participation—and full-time employment—at any given time. It may be especially unreliable in cases where men's and women's labor market involvement—and involvement in full-time work—is linked to hypothetical wages. As research on the gender wage gap in eastern Europe has demonstrated, when low-earning women exit the labor force in disproportionate numbers, we overstate women's economic gains (Brainerd 2000). Alternatively, if women who would earn high wages leave the paid labor force in disproportionate numbers, the gender wage gap understates women's economic standing.

We demonstrated in chapters 3 and 4 that women's employment and involvement in full- and part-time work is associated with their education and having children. In chapter 5, we saw that how women are included in or excluded from the paid labor market has an impact on gender segregation in occupations. When women are employed in part-time work, they are more likely to be segregated in the labor market into feminized jobs. When women are generally excluded from the market and have a disproportionate share of household responsibilities, the few women who "get through" and maintain employment are more likely to be found in full-time, gender-integrated jobs.

To understand how these processes of labor market inclusion and exclusion affect the gender gap in wages, we examine wages among women and men with different levels of connection to the paid labor force. We construct estimates of the gender wage gap that include part-time workers and estimate the hypothetical wages of those currently not employed. Attention to the wages of full-time and part-time workers and the expected wages of nonworkers provides a more complete portrait of gender inequality in wages and earned income by illustrating how gender differences in employment rates

Figure 6.2   Comparison of the Relative Hourly Wages of Women and Men, for All Adults and for Employed Workers, Mid-1990s

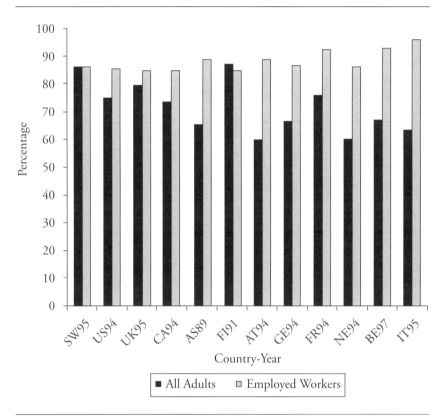

Source: Luxembourg Income Study (LIS 2003).
Note: See country abbreviations in figure A.1.

and hours worked shape the share of total income earned by women. Women's relative wages—and conventional scholarly accounts thereof—are influenced by the same factors that affect the division of household labor and the composition of the labor force.

Figure 6.2 illustrates how measures of relative wages that do and do not include the unemployed and those not in the labor force generate different accounts of gender wage inequality for LIS countries in the 1990s. The gray bar to the left shows relative wages for all women and men age eighteen to sixty-four, whether they were in the labor force, using the observed wages for those employed and estimating the wages of those not employed as zero. The lowest levels are those of countries where fewer women were earning a wage—Austria, Italy, and the Netherlands—that is, where inclusion was most limited. The black bar to the right shows relative wages for employed women and men, indicating the degree of equality for those who had observed wages in the labor market.

A key observation is that in some countries there is a large difference between bars, and in some countries there is no difference. For example, Finland and Sweden show almost no difference in the relative wages of all women and men versus employed women and men. In contrast, most conservative-corporatist countries show a large difference between the two measures. For example, Italy posts more than a thirty-percentage-point difference in the mid-1990s. Although the difference between all women and men and just their employed counterparts is largest in conservative-corporatist countries, these same countries post the highest levels of wage equality between women and men in the labor market. Again returning to the example of Italy, working women earn 93 percent of what working men earn.

The processes of inclusion in or exclusion from the labor force and the sorting of women and men into different occupations affect our understanding of cross-national variation in the relative economic status of women as measured by wages. This is especially the case when opportunities in the labor force are dictated not only by economic considerations but also by the institutionalization of gendered expectations surrounding domestic labor and the care of children.

WAGES OVER THE LIFE COURSE

The gender wage gap is a summary measure of the mean wages of working women compared to the mean wages of working men. Although it does not account for differences in labor market participation, involvement in full-time or part-time work, or occupational sex segregation, it does reflect the average value of work for women and men in the paid labor force. Again, both supply and demand explanations have been offered for understanding the relative wages of women and men. Economists typically emphasize skill-based explanations for the level and trend in the gender wage gap. That is, it is common to look at economic standing measured by the wage gap as a consequence of differential investments in experience and skills or training. To the extent that women have increased their investments in workplace skills and competencies, we would expect a narrowing of the gender wage gap.

Alternatively, the gender wage gap may reflect demand-side processes—attributions by employers about the perceived productivity of workers or reflections of employer bias against women or mothers. Recent research has found striking differences in how people evaluate prospective employees. Experimental studies show that mothers face a stiff earnings penalty and that fatherhood carries a wage premium (Correll, Benard, and Paik 2007).

Table 6.1 compares women's hourly wages relative to men's, drawing distinctions between estimates that include all women and men (those employed and not) and those that are limited to employed workers, and it displays the difference between the two measures. The table includes estimates of women's average hourly wage as a percentage of men's average hourly wage for all women and men age eighteen to sixty-four and women's and men's distribution across other social and demographic groups (for example, highly educated, parents of young children, parents of older children) in the LIS countries observed in the 1990s. (Table A.6 reports all LIS years.) On average, these data show that among women and men of working ages, women earn approximately 72 percent of men's wages. Women's hourly wages increase to 88 percent of men's when we examine only employed women and men.

The difference in relative wages between all women and men and employed workers is due to differences in employment between women and men. Where women's employment rates are significantly lower than men's, the gap is largest between the wages of all women relative to men, and of working women relative to working men (for example, Italy, the Netherlands, and Belgium). Where there are small differences in the employment of women and men, there is little difference in the relative wages between all women and men and only workers (for example, Finland and Sweden).

Table 6.1 also shows mean relative wages for highly educated women and men, parents of young children, and parents of older children. Among the highly educated, women's wages averaged 85 percent of men's, constituting a gender wage gap of 15 percent. The wage gap among highly educated workers is five percentage points lower, or 10 percent. This signals two things. First, highly educated women and men have more similar employment prospects than do women and men in general. Second, higher education does little to close the gender wage gap. In most countries, but not all, highly edu-

Table 6.1   Women's Wages Relative to Men's, by Parental Status and
             Education, Mid-1990s

		All Adults			Highly Educated		
Country	Year	All (1)	Workers (2)	Difference (2–1)	All (1)	Workers (2)	Difference (2–1)
Austria	1994	60%	89%	29%	91%	102%	11%
Australia	1989	66	89	23	69	85	16
Belgium	1997	67	93	26	91	93	1
Canada	1994	74	85	12	81	87	6
Finland	1991	87	85	–2	88	85	–3
France	1994	76	93	17	87	94	7
Germany	1994	67	87	20	72	84	12
Italy	1995	63	96	33	112	100	–12
Netherlands	1994	60	87	27	78	90	11
Sweden	1995	86	86	0	89	84	–4
United Kingdom	1995	79	85	6	85	87	2
United States	1994	75	85	10	82	87	5
Mean		72	88	17	85	90	4

Source: Luxembourg Income Study (LIS 2003).

cated women close the gender wage gap by a couple of percentage points. In some countries, however, highly educated women appear to compare to highly educated men less favorably than all women compare to all men.

A different pattern emerges when we look at wages among mothers and fathers. The gender wage gap for parents of young children is much larger than the gap among all women and men. The earnings of women with children age six or younger relative to those of men with young children range from a low of 33 percent in Germany to a high of 74 percent in Finland. This gap among all parents reflects the exclusion of many mothers with small children from the labor market. If we restrict our focus to working parents of small children, the results are much more similar to what we see for all women and men. In fact, the mean is the same with women earning 88 percent of men's earnings.

This provides an interesting contrast with the gender wage gap among parents with older children and reflects women's return to the labor force.

	Young Children Age Zero to Six			Older Children Age Seven to Seventeen		
All (1)	Workers (2)	Difference (2–1)	All (1)	Workers (2)	Difference (2–1)
36%	88%	52%	62%	89%	27%
42	90	48	68	85	17
71	97	27	69	93	24
55	82	27	72	80	8
74	86	12	86	80	–7
66	94	28	77	90	12
33	83	50	65	84	19
54	96	42	59	93	34
47	93	47	50	78	28
63	81	18	76	82	6
54	85	31	73	80	7
61	83	21	72	79	7
55	88	33	69	84	15

Among all parents with older children, the wage gap is less severe: women's relative wages move from a mean of 55 percent of men's for parents with young children to 69 percent for parents with older children. When we restrict our focus to workers, however, women's relative wages do not similarly improve. For working parents, women's relative wages are 88 percent of men's for parents with young children and 84 percent for parents with older children. This reflects the less select nature of women with older children in the labor force relative to women with younger children and may also be an indication of a penalty for interrupted employment during the prime childbearing years.

Table 6.2 reports the mean effects of education and child-rearing on women's and men's wages in a regression framework. Recall that the regression framework allows us to examine the specific effects of education and children on wages while holding other relevant information (such as age and marital status) constant. Beginning with education, we see similar effects of

Table 6.2   Cross-National Variability in Linear Regression Predicting Hourly Wages

	Women			Men		
	Highly Educated	Youngest Child Age Zero to Three	Number of Children	Highly Educated	Youngest Child Age Zero to Three	Number of Children
Mean	0.33	0.05	−0.03	0.28	0.01	−0.01
Median	0.33 (IT91)	0.06 (GE89)	−0.04 (GE00)	0.27 (IT91)	0.01 (IT95)	−0.01 (SW92)
Minimum	0.14 (GE94)	−0.20 (SW95)	−0.08 (NE91)	0.14 (GE94)	−0.07 (SW95)	−0.03 (AT97)
Maximum	0.52 (IT95)	0.21 (NE94)	0.01 (BE97)	0.46 (IT95)	0.11 (GE94)	0.01 (GE00)

Source: Luxembourg Income Study (LIS 2003).

Note: Models also include age, age-squared, medium education, marriage, and youngest child age four to six. See country abbreviations in figure A.1.

higher education on wages for both women and men. Consistent with microeconomic explanations, the effect of education on wages is positive in all countries and years. There is variation, however, suggesting that in some countries education has larger returns in the labor market than in others. For example, wage returns to education were smallest for both women and men in Germany in 1994 and largest in Italy in 1995.

The effect of having a very young child on wages is less consistent in direction for both women and men. That is, in some countries the influence of living with an infant or toddler is positive on wages, and in some it is negative. Overall, living with very young children shows a small positive influence on women's wages. There is large variability, however, in this effect: the effect on women's wages in Sweden in 1995 was large and negative, but large and positive in the Netherlands in 1994. In Sweden, mothers with very young children are less likely to exit the labor force than are mothers with very young children in the Netherlands. In contrast, the effect of very young children on men's wages shows less variability and is close to zero at the mean.

The effect of the number of children on wages is much less variable. At the mean, the effect of the number of children on women's wages is negative. This echoes the descriptive analyses shown in table 6.1, which illustrates that the less select nature of women with children—especially older children—in the labor market counteracts the wage bonus that women with very young children appear to receive. The effect of the number of children on men's wages shows almost no variability and is close to zero at the mean.

Differences in the individual-level correlates of employment, hours worked, occupational location, and wages across countries reveal how our understanding of the relative economic status of women is affected by the degree of their inclusion in the paid labor force. While women with children—and women with very young children—are more likely to be employed in the paid labor force in Denmark and Sweden than in Italy, they are more likely to be involved in part-time work and more likely to work in professional occupations and clerical, sales, and service occupations. As a result, it is not surprising that the effects of having children for women in the paid labor force are negative in Sweden and positive in Italy. It is likely that the women who remain in the paid labor force in Italy are a highly selective group who maintain connections to the paid labor force exactly because they expect high returns. If such a mechanism is at work, then there is reason to believe that our estimates of the effects of child-rearing, and possibly education, on women workers are biased because we observe only the experiences of highly select workers in countries where women's labor force participation is low.

CROSS-NATIONAL VARIABILITY IN WAGES

Country-level conditions contribute to cross-national variation in the gender wage gap. Table 6.3 displays the associations between national-level conditions and women's average wages as a percentage of men's. We report effects for all women and men and for workers only, as well as the difference between the two measures. Comparing the three columns, we see that across countries working women earn, on average, close to 80 percent of the wages of working men. Including nonworkers widens the wage gap considerably, since women are much more likely than men to be unemployed or not in the labor force.

Looking at the effects of year, we see consistent evidence of aggregate improvements in women's economic standing. The size of the gender wage gap declines over time among workers, and even more dramatically among all women and men. The more dramatic effect for all women and men shows that women's increased employment rates have garnered them a larger share of total earnings.

With the exception of part-time employment, mechanisms of inclusion and exclusion have little influence on the aggregate gender wage gap. The availability of part-time work is negatively associated with the relative economic standing of women workers and positively associated with the larger wage gaps among all women and men that account for gender differences in employment. The relationship between part-time work and higher gender wage gaps among workers exposes contradictions between economic inclusion and economic equality. When women are incorporated into the economy through part-time work, economic inequalities in pay are magnified.

There are a couple of important explanations for the relationship between part-time work and gender inequality. One suggests that the quality of part-time work is poor and thus poorly compensated. Another suggests that involvement in part-time work disadvantages workers who work part-time (and who are mostly women) through declines in accumulated work experience or access to the highly paid jobs that are typically full-time. Attention to how the wages of specific social and demographic groups—workers with children and workers with higher levels of education—correlate with rates of part-time work may help clarify the mechanisms that link part-time work with low

Table 6.3   The Association Between National Conditions and
Women's Hourly Wages Relative to Men's

	All	Workers	Difference
Intercept	32.673	79.689*	47.324[+]
Year	1.422*	0.376*	−1.063[+]
Gender egalitarianism			
Women in parliament	−25.230	−4.514	18.402
Economic conditions			
Unemployment	−54.836	44.699	96.171
Service-sector growth	94.691	−60.961	−150.128
Per capita GDP growth	−151.238	67.872	225.288[+]
Mechanisms of inclusion			
Maternity leave	20.788	−4.136	−23.126
and inequality			
Part-time employment	29.692	−25.845*	−55.598
and equality			
Child care	57.139	3.241	−54.829
Mechanisms of exclusion			
and equality			
Union density	−2.911	3.751	6.830
and inequality			
Parental leave	−4.633	−0.214	4.828
Adjusted R-squared	0.366	0.010	0.185

Source: Luxembourg Income Study (LIS 2003).
* T-ratio $\geq$ 2; [+] T-ratio $\geq$ 1.8

wages. It is also quite possible that state policies and conditions that do not affect the overall level of women's economic standing as reflected by the gender wage gap differentially affect the wages of particular social and demographic groups. We investigate these issues in the next section.

INSTITUTIONALIZING GENDER INEQUALITY IN WAGES

Table 6.4 summarizes results from models that examine how the effects of social and demographic characteristics at the individual level vary with national context. Specifically, models test how the effects of education and the presence and age of children in the household depend on mechanisms of inclusion and exclusion and other national conditions. The first column in table 6.4 shows the relationship between national conditions and the effect of high levels of education on women's wages. The intercept shows a positive relationship, increasing over time, between high education and women's wages. Comparing results for women and men indicates that the effect of high education on wages has increased over time for both women and men. These results are consistent with research showing that the wages of those with high education have diverged from the wages of those with less education over time (Katz and Murphy 1992).

The effect of having more education on women's wages is also sensitive to mechanisms of inclusion. The level of part-time employment is negatively associated with education's effect on wages: where the part-time workforce is larger, the positive effect of high education is dampened. Although large part-time workforces may promote women's labor market participation, these gains are often offset by the caregiving demands experienced by many part-time women workers, compressing wages across the educational spectrum.

Mechanisms of exclusion are also negatively associated with the effect of education on women's wages. Where union density is higher, the effect of education is less positive for both men and women. High levels of union density, not surprisingly, serve to shrink the pay gap between highly educated and less-educated workers of both sexes. The wage-equalizing effects of unionization and other indicators of centralized bargaining are well established in comparative research (see, for example, Kenworthy 2004; Blau and Kahn 2002). These results emphasize that wage-setting institutions like labor unions may simultaneously exclude certain groups from work while effecting greater equality among workers within the labor market.

Long parental leaves are also associated with greater wage equality by education among workers. Similar to the exclusionary effects of unionization, parental leave exacerbates inequality in the effects of education on employment but results in greater equality among workers. Long parental leaves are associated with declines in the effect of education on women's wages. They are unlikely to raise the wages of women with low levels of education; it is more likely that they retard wage growth among well-educated women over the life course. Linked to the wholesale exit of women (including those with more education) from paid work, long parental leaves exacerbate the inequality associated with child-rearing while reducing the inequality associated with

Table 6.4   The Association Between National Conditions and Factors Predicting Hourly Wages

	Women			Men		
	Highly Educated	Youngest Child Age Zero to Three	Number of Children	Highly Educated	Youngest Child Age Zero to Three	Number of Children
Intercept	0.803*	0.239	0.033	0.552*	0.033	−0.020
Year	0.007+	−0.001	0.001	0.010*	−0.001	0.000
Part-time employment	−0.579*	0.419+	−0.126*	−0.144	0.086	−0.048+
Child care	0.042	0.093	0.171*	0.311	−0.221+	0.038
Union density	−0.569*	−0.170	−0.056*	−0.356*	0.009	−0.005
Parental leave	−0.118*	−0.044	−0.019*	−0.058	0.029	−0.006

Source: Luxembourg Income Study (LIS 2003).

Note: Models also include age, age-squared, medium education, marriage, and youngest child age four to six at the individual level and women's employment, service-sector growth, per capita GDP, unemployment, maternity leave, women in parliament, and year at the country level.

T-ratio ≥ 2; +*T*-ratio ≥ 1.8

education. We now examine how national conditions interact with the effects of having children.

Mechanisms of inclusion are important for understanding variability in the effect of very young children on women's wages. Where part-time employment is greater, the positive effect of living with an infant or toddler on wages is larger. That is, women with very young children earn a premium in countries with large part-time workforces compared to women in countries with smaller part-time workforces. It may be the case that these women represent a distinct group with particularly strong labor force attachments that are rewarded in the paid labor market.

Whereas part-time employment has a negative effect on the wages of women living with children, publicly funded child care has a positive effect on their wages. These results highlight that the particular mechanism of inclusion has consequences for inequality measured within the labor market. For example, countries with high rates of part-time employment do a better job of incorporating mothers—especially those with older children—into the labor market. Yet, if mothers are incorporated into the labor market through part-time work, their occupation and wage fortunes are distinct from those of other workers. It is likely that they continue to devote disproportionate time to domestic labor (or their employers perceive that they do), and they earn less as a result.

In contrast, countries with higher rates of public support for child care reward the labor force attachment of mothers. Mothers who maintain a connection to the labor force receive higher wages. It may be the case that public support for child care enables mothers to maintain connections to the labor market and therefore not risk the wage losses associated with child-rearing. It is also likely that public support for child care reduces the likelihood that employers will discriminate specifically against women for having children.

Mechanisms of exclusion—union density and parental leave—are associated with lower wages for women with children. Employed mothers living in countries with high levels of unionization and long parental leaves earn less relative to mothers in other countries. We suspect that these effects are driven by the high degree of gender specialization associated with high rates of unionization and long parental leaves. That is, these conditions encourage mothers to decrease the intensity of their labor market involvement, while simultaneously encouraging fathers to increase the intensity of their involvement. The decreased intensity of labor force involvement among workers who are mothers, or even employers' perceptions of decreased intensity, could retard their wages. It is possible that mothers in these countries suffer both from losing labor market experience and from failing to meet employer expectations of an ideal worker.

SPOTLIGHT: TRENDS IN WOMEN'S WAGES IN THE UNITED STATES AND WEST GERMANY

In this section, we explore trends in women's wages in the United States and West Germany. Figure 6.3 shows trends in women's wages relative to men's among all women and men and among working women and men. In the United States, the gender pay gap between all women and men and among workers only narrows over time. The difference between all women and men

Figure 6.3   Trends in Women's Hourly Wages Relative to Men's for All Adults and for Employed Workers, in the United States and West Germany

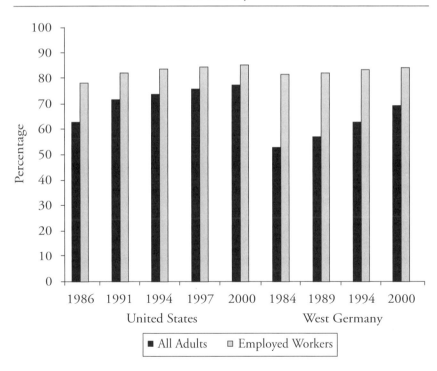

Source: Luxembourg Income Study (LIS 2003).

Table 6.5   Trends in Women's Hourly Wages Relative to Men's in the
            United States and West Germany

	All Adults			Highly Educated		
	All (1)	Workers (2)	Difference (2–1)	All (1)	Workers (2)	Difference (2–1)
United States						
1986	63%	79%	16%	72%	81%	9%
1991	72	83	11	81	86	5
1994	75	85	10	82	87	5
1997	77	86	9	83	87	5
2000	79	87	8	84	88	4
West Germany						
1984	54	84	29	75	96	21
1989	58	83	26	71	91	19
1994	64	85	21	64	83	19
2000	71	86	14	76	85	8

Source: Luxembourg Income Study (LIS 2003).

and workers also decreases. The trend for the United States, however, does not appear linear. There was a substantial convergence in the gender wage gap among all working-age women and men from 1986 to 1991. This narrowing may reflect changes in women's and men's relative standing with the recession of the early 1990s.

West Germany displays a somewhat different pattern. The gender wage gap among all women and men narrows over time, but the gap among working women and men remains fairly constant. In the United States, the incorporation of women into the labor market has been accompanied by corresponding increases in wage gains among women in the labor market. In West Germany, however, women's incorporation into paid work has not coincided with changes in wage equality among the employed.

Table 6.5 displays trends in women's wages relative to men's for specific social and demographic groups. We start with the gender wage gap among highly educated men and women in the United States. Here we see a trend similar to that for all men and women—a narrowing of the gap over time, with a pronounced shift toward equality from 1986 to 1991. We also see de-

Young Children Age Zero to Six			Older Children Age Seven to Seventeen		
All (1)	Workers (2)	Difference (2–1)	All (1)	Workers (2)	Difference (2–1)
45%	77%	32%	61%	74%	13%
57	79	22	70	77	7
61	83	21	72	79	7
64	82	18	74	81	7
64	82	18	78	83	5
32	83	52	50	78	28
31	81	50	55	80	25
30	82	53	59	81	23
34	82	49	70	81	11

clines in the gender wage gap associated with having children. In terms of absolute difference, parents with children age zero to six saw the greatest change. In 1986, among all parents with young children, women's wages were 45 percent of men's; they had increased to 57 percent by 1991, and 64 percent by 2000. The gender wage gap among employed parents with young children closed as well, but by only five percentage points. We see a similar pattern for parents of children age seven to seventeen, but more change in the gender wage gap among the employed. The gender wage gap for employed parents of older children narrowed by nine percentage points.

We now review trends in West Germany, where the gender wage gap among highly educated women and men shows a surprising pattern. Unlike in the United States, highly educated German women have not closed the gender wage gap with highly educated German men. In fact, among the employed, highly educated women appear to have lost ground since the 1980s, posting relative wages of 96 percent of men's in 1984 and 85 percent of men's in 2000. Parents of young children show a similar level of stagnation in the gender wage gap. Among parents with children age zero to six, women's rela-

Table 6.6 Linear Regression Predicting Women's Hourly Wages in the United States and West Germany

	High Education		Youngest Child Age Zero to Three		Number of Children	
	Estimate	95 Percent Confidence Interval	Estimate	95 Percent Confidence Interval	Estimate	95 Percent Confidence Interval
United States						
1986	0.38*	0.33 0.43	0.06*	0.00 0.11	-0.05*	-0.07 -0.03
1991	0.42*	0.40 0.43	0.09*	0.07 0.11	-0.05*	-0.05 -0.04
1994	0.42*	0.40 0.44	0.07*	0.05 0.09	-0.04*	-0.04 -0.03
1997	0.43*	0.41 0.45	0.07*	0.05 0.09	-0.04*	-0.05 -0.03
2000	0.45*	0.43 0.47	0.06*	0.04 0.08	-0.04*	-0.04 -0.03
West Germany						
1984	0.42*	0.35 0.49	0.17*	0.07 0.27	-0.05*	-0.08 -0.02
1989	0.36*	0.28 0.43	0.06	-0.03 0.15	-0.02	-0.05 0.01
1994	0.19*	0.12 0.26	0.06	-0.09 0.21	-0.02	-0.06 0.01
2000	0.28*	0.23 0.33	0.14*	0.04 0.24	-0.04*	-0.07 -0.01

Source: Luxembourg Income Study (LIS 2003).

Note: Models also include age, age-squared, medium education, marriage, and youngest child age four to six.

$*p < .05$

tive wages stood at 32 percent of men's in 1984 and 34 percent in 2000, and for employed parents women earned 83 percent of men's wages in 1984 and 82 percent in 2000. The only appreciable narrowing of the gender wage gap is in fact rather sizable: among all working-age parents with older children, West German women closed the gap by twenty percentage points, with a large jump from 1994 to 2000.

Table 6.6 shows trends in the individual correlates of women's wages in the United States from 1986 to 2000 generated by regression analysis. The effect of high levels of education on women's wages becomes more positive over time. There is little change in the positive effect of very young children or the negative effect of the number of children on women's wages. We do, however, observe an irregularity in the effect of having a very young child on women's wages in 1991. The effect is larger in 1991 than in other years, although the difference is not statistically significant. Recall from chapter 3 that during the recession of 1991 women with very young children were less likely to be in the labor force. This larger positive effect on wages probably reflects the more select nature of mothers with very young children who remained in the labor force during this time.

Table 6.6 also shows trends in the individual correlates of women's wages in West Germany from 1984 to 2000 generated by regression analysis. Unlike the effect of greater education on the wages of U.S. women, we observe that the effect of greater education on German women's wages is less positive over time. One possible explanation for this pattern is the increasing length of parental leave during this time period. Parental leave is associated with less positive effects of education on women's wages. Similar to their U.S. counterparts, German women experience little change in either the positive effect of having very young children or the negative effect of the number of children on their wages.

CONCLUSION

Estimates of the gender wage gap across countries show that women have experienced economic gains relative to men over the last thirty years. Most recent estimates suggest that women's wages are between 75 and 80 percent of men's. Further, recent data reveal a convergence (or declining cross-national variation) in the gender wage gap across countries.

Education is a strong—and increasingly important—predictor of wages, and women's gains in education help to explain their overall economic gains. Yet the persistence of gender inequality in wages is connected to gender inequalities in the domestic obligations associated with child-rearing. More-over, while a number of national conditions directly affect our understanding of the gender wage gap, they also influence women's economic standing indi-rectly through their effects on the domestic division of labor by shaping both labor supply and employer perceptions about women's work in the paid labor force.

Mechanisms of inclusion and exclusion influence employment in ways that are consequential for estimates of the gender wage gap. The relative eco-nomic standing of women is structured by differential access to paid employ-ment, full- and part-time work, and particular occupations in relation to pub-licly provided child care and parental leave.

Furthermore, mechanisms of inclusion and exclusion may exacerbate wage inequality over the life course through one or both of the following mecha-nisms. First, they may affect labor market involvement over the life course and the resultant accumulation of work experience. Second, they may affect employer perceptions of the suitability of mothers or fathers for waged work.

Although labor market exclusion may be associated with strong economic performance among working women in the short term, if women maintain a disproportionate share of domestic responsibilities, gender inequality in wages will endure. Decreases in the gender wage gap provide little cause for celebration of women's economic progress if they are driven by the exclusion of women from the labor market, particularly to the extent that such exclu-sion is associated with the demands of child-rearing.

CHAPTER 7

Inequality in Employment, Hours Worked, Occupation, and Wages in the United States and Germany

Up to now, this book has focused on gender inequality cross-nationally. This chapter shifts the focus to examine heterogeneity among women within countries, offering additional detail on how the dynamics of labor market inclusion and workers' attachment to the paid labor force influence inequality for different groups of women within single-country settings. The aim of this chapter is to apply some of the insights generated from cross-national accounts of gender inequality in the labor market to the study of inequality between women of different races, ethnicities, and nationalities within countries.

The processes that generate inequality are situated at both the individual and group levels and operate in relation to the structural and institutional conditions that affect domestic work and work in the paid labor force. In this chapter, we examine the extent to which education and child-rearing affect the labor market involvement and concentration in different occupations of women from different racial and ethnic groups in the United States and of different nationalities in Germany. We also consider how employment patterns affect our estimates of wage inequality. We are keenly aware of the limitations of focusing on only two cases, but no other LIS countries offer sufficient data to examine employment, hours worked, occupation, and wages by race, ethnicity, and nationality. We believe these results are illustrative, and we encourage future scholars to examine more carefully how state-level social policies and employment conditions structure tradeoffs between home and work differently across social and demographic groups in other countries.

Previous chapters have highlighted the importance of education and child-rearing for understanding inequality between women and men within countries. These same characteristics may be associated with inequality between different groups of women within the same country. On the one hand, different groups of women may have different levels of educational attainment or family obligations. Inequality in economic outcomes between groups of women may be explained by differences in the composition of the group (for example, level of education and domestic responsibilities associated with child-rearing). On the other hand, variation in the economic outcomes of different groups of women may be explained by the varying salience of factors like education and child-rearing for labor market outcomes. Institutional designs may magnify or dampen inequality between groups.

The previous chapter spotlights on the United States and West Germany (this chapter considers Germany as a whole after reunification) have highlighted the importance of economic conditions for understanding women's employment outcomes in the United States, and of family policy for Germany. These findings draw our attention to the key role played by education in inequality among women in the United States and the importance of family obligations in Germany. National-level social policies and employment conditions in each country are likely to shape the way in which social and demographic characteristics, such as education and child-rearing, are linked to the labor market outcomes of different racial or ethnic groups or different nationalities.

For example, in the United States the provision of paid parental leave is generally left to the discretion of individual employers. Women working in professional occupations are not only much more likely to be able to afford to take time off from work but also much more likely than women working in service occupations to have employers that offer paid leave. Thus, American women who work in professional jobs may be able to take parental leave with the expectation of job security and without significant loss of income. American women who work in service jobs, however, are much less likely to receive parental leave benefits, and even if their employers offer job security during parental leave, they may not be able to afford the time off from work. The absence of paid parental leave therefore may increase inequality between different classes of workers. To the extent that this class cleavage is aligned with cleavages by race and ethnicity, we can expect inequality between race and ethnic groups to be magnified. In contrast, in Germany the provision of extensive paid parental leave may exacerbate inequality between women and men, but decrease inequality between groups of women by locating inequality around motherhood rather than class.

CLEAVAGES IN THE UNITED STATES

In the United States, we focus on economic divisions by race and ethnicity, examining differences among non-Hispanic white, non-Hispanic black, and Hispanic women. Having historically held a marginalized place in the U.S. economic and social structure, black women made strong relative wage gains through the 1950s and 1960s, only to see them stall in more recent years (Pettit and Ewert, forthcoming). Increases in the educational attainment of black Americans relative to their white counterparts through the 1950s and 1960s, as well as occupational shifts and antidiscrimination laws, fueled black economic progress (Freeman 1973; Brown 1984; Darity and Mason 1998). A movement away from domestic service and into better-paying occupations was particularly advantageous for older cohorts of black women workers (Goldin 1990; Blau and Beller 1992). Affirmative action and antidiscrimination laws helped blacks secure employment in government jobs and professional occupations and spurred declines in overt wage discrimination (Darity and Mason 1998; Grodsky and Pager 2001).

Since the 1980s, however, black women's relative wages have declined. Black women today have lower levels of education than white women, are more likely to be unemployed, and are disproportionately concentrated in low-skill sectors of the economy (Browne and Misra 2003; McCall 2005). Research has documented growing wage inequality by education among women (Bernhardt et al. 2001; McCall 2000), important wage differentials by family structure (Budig and England 2001), and growing inequality by occupation (Autor, Katz, and Kearney 2004; Katz and Autor 1999). Increasing returns to education and growing wage inequality by occupation may particularly disadvantage black women given their structural location in the economy and society.

The economic disadvantage of black women in the United States is shared by Hispanic women. Hispanic women are less likely to be employed and more likely to receive lower wages than white women. There is variation in the labor force participation and outcomes among Hispanic women related to country of origin and immigration status. In relation to whites, for example, Cuban women fare best, followed by Puerto Rican women and then by Mexican-origin women. (U.S.-born Mexican Americans fare better than their Mexican-born counterparts.) Mexican-origin women make up the largest share—about two-thirds—of Hispanic women. As a group, the labor market fortunes of Mexican-origin women have been hampered by a continuous immigration flow, low levels of education, and geographic concentration in economically depressed areas (Misra 1999; Corcoran, Heflin, and Reyes 1999). Thus, the group with the worst outcomes is also the largest subgroup of Hispanic women.

CLEAVAGES IN GERMANY

In Germany, we focus on nationality and examine three groups: German nationals, Turkish nationals, and other foreign nationals. Research on racial and ethnic cleavages in Germany is complicated because German official statistics distinguish residents only by nationality (Liebig 2007). In statistics, ethnic Germans and other immigrants granted nationality become "German nationals" and first- and second-generation immigrants who have not achieved German nationality remain foreigners and are identified by their country of nationality. Thus, our category "German national" includes native-born ethnic Germans, foreign-born ethnic Germans, and non-ethnic Germans who are native- or foreign-born but have been naturalized. Consistent with prior research, we examine Turkish nationals as the largest immigrant group. For a third group, we examine foreign nationals from non-Turkish guest-worker-sending countries (primarily Greece, Spain, Italy, and the former Yugoslavia), and nationals of eastern Europe and Russia. Foreign nationals make up about 9 percent of Germany's population; among foreign nationals, Turks are the largest group, at 26 percent (Trzcinski 2006).

There have been three main sources of immigration to Germany: guest-worker migrants, ethnic German migrants, and humanitarian migrants. In response to a short supply of low-wage workers, guest-worker recruitment treaties were signed between 1955 and 1968 with Italy, Greece, Spain, Turkey, Morocco, Portugal, Tunisia, and Yugoslavia (Liebig 2007). Both men and women were recruited; approximately one-quarter of guest workers were women recruited by Germany "to work in the least attractive jobs in its harshest industries" (Wilpert 1990, 7). Most female guest workers were employed in manufacturing, and most of these women were from Turkey or Yugoslavia (Wilpert 1990).

Although the recruitment of guest workers ended in 1973, family reunification was a continued source of migrants from these countries. Spouses of guest workers, mostly women, did not automatically obtain access to the labor market (Liebig 2007). Although Germany allowed family unification, there was no attempt to integrate guest workers and their families into German society. Policies opposed naturalization and encouraged return to the sending country.

Nationality is not granted by virtue of birth in Germany; hence, many second-generation immigrants are nationals of their parent's country of origin. It was not until the 1990s that policies were changed to allow application for German nationality after fifteen years in the country; further reforms followed in 2000 and 2005 (Euwals et al. 2007). Despite liberalizations in the 1990s, most guest workers and their families have not obtained nationality. Those who have done so tend to be a more select group with higher educational credentials and a better command of German (Liebig 2007).

Germany's strict policy on naturalization does not apply to ethnic German migrants. Until recently, Germany granted automatic nationality to anyone who could document a German bloodline. The immigration of ethnic Germans, primarily from eastern Europe, peaked in 1989 to 1990. Not only were ethnic Germans granted citizenship, but they received considerable assistance to integrate. Those from the former Soviet Union received a cash payment as an "integration allowance." Humanitarian migrants are the most recent source of immigration to Germany. Many humanitarian migrants are from the former Yugoslavia (now Bosnia and Herzegovina, Croatia, the Republic of Macedonia, Montenegro, Serbia, and Slovenia) (Liebig 2007).

Foreign-born women, especially Turkish nationals, are disadvantaged in the labor market. This disadvantage is largely explained, however, by differences in age, education, and family-status characteristics. Comparing native-born and foreign-born women, foreign-born women are much more likely to have low levels of education and thus are especially vulnerable to unemployment and economic downturns (Liebig 2007). Compared to German nationals, Turkish nationals are much less likely to be employed. Among women with the least education, however, Turkish women are slightly more likely to be employed than are German nationals (Euwals et al. 2007; Liebig 2007). The employment rate of non-Turkish immigrants lags behind the employment rate of German women, but is higher than the rate of Turkish women; again, differences are largely explained by women's social and demographic characteristics (Trzcinski 2006).

In summary, there are clearly racial and ethnic cleavages among women in both countries. These cleavages are, at least in part, compositional. That is, different groups of women bring different sets of human capital to the labor market and may have different levels of family obligations. But also, the mechanisms relating these social and demographic characteristics to labor market outcomes may vary by group. In this chapter, we examine the social and demographic correlates of economic inequality between women within countries and in relation to race, ethnicity, and nationality.

EMPLOYMENT

Previous chapters documented variation in women's employment across countries. Table 7.1 shows women's employment by race and ethnicity in the United States and by nationality in Germany in the mid to late 1990s. Although we focus here on differences among women within Germany and the United States, there are some illuminating comparisons across these two countries. First, employment, including full-time employment, is higher for all groups in the United States than in Germany. Employment ranges from 63 to 78 percent in the United States, compared to 33 to 61 percent in Germany. Hispanic women, the group with the lowest level of employment in the United States, have greater labor market involvement than do German nationals, the group with the highest level of employment in Germany.

Despite these differences, both countries exhibit similar patterns of labor force participation. In both countries, women from the majority are the least likely to be out of the labor force. White women in the United States and German nationals have employment rates that are five to nine percentage points higher than those of black women in the United States or other nationals in Germany, respectively. Majority women are also the most likely to be employed part-time. Minority groups share some similarities as well. Hispanic women in the United States and Turkish nationals in Germany appear particularly disadvantaged in employment rates. The groups in the midrange—black women in the United States and other nationals in Germany—appear more similar in employment rates to the majority group than to Hispanic women or Turkish nationals.

Table 7.1   Employment Rates of Women in the United States and
Germany, Age Eighteen to Sixty-Four, by Subgroup

	United States: Race-Ethnicity			Germany: Nationality		
	White	Black	Hispanic	German	Other	Turkish
All women						
Not in labor force	22%	27%	37%	39%	48%	67%
Part-time	20	13	15	22	21	10
Full-time	58	60	48	39	31	24
Highly educated						
Not in labor force	16	17	21	24	46	53
Part-time	21	12	19	22	29	12
Full-time	63	71	60	54	25	35
Young children						
(Age zero to six)						
Not in labor force	27	30	45	58	69	82
Part-time	24	14	13	26	21	7
Full-time	49	56	42	16	10	11
Older children						
(Age seven to seventeen)						
Not in labor force	18	23	32	30	46	65
Part-time	25	14	17	33	22	8
Full-time	57	63	51	37	32	27
Number of observations	85,982	12,624	18,364	12,063	959	638

Source: Luxembourg Income Study (LIS 2003).

Differences in employment rates between racial, ethnic, and nationality groups vary dramatically between the United States and Germany. The spread in employment rates by nationality in Germany is much greater than the spread in the United States by race and ethnicity. In Germany, Turkish women stand out as especially different from other nationals in employment rates. The employment rate of Turkish women, at 33 percent, lags behind that of German nationals by twenty-seven percentage points, compared to

Hispanic women in the United States, whose employment rate lags behind that of white women by fifteen points.

We now look at variation in the effects of individual-level characteristics for different groups of women, starting with education. As expected, more highly educated women are more likely to be employed and to work full-time across all groups in the United States. Minority women, however, appear to get more of an employment boost from higher levels of education than do white women. The employment rate for Hispanic women increases from 63 to 79 percent among highly educated women. And highly educated black women's full-time employment rate outpaces that of highly educated white women by eight percentage points—71 percent compared to 63 percent.

This contrasts with the German case, where German nationals appear to get the biggest boost from more education, which increases their employment rate from 61 to 76 percent. Other nationals show no significant change. Although Turkish nationals increase their participation with education, only 35 percent of highly educated Turkish national women work full-time.

We now examine the effects of having children on the employment of women from different ethnic and racial groups. As we have seen in other chapters, family obligations depress women's employment rates in Germany more than in the United States. Comparing all working-age women (age eighteen to sixty-four) in the United States to women with young children, mothers of children six years old or younger show employment rates that are three to eight percentage points lower than rates for all women. Hispanic women with young children show the largest drop, at eight points, and black mothers of young children show the smallest drop, at three points. For white women with young children, we observe a larger drop in full-time employment but an associated shift to part-time employment. Employment rates for women with older children resemble overall rates.

In Germany, the drop in employment rates for women with young children is much more pronounced. Women with young children are employed at rates fifteen to twenty-one percentage points lower, depending on nationality, than the rates of all working-age women (age eighteen to sixty-four). Full-time employment rates for mothers of children age six or younger range from 10 percent for other nationals to 16 percent for German nationals. Employment rates rebound for women with older children.

Next we try to understand these differences in employment rates by examining whether education and child-rearing affect the employment of different groups in the same way. Table 7.2 displays the effects of education and children on employment from regression models that hold other relevant information constant. The panels illustrate important similarities and differences by race and ethnicity in the United States and by nationality in Germany. Similar to the findings in chapter 3, education is positively related to employment. This is especially true in the United States, where having a high level of education exerts a strong influence on employment. The positive effect of education is even greater for black women than it is for white or Hispanic women.

Differences are harder to detect in Germany because of the smaller sample size, but some clear patterns emerge. Education is important, but to a lesser extent. There is a strong positive effect of higher levels of education on employment for German nationals, but it is smaller in magnitude than in the United States, and education is not as important for Turkish and other nationals. This suggests that education does not sort women into and out of employment as strongly in Germany as it does in the United States.

In contrast, the family obligations associated with having children appear to be a stronger sorting mechanism in Germany than in the United States. In the United States, having a very young child reduces the labor force participation of white and Hispanic women. Black women, however, exhibit a different pattern: they are not less likely to be employed if they have an infant or toddler at home. Germany shows even stronger effects for family obligations on women's employment. Children, especially very young children, reduce women's employment. In sum, women in the United States are strongly sorted into or out of the labor force by education, whereas in Germany women are strongly sorted by family obligations.

Table 7.3 shows the extent to which the non-employed differ from employed workers on education and family obligations. We show these differences because they reveal how women employed in the labor market differ from women outside it. Given the results in table 7.2, we expect that on average women in the labor market will be more likely to have high levels of education and less likely to have very young children. Table 7.2 suggests, however, that there are deviations from this pattern based on race, ethnicity, and nationality.

The difference in educational levels between employed and non-employed women is not nearly as large in Germany as it is in the United States. In the United States, employed women are much more likely to have high levels of

Table 7.2　Logistic Regression Predicting Women's Employment in the United States and Germany, by Subgroup, Odds Ratios

	High Education	95 Percent Confidence Interval		Youngest Child Age Zero to Three	95 Percent Confidence Interval		Number of Children	95 Percent Confidence Interval	
	Estimate			Estimate			Estimate		
United States									
White	3.55*	3.34	3.77	0.56*	0.53	0.59	0.83*	0.81	0.85
Black	3.86*	3.43	4.33	0.90	0.79	1.02	0.83*	0.80	0.87
Hispanic	3.28*	3.01	3.57	0.61*	0.55	0.67	0.88*	0.85	0.91
Germany									
German national	2.69*	2.24	3.24	0.18*	0.14	0.23	0.66*	0.60	0.71
Other national	0.78	0.44	1.39	0.29*	0.12	0.72	0.56*	0.43	0.73
Turkish national	1.76	0.72	4.32	0.42*	0.18	1.00	0.99	0.67	1.46

Source: Luxembourg Income Study (LIS 2003).

Note: Models also include age, age-squared, medium education, marriage, youngest child age four to six, and other household income.

*p < .05

Table 7.3   Differences in Education and Family Status Between
Employed Workers and Non-Employed in the United
States and Germany, by Subgroup

	High Education	Youngest Child Age Zero to Three	Number of Children
United States			
White	0.19	–0.06	–0.15
Black	0.24	–0.06	–0.24
Hispanic	0.21	–0.13	–0.42
Germany			
German national	0.11	–0.11	–0.12
Other national	0.01	–0.14	–0.44
Turkish national	0.08	–0.19	–.32

Source: Luxembourg Income Study (LIS 2003).

education than are women who are unemployed or not in the labor force. This is true across all groups, but especially among black women, whose employment rates increase the most of all groups. Comparing employed women to non-employed women, the difference in the percentage of women with high levels of education ranges from one percentage point for other nationals to eleven percentage points for German nationals. (In contrast, the range in the United States is from nineteen percentage points for white women to twenty-four for black women.)

Family obligations play a larger role in structuring employment in Germany, most notably among Turkish women. In the United States, women with children are less likely to be employed, especially Hispanic women. Employed Hispanic women have 0.4 fewer children than non-employed Hispanic women, and they are much less likely to have a young child at home. Thus, family obligations sort Hispanic women into and out of the labor market more strongly than they do white and black women. In Germany, the gap in the average number of children of employed versus non-employed women is similar to the gap in the United States. But the difference in the proportion of employed versus non-employed women who have a child age six or younger is much larger in Germany than in the United States, and it is especially large for Turkish women.

There are strong similarities between the majority groups of each country—white women in the United States and German nationals. They differ significantly, however, in terms of the relationship between education and employment (in the United States) and the effects of having young children on women's employment (in Germany). In Germany, the majority group's employment is increased the most by education, whereas in the United States the majority group benefits the least. Hispanic women in the United States share some similarities with Turkish and other nationals in Germany in that family obligations have significant implications for their employment. In both the United States and Germany, family obligations have a greater impact on the employment of minority groups than on that of whites or German nationals.

These descriptive differences foreshadow that black and Hispanic women outside the labor force should expect worse returns to employment than black and Hispanic women inside the labor force. Germany is an interesting case because employed German nationals are more likely to be highly educated than German nationals who are not employed, but employed and non-employed German nationals have, on average, similar family obligations, as indicated by the number and ages of their children. Turkish and other nationals who are out of the labor force differ from their employed counterparts in relation to family obligations but do not differ substantially on educational qualifications, suggesting that the returns to employment that unemployed women or those out of the labor force in these groups could expect may compare well with the returns received by employed women of the same nationality.

OCCUPATION

To understand within-country economic inequality by ethnicity, race, and national status, it is important to consider not only how many and which women in each group are working but in what occupations they are employed. Segregation by race and ethnicity is not as severe as segregation by sex, at least in the United States, but it is a central divide. In the United States, for example, 52 percent of women would have to change occupations to integrate with men, but only 27 percent of white women would have to change occupations to integrate with black women (Padavic and Reskin 2002). In general, white women can be found in clerical and professional-technical jobs, black and Mexican American women can be found in clerical and ser-

Figure 7.1   Occupational Location of Women in the United States and Germany, by Subgroup

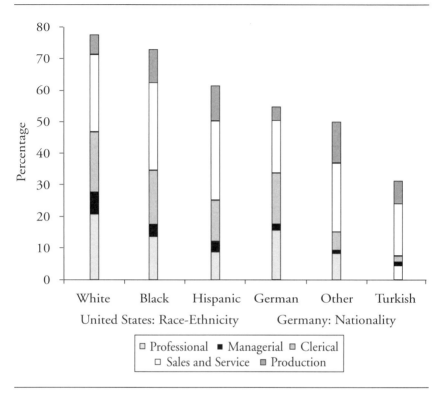

Source: Luxembourg Income Study (LIS 2003).

vice jobs, and Mexican-born women can be found working in service and production jobs (Misra 1999). Recent declines in segregation have benefited educated women more than their less-educated counterparts (Jacobs 1999), which may help explain why black and Mexican-born women's wages fell in the 1980s while white women's increased, widening the wage gap between racial-ethnic groups (Misra 1999).

Figure 7.1 shows women's occupational location in the United States by racial-ethnic group and in Germany by nationality in the mid to late 1990s. The bar height represents the total employment rate. In both countries, majority women have greater representation in professional and managerial occupations and minority women have greater representation in production and sales and service occupations. In the United States, women are evenly represented in clerical positions. Comparing black and Hispanic women, Hispanic women are more likely to be in production and sales and service, whereas black women are more likely to be in professional occupations.

German nationals have a much larger presence in clerical occupations, and minority women's concentration in production occupations is especially striking. This is consistent with Germany's immigration policy that explicitly recruited women from abroad for work in manufacturing. Unlike the United States, where the occupations of blacks and Hispanics diverge, minority groups in Germany share a similar occupational profile. Turkish and other nationals are similarly represented across occupational groups.

Table 7.4 shows the occupational distribution for employed women by education and family obligations. Employed, highly educated women from all groups are more likely than all women to be in professional and managerial occupations. In the United States, highly educated white women, however, are more concentrated in these positions, and highly educated black and Hispanic women have greater representation in clerical, sales and service, and production work than do white women. In Germany, highly educated women from all groups are more likely to be in professional occupations relative to all employed women. Similar to their U.S. counterparts, highly educated German nationals are more concentrated in professional positions, and highly educated Turkish and other nationals have greater representation in sales and service and production jobs than do German nationals. Strikingly, 43 percent of employed, highly educated Turkish nationals work in sales and service occupations.

Among employed women with young children age six or younger, we find that in the United States all subgroups are slightly more likely to be in sales and service and production jobs than American women without young children. This is most pronounced for black women. In contrast, other national and German women with young children are more likely to be in professional occupations than those without children, indicating that they are a select group. Turkish women with young children, however, are more likely to be in sales and service and production occupations, indicating that Turkish nationals' employment prospects are diminished. Unlike the analyses of employment, we do not use regression analysis to examine the effects of education and child-rearing on occupational location because our sample size for minority groups in Germany is too small.

Table 7.4   Occupational Segregation of Women in the United States and Germany, by Subgroup

	United States: Race-Ethnicity			Germany: Nationality		
	White	Black	Hispanic	German	Other	Turkish
All workers						
Professional	27%	19%	14%	28%	17%	18%
Managerial	9	4	4	3	0	0
Clerical	25	24	22	30	13	8
Sales and service	31	38	39	29	43	48
Production	8	14	18	8	26	25
Highly educated						
Professional	39	31	30	62	37	32
Managerial	11	7	8	4	0	0
Clerical	22	30	28	18	21	10
Sales and service	23	25	28	11	28	43
Production	4	7	5	4	11	15
Young children						
(Age zero to six)						
Professional	27	16	12	35	40	0
Managerial	8	3	4	2	0	0
Clerical	23	23	21	28	10	3
Sales and service	33	42	39	26	35	67
Production	9	16	21	8	15	30
Older children						
(Age seven to seventeen)						
Professional	27	19	13	28	11	12
Managerial	8	4	4	2	0	0
Clerical	25	26	21	29	10	10
Sales and service	31	37	40	31	44	49
Production	8	14	19	9	34	28

Source: Luxembourg Income Study (LIS 2003).

WAGES

Differences in employment and occupational location across groups suggest associated wage differentials. Table 7.5 shows estimated mean hourly wages for all women as a percentage of the mean wage for employed women from each country's majority group. Again, we see an across-the-board education payoff in the United States: highly educated black, white, and Hispanic working women fare better than their *less*-educated counterparts. Comparing the effects of education by group relative to baseline levels of white women's employment, highly educated white women make 10 percent more, and highly educated black women make 4 percent more, than all white women, whereas highly educated Hispanic women make the same as all employed white women. This contrasts sharply with Germany, where highly educated German nationals make 14 percent more, but highly educated other nationals make 13 percent less, and highly educated Turkish nationals make 24 percent less than all employed German national women. Furthermore, beyond not "catching up" minority workers to German nationals, education does not boost other nationals' wages and carries a wage penalty for Turkish nationals. Highly educated Turkish nationals do not earn more, and some even earn less, than their less-educated counterparts.

In terms of the effects on wages, black women in the United States stand apart from white and Hispanic women as especially disadvantaged by having young children. Employed black women with young children earn seven percentage points less than all employed black women. The figures for employed white and Hispanic women with young children are two and three points less, respectively. In contrast, having older children does not dramatically reduce wages for any group. We see a similar pattern for the wages of Turkish national women in Germany. Employed Turkish women with young children appear to disproportionately bear a wage penalty compared to Turkish women without young children, German nationals, and other nationals.

Table 7.6 presents estimates of the effects of education and family obligations on the wages of women by race, ethnicity, and nationality from regression models that hold other relevant information constant. In the United States, high education has a positive effect on wages for all groups. It appears, however, that high education is more positively related to wages for Hispanic women than for black women. In regards to family obligations, white and Hispanic women show a positive association between having a very young

Table 7.5   Mean Hourly Wages of Women in the United States and Germany, by Subgroup, as a Percentage of Majority Workers' Hourly Wage

	United States: Race-Ethnicity			Germany: Nationality		
	White	Black	Hispanic	German	Other	Turkish
All women						
All	0.73	0.65	0.50	0.52	0.40	0.22
Highly educated	0.87	0.84	0.75	0.73	0.43	0.31
Young children						
(Age zero to six)	0.66	0.57	0.42	0.32	0.26	0.08
Older children						
(Age seven to seventeen)	0.75	0.68	0.53	0.58	0.44	0.23
Workers						
All	1.00	0.92	0.83	1.00	0.86	0.80
Highly educated	1.10	1.04	1.00	1.14	0.87	0.76
Young children						
(Age zero to six)	0.98	0.85	0.80	0.98	0.86	0.67
Older children						
(Age seven to seventeen)	0.98	0.91	0.82	0.97	0.89	0.84

Source: Luxembourg Income Study (LIS 2003).

child and wages. Recall that white and Hispanic women with young children are more likely to be unemployed or out of the labor force than black women with young children. This suggests that among white and Hispanic women, mothers with very young children who can command higher wages (and who thus either face larger opportunity costs to leaving the labor force or can simply pay for child care) are more likely to remain in the labor force than women who command lower wages.

In Germany, Turkish and other nationals do not receive the same return to high education that German nationals do. This may help explain why high levels of education do not have as large a positive effect on employment for these groups. It is possible that non-German nationals have difficulty translating their education into high-wage jobs. The small sample in Germany makes differences hard to detect, but there is some evidence that the selection of Turkish and other nationals with very young children into the labor mar-

Table 7.6 Linear Regression Predicting Women's Hourly Wages in the United States and Germany, by Subgroup

	High Education		Youngest Child Age Zero to Three		Number of Children	
	Estimate	95 Percent Confidence Interval	Estimate	95 Percent Confidence Interval	Estimate	95 Percent Confidence Interval
United States						
White	0.40*	0.38 0.42	0.08*	0.07 0.10	-0.03*	-0.04 -0.03
Black	0.38*	0.34 0.41	0.01	-0.02 0.04	-0.04*	-0.05 -0.02
Hispanic	0.43*	0.41 0.46	0.04*	0.02 0.07	-0.03*	-0.04 -0.02
Germany						
German national	0.24*	0.20 0.28	0.10*	0.02 0.18	-0.05*	-0.07 -0.03
Other national	0.09	-0.03 0.21	0.03	-0.42 0.47	0.06	-0.02 0.13
Turkish national	-0.04	-0.21 0.13	-0.24	-0.55 0.08	0.04	0.00 0.09

Source: Luxembourg Income Study (LIS 2003).

Note: Models also include age, age-squared, medium education, marriage, and youngest child age four to six.

*$p < .05$

ket is not related to expected wage returns. For German nationals—but not Turkish and other nationals—having a very young child is positively associated with wages. This suggests that, unlike German nationals, minority women with very young children do not have unusually good employment prospects in the labor market.

Our understanding of inequality using a measure like wages depends not only on the relative wages of groups of women participating in the paid labor force but also on exactly how many women from each group are employed in the paid labor force, and how they compare to women who are unemployed or not in the paid labor force. Important compositional differences between the employed and the non-employed may cause us to over- or underestimate the wage gap between groups of women. To examine this selectivity argument we must consider how inequality in wages relates to the proportion of the population employed and how workers in the paid labor force differ from people not observed in the paid labor force (that is, the selectivity of workers). A comprehensive assessment of how well the observed wage gap reflects differences in economic potential in the population must take account of the differential employment of groups of women.

We have already seen in table 7.3 that nonworkers are likely to differ from workers on observable characteristics, but the extent to which workers differ from nonworkers varies by race and ethnicity in the United States and by nationality in Germany. For example, in the United States the difference in the educational level of black women inside and outside the labor force is larger than is the difference for other groups. That is, black women are more positively selected on education than are white or Hispanic women.

Table 7.7 shows estimates of the wage gap between race and ethnic groups by generating hypothetical wages for women who are not observed working in the paid labor force. In the United States in the mid-1990s, when our data were collected, conventional labor force statistics estimated the white-black wage gap at 13 percent and the white-Hispanic wage gap at nearly 25 percent. These figures overstate black and Hispanic women's relative economic standing because black and Hispanic women outside the labor force would expect to earn significantly less than would white women not in the paid labor force. Assuming jobless women would earn wages comparable to those of women of the same race, ethnicity, and education level employed in the paid labor force, the wage gaps between race and ethnic groups among women would be even greater—over 15 percent for blacks and 28 percent for Hispanics. This strik-

Table 7.7   Observed and Adjusted Hourly Wage Gaps in the United States and Germany, by Subgroup

	Observed	Adjusted
United States		
White—Black	12.9%	15.4%
White—Hispanic	24.5	28.0
Germany		
German—other national	15.4	13.7
German—Turkish national	27.8	27.8

Source: Luxembourg Income Study (LIS 2003).

ing finding suggests that, contrary to some well-publicized assumptions, measured estimates of the black-white wage gap among women provide optimistic accounts of the relative economic standing of blacks.

In Germany, however, adjusted wage gaps are the same or smaller than the observed gap. Conventional labor force statistics indicate that German nationals out-earned other nationals by over 15 percent and out-earned Turkish nationals by about 28 percent between 1994 and 2000, when our data were collected. The adjusted gaps show that accounting for differences in labor force participation does not change the wage gap between German and Turkish nationals and actually decreases the gap between German and other nationals to 14 percent. If employed, other nationals outside the labor force would command greater wages than German nationals outside the labor force, based on estimated wage returns to observed social and demographic characteristics.

Comparing the United States with Germany highlights the consequences of employment sorting mechanisms for understanding inequality in wages by race, ethnicity, and nationality within countries. In the United States, adjusted wage gaps are considerably higher because race and ethnic inequality in the U.S. labor market is strongly tied to education. In Germany, education is clearly important, but not nearly as relevant as family obligations for sorting workers into or out of the labor market. Because family obligations tell us less about expected returns to employment for non-employed women than does education, wage gap adjustments among women in Germany are small. When the labor market is sorted by family obligations and not education, inequality among women may be dampened, but inequality between women and men may be heightened.

CONCLUSION

This chapter examines heterogeneity in employment, occupation, and wages within two countries. The U.S. and German cases highlight how the composition of the labor force varies dramatically both across and within countries, affecting estimates of occupational segregation and the wage gap. In the United States, minority women out of the labor market can expect worse returns to employment than majority women outside the labor force; thus, estimates of racial-ethnic wage gaps underestimate the extent of inequality in pay. This contrasts with Germany, where minority women outside the labor force can expect the same or better returns to employment than majority women out of the labor force, making estimates of racial-ethnic wage gaps among workers a reasonable gauge of inequality in wages.

These results point to the mechanisms undergirding race and ethnic inequality among women within countries. In the United States, where wages are strongly linked to education, differences in educational attainment across racial and ethnic groups highlight the importance of education in shaping inequalities. Family obligations play a relatively small role in the United States, in part owing to the lack of public supports for parents to stay home and care for their children when they are young (see, for example, Morgan and Zippel 2003).

In Germany, educational attainment plays a secondary role to family obligations in shaping economic inequality by nationality. Two possible explanations for this are Germany's long parental leave policies and a scarcity of private child care options. Mothers of all nationalities in Germany are more likely to exit the labor market than are mothers in the United States when their children are young. The number of German mothers who remain in paid employment when their children are young is too small for us to generate a reliable statistical profile of them and their experiences. Evidence suggests, however, that gender inequality in both domestic production and child care is entrenched through national policies and conditions that reinforce women as primary caregivers of children.

Although this chapter has focused on inequality within two countries, its findings draw attention to the same mechanisms of inclusion and exclusion that guided our examination of gender inequality across countries. The laissez-faire approach to tensions between home and work in the United States leaves them to play out within the marketplace. As a result, the outsourcing of domestic work has become a key feature that distinguishes the economic fortunes of families (and women) who cook, clean, and care for others' children from families (and women) who outsource domestic responsibilities such as cooking, cleaning, and child care. Not surprisingly, minority women and those with relatively low levels of education are heavily concentrated in occupations and jobs that provide domestic labor. Inclusion, in this case, is coupled with high levels of inequality between women.

In contrast, German youth need not attain very high levels of education in order to be employed, have jobs with benefits, and earn good wages. However, strong expectations that women will care for their own children result in sometimes irreconcilable tensions between home and work. In Germany, the expectations and rewards of motherhood are at odds with the demands of the workplace. The exclusionary effects of long parental leaves transcend the boundaries of education and nationality and reinforce gender inequalities in economic outcomes. Even women who have the means to outsource domestic obligations encounter an insufficiently developed service sector that is unable to fully meet the demands of employed mothers. Across the social spectrum, gender inequality is deeply entrenched in the domestic obligations associated with rearing children.

Our conclusions would certainly be strengthened if this analysis had included additional countries with varying policy arrangements and social conditions. Ideally, we would have liked to compare findings on within-country heterogeneity from the United States and Germany with findings from other kinds of countries—for example, a representative social democratic country. No other LIS countries offer sufficient data, however, to conduct a similar analysis of racial and ethnic subgroups. In addition, our analysis does not specifically investigate how social policies and employment conditions structure inequality in relation to marital status. Single mothers may be uniquely affected by the sort of conditions we consider here. This is a vital area of research that we leave for future scholars. Nonetheless, we believe that our findings offer important clues to how the same mechanisms of inclusion and exclusion that structure gender inequality across countries shape within-country differences in the employment prospects and outcomes of minority and majority women in relation to education and child-rearing.

CHAPTER 8

The Institutionalization of Gender Inequality in the Workplace

Women's economic fortunes are highly variable across countries. Women in Sweden, Denmark, and Finland lead the world in levels of employment; women in Belgium and the Netherlands are the most likely to work alongside men in similar occupations; and working women in Italy have reached near-parity in wages with men. No single explanation can account for gender inequality in employment, occupational sex segregation, and wages across countries, but political foundations lie beneath gender inequality in the workplace. Inequality between women and men in the workplace is rooted in societal conceptions of gender and family obligations, and it is institutionalized through social policies and employment conditions that regulate, routinize, and reinforce gender differences in home production and market work.

The evidence to support this picture was pieced together using multiple data sources and four measures of gender inequality in economic outcomes. Analyses of the Luxembourg Income Study (LIS) data, along with country-level measures of national political and economic conditions—including mechanisms of inclusion and exclusion—generate three key insights. First, accounts of gender inequality in the economy are keenly affected by what we measure and how we measure it. Second, differences in how women and men fulfill their gender and family responsibilities and in how states and markets support those responsibilities are clearly implicated in cross-national accounts of gender inequality in the labor market. Third, the very nature of the trade-off between labor market inclusion and equality within the market obscures our understanding of the significance and extent of gender inequality.

This book has focused on four key indicators of economic inequality because, as chapter 1 demonstrated, countries vary considerably in how they rank on measures of women's inclusion in the labor market, hours worked, occupational sex segregation, and gender inequality in wages. Where women have made significant inroads into the paid labor force, they often encounter relatively high levels of occupational sex segregation and relatively low wages. In contrast, where women's employment levels are low, women who remain in the workforce often fare better on measures of occupational and wage inequality. A focus on only one outcome or only one country obscures the complex nature and underpinnings of gender inequality. An analysis of several indicators from multiple countries is required to understand the complex mechanisms and key individual characteristics and country conditions that affect employment in the paid labor market and gender inequality in hours worked, occupation, and wages. Efforts to further understand women's labor market position therefore require that we pay attention to multiple indicators of inequality and adopt a multifaceted approach that considers the individual, household, and societal factors that structure gender inequality.

Attention to multiple indicators of gender inequality is necessary because inequality in one domain has implications for inequality in another. For example, inclusionary mechanisms—part-time work and public child care—facilitate the employment of women, and of mothers in particular. Yet they do so in very different ways. Women's economic inclusion, when keyed to part-time work, is associated with segregation into female-dominated occupations. When women's employment is coupled with more gender equality in household labor—as is the case with publicly funded child care—occupational sex segregation is less severe because women, and especially mothers, are better integrated into the labor market.

Rearing children fundamentally cleaves the wages of women from those of men, though country-level conditions (and the employment patterns they support) can go a long way toward mitigating the negative effects of children on women's wages. Although mechanisms of exclusion are associated with lower rates of employment among women and mothers, they are also associated with greater gender equality in wages for those who remain in the labor market. Unionization and long parental leaves may lead to a highly selective workforce, driving up wages among women in the labor market. It is also the case that strong unions can promote greater wage equality, both reducing the wage penalties associated with motherhood and the wage premiums associated with fatherhood (and childlessness among women).

Institutional conditions also frame economic inequality within racial and ethnic groups in the United States and by nationality in Germany. Black and Hispanic women fare poorly economically compared to white women in the United States. German nationals fare better on economic outcomes than foreign nationals living in Germany. There are important racial and ethnic disparities in the United States in key predictors of employment, occupation, and wages. Black and Hispanic women still trail whites in years of school completed and also differ from whites in relation to other social and demographic characteristics associated with labor market outcomes. Similar differences are found in Germany between German nationals and Turkish women or women of other nationalities. While majority-group members are much more likely to be employed in both the United States and Germany, minority-group members are more likely to be concentrated in sectors of the economy where wages have lagged behind those of majority-group members.

Institutional factors undergird racial and ethnic inequality in the United States and inequality by nationality in Germany. We have shown that certain features of the political and economic landscape in both countries shape the economic fortunes of ethnic and racial groups. While differences in education drive racial and ethnic economic inequality in the United States, in Germany education is secondary to the effects of family obligations in fostering inequalities for different national groups.

There is no easy remedy for gender inequality in the household and the labor market. It is critical, however, to clarify how alternative indicators of labor market inequality generate different estimates of the relative standing of women across countries. Different measures of gender inequality reflect gender differences in power and resources at home and work. The fact that countries perform inconsistently across our four measures of economic inequality reveals that differential rates of employment are critical in determining occupational sex segregation and the gender wage gap among workers.

We close by returning to some of the central questions that have motivated this research. First, we ask whether there is a necessary tradeoff between women's labor market inclusion and economic equality within the market. Do high levels of women's employment necessarily bring high levels of occupational sex segregation, and must high employment levels among women always be accompanied by low relative wages? Surely the answer is no: women across many countries have exhibited strong gains in employment along with gains in occupational integration and wages. Yet we struggle to identify even one country where women can have children without risking their economic fortunes. Nonetheless, this exercise points to the key causal processes undergirding gender inequality in the labor market.

Second, we discuss the implications of gender inequality in employment, hours worked, occupation, and wages. As we have seen, women's economic fortunes are shaped by the domestic demands associated with child-rearing and the manner in which states relieve or concentrate caregiving within households and in the hands of women. We discuss how gender inequalities in households and the economy reverberate over the life course and across generations through their effects on economic security and fertility.

THE INCLUSION-EQUALITY TRADEOFF

Gender inequalities in employment and especially wages, occupational sex segregation, and involvement in part-time work primarily manifest for women and men with children. Although the gender divide in work and family obligations is by no means determinate, as long as women's and men's family responsibilities differ, there is likely to be a tradeoff between labor market inclusion and economic equality measured within the marketplace.

Table 8.1 revisits the theoretical model articulated in chapter 2, noting the ways in which tradeoffs between labor market inclusion and other indicators of economic equality are borne by different social and demographic groups. State policies and conditions can alleviate the tensions between gender, family, and work. Their effects vary, however, across cases and within countries, and also differentially by measures of gender equality. For example, chapter 3 demonstrated that the availability of part-time work and the provision of publicly supported child care foster high levels of employment among women, although in different ways. Some countries enable mothers to combine work and family by relieving the domestic demands associated with children through publicly provided child care, thereby reducing inequality in employment between mothers and childless women. At the same time, however, publicly provided child care is associated with greater inequality in employ-

Table 8.1   Results in Relation to the Theoretical Framework

	Inclusion	Exclusion
Equality	Conditions that foster high levels of female employment by relieving the demands of child-rearing are associated with larger differences in employment by education. Although reduced domestic demands foster equality in hours worked and occupation, they are associated with the concentration of highly educated women in paid employment (especially full-time work) and greater concentrations of highly educated women in professional jobs.	Conditions that foster low levels of female employment by establishing ideal-worker norms inconsistent with the demands of child-rearing are associated with smaller gaps in employment by education. Employment protections foster equality by education in hours worked and pay among the employed.
Inequality	Conditions that foster high levels of female employment by promoting flexible working arrangements that allow women to combine employment with disproportionate responsibility for the demands of child-rearing are associated with relatively low rates of employment among women who specialize in home production, as signaled by more children. Expectations of gender specialization at home and at work are associated with the concentration of highly educated women in full-time employment and less-educated women in part-time employment, lower educational inequalities in wages, and larger wage gaps between childless women and those with more than one child. Women with very young children, however, are relatively well compensated.	Conditions that foster low levels of female employment by concentrating the demands of child-rearing within the home are associated with the exclusion of women with very young children from work in the paid labor force. Expectations of gender specialization at home and at work are associated with relatively small wage differences by education but relatively large wage differences between mothers and childless women. Greater investments in domestic work, signaled by more children, are associated with relatively low wages.

Source: Authors' compilation.

ment between highly educated women and those with less education. Other countries enable mothers to combine work and family by emphasizing work hours that are compatible with child-rearing demands through widely available part-time employment. The availability of part-time work, however, is associated with cleavages in employment between mothers with very young children and other mothers.

Chapter 4 confirmed some of the insights in chapter 3, although with a focus on a smaller subset of fifteen countries that enabled us to examine patterns of part-time employment. Policies that relieve the domestic demands of child-rearing not only foster mother's employment but enable them to secure full-time jobs. However, while mothers with very young children exhibit higher employment rates in countries with generous child-care provision, less-educated women are more likely to be excluded from employment in the paid labor force. Conditions that concentrate the demands of caregiving within households often lead to the exclusion of women—and mothers—from both full- and part-time jobs in the paid labor force. Interestingly, high levels of part-time work are associated with a bifurcation of women into full- and part-time jobs, with highly educated women concentrated in full-time jobs and part-time jobs reserved for women with less education. Workplace protections, indicated in our analysis by high levels of unionization, help incorporate women with low levels of education into both full- and part-time work.

Gender differences in employment and hours worked that are associated with child-rearing have implications for other indicators of inequality. For example, chapter 5 illustrated that high rates of women's labor market involvement do little to remedy occupational sex segregation if gender inequalities in the domestic work associated with children are not relieved. In countries where family policies enable parents to stay home with young children and workplaces incorporate workers through part-time employment, occupational sex segregation remains high because of enduring gender inequality in household divisions of labor. Women continue to be the primary caregivers for children and work in occupations that enable them to manage domestic responsibilities. High rates of part-time employment often fuel occupational sex segregation and increasingly differentiate jobs that enable workers to provide for their families from those that enable workers to manage competing work and family obligations. In countries where women's labor force participation rates are low, evidence suggests that women who remain in the paid labor force represent a particularly educated lot who have made important inroads into male-dominated and managerial occupations. But even policies that relieve the domestic demands of child-rearing appear to heighten educational inequalities among women. Although generous support for public child care is associated with reductions in sex segregation across occupations, it is also coupled with the disproportionate concentration of highly educated women in professional occupations and not clerical, sales, and service occupations.

Differential employment—especially in relation to child-rearing—also helps to explain why the gender wage gap is low in countries with low levels of women's employment and relatively high in countries where women exhibit high employment rates. Gender divides in part-time and full-time jobs, in occupations with strong earnings trajectories and those with flat earnings profiles, and in jobs that value experience and those that do not, all help to explain the persistence of gender inequality in wages. Women and men fall into well-worn labor market trajectories that enable them to fulfill their gender expectations and family responsibilities. Countries with the smallest gender wage gap typically have highly selective labor forces or include a high proportion of full-time workers. In some cases, like Italy, women in the paid labor force are both highly selective and likely to work full-time. Although many Italian women exit the labor market when they marry and have children, those who stay in the labor market are a particularly skilled and committed group and earn wages nearly commensurate with those of men.

The theoretical framework we articulated in chapter 2 illustrates the tensions between labor market inclusion and equality. In all twenty-one countries we study, we find some degree of an inclusion-equality tradeoff. High levels of women's labor force participation are typically associated with significant gender differences in hours worked, occupation, and pay. Low levels of women's employment are generally coupled with greater representation of women in full-time work, occupational integration, and gender equality in pay among employed workers.

But the specific contours of inequality across and within countries are shaped by the policies and conditions that influence both the domestic division of labor and the allocation of workplace rewards. Conditions that incorporate women into the labor market but maintain specialization in the domestic sphere reinforce gender divisions and expose significant inequalities between mothers and childless women and men in general. Our evidence also suggests that even where women are relieved of the domestic demands associated with children, social policies and employment conditions can perpetuate inequality by class. We find several instances where exclusion and equality are generated through a selection mechanism in which employed women eschew child-rearing. This may be accomplished either through childlessness or the purchase of substitutes for domestic labor. We also find, however, that other conditions associated with low employment rates among women—such as high rates of unionization—generally accompany reductions in occupational and wage inequality.

Failing to take full account of these important features of the labor market and the multiple dimensions of labor market inequality obscures contemporary accounts of gender inequality within the labor market. Institutional conditions such as family policy influence gender inequality in the labor market directly and indirectly through labor supply and demand effects. Moreover, gender differences in employment and involvement in segmented labor markets may perpetuate inequality over the life course by cleaving the work experiences of women from those of men and the work experiences of mothers from those of fathers.

Is there a necessary tradeoff between labor market inclusion and economic equality within the market? The answer is rooted in gender inequalities in household labor and child care. Women can do as well as men in the marketplace. This is especially true if women act more "like men" in the labor market. Single women, women with no children, and women who maintain full-time work generally do as well as similarly skilled men across countries. However, when women fulfill gender-normative expectations associated with child-rearing, they often fare worse in the paid labor force than women without domestic obligations, and worse than men. Some countries go to great lengths to help women and families accommodate competing work and family demands, yet the persistence of inequalities in domestic responsibilities continues to structure inequality within the market.

MEASURING GENDER INEQUALITY

The cross-national comparative research on gender inequality is dominated by studies of a particular outcome like employment, hours worked, occupational sex segregation, or wages. Previous studies have not reconciled inconsistencies in women's economic standing within countries or within welfare state regime types across measures. For example, although the social democratic countries of Sweden, Denmark, and Finland continually post the highest rates of women's employment, they also have relatively high rates of occupational sex segregation and relatively low wages. These inconsistencies in gender inequality defy a single causal explanation and point to the complexity of gender inequality across countries. Attending to both individual-level characteristics and national context reveals important individual, household, and national-level conditions that influence gender inequalities in economic outcomes. Accounts of gender inequality in the economy must address the institutional conditions that influence both household commitments and labor market outcomes.

Heterogeneity in women's economic standing within welfare state regime types draws attention to the particular national-level factors that influence gender inequality across countries. Employment rates are typically low among women in conservative-corporatist economies. A consistent exception, however, is France, which posts moderately high employment rates among women and particularly high employment rates among women with children. Austria also has relatively high female employment rates in comparison to other conservative-corporatist countries. These exceptions invite a more nuanced examination of the specific policies and conditions at the national level that frame gender and work.

How the specific contours of family policy directly influence labor supply and demand has important consequences for other indicators of inequality. Restricting analyses to the effects of broad family policy packages may be as limiting as restricting examinations to differences across welfare state regime types. Specific features of states—both their social policies and their employment conditions—have different implications for employment, hours worked, occupational segregation, and wages. As states continue to refashion their family policies in response to the shifting political and economic terrain, it is imperative that research pay closer attention to the unique effects of different policy conditions. Specific policies can exacerbate or ameliorate gender inequality.

Gender divides in the workplace are strongly related to gendered expectations surrounding domestic work and the care of children. Women's economic advancement is deeply intertwined with men's involvement in home production. Policies and conditions that support men's home production may further women's economic standing. Reductions in work hours and "use it or lose it" paternity leave schemes are two examples of efforts to encourage men's involvement in the domestic sphere.

Supporting women as workers and mothers is also critical for advancing women's economic opportunities, enabling them to make choices about how to allocate their time, and shaping normative expectations about the appropriateness of the employment of women and mothers. Publicly supported child care, extended school days, and flexible working arrangements may allow women to combine work and family, should they choose to do so.

Recent work confirms the relevance of these policies and conditions for gender differences in time spent on domestic work. Men spend more time on domestic work where aggregate levels of women's employment are higher and where women work longer hours. Women's and men's domestic work is also linked to specific policies and conditions. Long work hours and lengthy parental leaves are associated with less housework for fathers and more housework for mothers, particularly in fixed housework tasks like cooking. Publicly funded child care, on the other hand, is associated with less housework for mothers (Hook 2006, 2010).

Within-market inequalities may be reduced by economic policies such as minimum-wage laws, restrictions on working hours, and wage protections for part-time workers that reduce overall levels of inequality. Although part-time work is commonly protected by equal wage laws, part-time employment often carries with it both short- and long-term consequences for wages and careers. Increasing attention should be paid to how involvement in part-time work and the lost work experience associated with labor force withdrawals during child-rearing generate gender inequality. It is critical that we look at the implications of segmented labor markets and the quality and consequences of part-time work if we are to understand women's economic marginalization.

THE FUTURE OF GENDER INEQUALITY

Gender inequality in measures of employment, hours worked, occupation, and wages has important implications for inequality in a host of other domains. Tensions between household obligations and economic opportunities may help explain very low fertility rates, especially among highly educated women in much of continental and southern Europe. Below-replacement fertility may be tightly connected to the implications of child-rearing for economic opportunities. Having increased their education, experience, and attachment to the labor force, women may be reluctant to take on the responsibilities associated with child-rearing, especially when it is difficult to combine work in the paid labor force with family obligations and responsibilities. Extending parental leaves may be exactly the wrong solution to increasing fertility when what working women want is child care supports or more accommodating workplaces.

At the same time, gender inequality in the economy is tightly coupled with inequality in other dimensions like education. Just as national-level policies and conditions differentially influence the work lives of women and men and mothers and fathers, they also differentiate the work lives of highly skilled women from those of less-skilled women. There is little evidence that highly skilled women opt out of the paid labor force, but there is some evidence that highly skilled women opt out of child-rearing. Either through forgoing childbearing altogether or by having other people care for their children, highly skilled women lead work lives that increasingly approximate those of men. This trend—coupled with low-skill, immigrant, and ethnic minority women's specialization in caregiving occupations—fuels gender inequalities in the domestic obligations associated with child-rearing and provides a new dimension to class inequality.

Although the future of gender inequality in the economy is uncertain, it is undoubtedly tied to other social inequalities. Declines in state support for families will probably exacerbate the tensions associated with the competing demands of work and family life, and the likely result will be greater demands on women's time. Increases in state support for families, especially policies that enable women and men to combine the demands of the workplace and the domestic sphere, are likely to advance the economic fortunes of women. Economic growth and wage protections for low-skill and part-time workers are likely to benefit women. Growing wage inequalities and economic downturns, however, are likely to disadvantage women, especially where they are marginalized and concentrated in low-wage sectors of the labor market. Regardless of the specific direction of future economic and policy trends, a careful account of gender inequality in the economy will continue to require that we look at a broad array of indicators and at all of the individual and country-level conditions that engender and sustain it.

METHODOLOGICAL APPENDIX

Description of Data and Measures

We examine gender inequality in the labor market using data from the Luxembourg Income Study (LIS). The LIS database is a collection of over one hundred household income surveys that provide demographic, income, and employment information for twenty-nine member countries (Luxembourg Income Study 2003). We include surveys that contain the demographic and employment information necessary, as well as those in which the most recent survey is comparable to the one conducted just prior to it.

We analyze up to sixty-three micro-level data sets, spanning the years 1969 to 2000, from twenty-one countries: Australia, Austria, Belgium, Canada, the Czech Republic, Denmark, Finland, France, Germany, Hungary, Italy, Luxembourg, the Netherlands, Norway, Poland, the Russian Federation, Slovenia, Spain, Sweden, the United Kingdom, and the United States. We restrict our analysis to women and men age eighteen to sixty-four.

We examine four dependent variables: employment, part-time employment, occupational location, and wage.

Employment is based on self-reported employment status. Any respondent who reported any level of employment is coded as employed.

Part-time employment is calculated from reports of usual hours worked (or hours worked in the previous week where usual hours are not available). Employment is classified as part-time when a respondent reports one to thirty hours of work per week. Full-time is thirty-one hours or more; not employed is less than one hour.

We code occupation into five broad categories following the International Standard Classification of Occupations (ISCO-1968) (Charles 1992; ILO 1986). The five categories are: professional, technical, and related; administrative (officials, legislators) and managerial; clerical and related; sales and service; and production and related, transport equipment operators, and laborers. Because we are unable to separate sales and service in most countries, we use one category. We omit the categories agricultural, animal husbandry and forestry, fishermen, and hunters, as well as military personnel. We are unable to use a finer classification with such a broad array of countries.

Hourly wage is calculated from reports of yearly gross (or net) wage divided by usual work hours multiplied by weeks worked per year. Prior to calculation, we top-code hours per week to ninety-nine. After calculation, we top-code wages to five times the median and recode wages below one unit of local currency to zero.

MACRO-LEVEL DATA SOURCES

We compile national-level information on mechanisms of inclusion and exclusion and other national political and economic conditions from several sources. All indicators are measured in the year prior to the LIS survey where possible. Table A.2 lists the country-level conditions measured in the mid-1990s.

Gender Egalitarianism

We include a national-level control to gauge norms about the status of women. The propensity of a citizenry to elect women to parliament provides a concrete measure of national norms. The percentage of parliamentary seats occupied by women is compiled from United Nations (1995, 2000).

Economic Conditions

To control for economic conditions, we include indicators of service-sector growth, gross domestic product (GDP) growth, and unemployment. We gathered information on service-sector growth, GDP growth, and unemployment from the World Bank (2002). Service-sector growth indicates the annual growth rate for value-added in services. It includes value-added in wholesale and retail trade (including hotels and restaurants), transport, and government, financial, professional, and personal services such as education, health care, and real estate services. GDP growth measures the annual growth rate of gross value-added to the economy. The national unemployment rate measures the percentage of the labor force seeking employment but without work.

Table A.1   Measures of Gender Equality, All Countries, All Years

Country	Year	Percentage of Women Employed	Percentage of Part-Time Workers	Occupational Segregation	Observed Wage Gap
Austria	1994	58%	29%	38%	18%
(AT)	1997	60	33	42	16
Australia	1985	54	36	39	17
(AU)	1989	60	36	39	18
	1994	59	38	40	—
Belgium	1985	41	30	—	—
(BE)	1988	45	34	—	—
	1992	49	33	—	—
	1997	48	34	29	13
Canada	1987	63	30	39	25
(CA)	1991	62	31	37	26
	1994	63	32	36	23
	1997	65	32	33	—
Czech Republic	1992	62	—	39	—
(CZ)	1996	63	8	39	—
Denmark	1987	73	—	38	—
(DE)	1992	69	—	42	—
Finland	1987	73	—	42	—
(FI)	1991	70	10	42	19
	1995	59	—	42	—
	2000	66	—	45	—
France	1989	53	—	45	—
(FR)	1994	56	29	45	15
Germany	1984	51	36	39	35
(GE)	1989	53	35	40	33
	1994	55	35	40	28
	2000	63	37	36	26
Hungary	1991	52	10	46	—
(HU)	1994	50	12	39	—
Italy	1991	41	23	—	06
(IT)	1995	41	28	—	06
	2000	42	29	—	03

Table A.1   (Continued)

Country	Year	Percentage of Women Employed	Percentage of Part-Time Workers	Occupational Segregation	Observed Wage Gap
Luxembourg	1985	36%	18%	53%	—%
(LX)	1991	46	27	—	—
	1994	48	32	—	—
	1997	56	34	47	—
	2000	60	33	38	—
Netherlands	1991	37	53	34	30
(NE)	1994	55	56	32	21
Norway	1986	62	—	—	—
(NO)	1991	63	—	—	—
	1995	65	—	—	—
	2000	68	—	—	—
Poland (PO)	1995	45	—	—	—
Russian Federation	1992	62	15	52	—
(RU)	1995	58	26	54	—
	2000	57	11	37	—
Slovenia	1997	55	—	32	—
(SL)	1999	55	—	33	—
Spain (SP)	1990	29	—	39	—
Sweden	1992	79	36	39	22
(SW)	1995	76	44	37	22
	2000	79	—	—	—
United Kingdom	1986	60	45	—	—
(UK)	1991	63	41	44	29
	1995	63	41	—	23
United States	1969	48	—	—	—
(US)	1974	49	29	—	42
	1986	63	26	37	33
	1991	65	26	35	30
	1994	67	26	34	25
	1997	69	24	34	23
	2000	75	22	34	22

Source: Luxembourg Income Study (LIS 2003).

Figure A.1   Map of Country Abbreviations

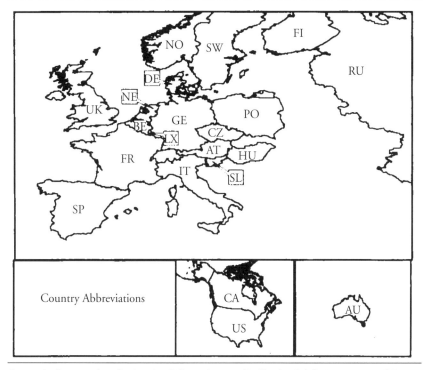

Source: Authors produced using ArcGIS, version 9.0 (Redlands, Calif.: Environmental Systems Research Institute).
AT = Austria, AU = Australia, BE = Belgium, CA = Canada, CZ = Czech Republic, DE = Denmark, FI = Finland, FR = France, GE = Germany, HU = Hungary, IT = Italy, LX = Luxembourg, NE = Netherlands, NO = Norway, PO = Poland, RU = Russian Federation, SL = Slovenia, SP = Spain, SW = Sweden, UK = United Kingdom, US = United States

Mechanisms of Inclusion and Exclusion

To gauge part-time work, we construct an estimate of the percentage of the workforce that is part-time. The measure of part-time work is drawn directly from the micro-level surveys. The measure of child care we have adopted represents the percentage of children age zero to two in publicly funded child care, in the year prior to the survey where possible. Our measure of publicly supported child care is drawn mainly from Gornick, Meyers, and Ross (1997), Meyers and Gornick (2000), and Gornick and Meyers (2003). Supplemental information is from Tietze and Cryer (1999), OECD (2001),

Table A.2   Macro-Level Conditions, All Countries, All Years

Country	Year	Percentage of Part-Time Workers	Percentage of Children Age Zero to Two in Public Child Care	Union Density	Parental Leave Weeks	Maternity Leave Weeks	Percentage of Women in Parliament	Service-Sector Growth	Per Capita GDP Growth	Unemployment Rate
Austria	1994	12.1%	3%	39%	112	16	12%	0.8	0.4	4.3%
(AT)	1997	12.6	3	37	112	16	27	2	2	5.3
Australia	1985	17.5	2	45	0	0	6	5.7	4.3	7.9
(AU)	1989	21.3	2	43	0	0	6	4.6	3.7	5.7
	1994	24.4	5	35	52	0	8	5.8	4.5	9.2
Belgium	1985	8.1	20	57	14	14	8	1	1.9	11.3
(BE)	1988	8.1	20	55	66	14	8	3.4	4.6	10.1
	1992	10.9	30	58	67	15	8	1.8	1.6	6.7
	1997	14	30	60	67	15	12	1.8	3.4	9
Canada	1987	16.8	5	32	17	15	10	3.8	4.1	8.8
(CA)	1991	17	5	33	25	15	13	0.2	-1.9	10.3
	1994	18.8	5	33	25	15	18	4	4.7	10.4
	1997	18.9	3	33	25	15	18	4	4.4	9.1
Czech Republic	1992	6.8	6	30	162	28	10	-5.2	-0.5	2.6
(CZ)	1996	6.1	1	30	214	28	15	-1.3	4.3	3.9
Denmark	1987	23.8	48	75	24	24	29	2	0	6.1
(DE)	1992	23.3	48	76	28	28	31	0.5	0.6	9

Finland	1987	7.7	32	71	160	43	32	4.6	4.2	5.2
(FI)	1991	7.2	32	75	160	44	32	−3.9	−6.3	6.6
	1995	8.2	21	79	164	52	34	4.3	3.8	15.5
	2000	11.6	12	79	164	52	37	3.2	5.7	9.8
France	1989	9.6	20	10	162	16	6	4.4	4.2	9.5
(FR)	1994	14.9	23	09	162	16	6	1.2	2.1	12.4
Germany	1984	12.6	2	31	14	14	21	3.7	3	7.1
(GE)	1989	12.6	2	30	57	14	15	3.5	3.5	5.7
	1994	15.8	11	27	162	14	21	1.7	2.3	8.4
	2000	16.5	7	24	162	14	31	3	1.9	8.7
Hungary	1991	5.4	8	20	160	24	21	−6.4	−11.9	8.5
(HU)	1994	5.4	9	20	160	24	11	1.9	2.9	10.7
Italy	1991	4.9	6	34	48	21	13	1.2	1.4	11
(IT)	1995	6.4	6	32	48	21	15	2.3	2.9	11.5
	2000	6.6	6	31	65	21	11	1.5	1.6	11.3
Luxembourg	1985	6.8	2	52	16	16	12	2.3	2.9	3
(LX)	1991	7	2	50	16	16	13	0.9	6.1	1.5
	1994	8	3	50	16	16	20	1.7	4.2	3.5
	1997	7.7	3	50	16	16	20	3.3	3.6	3.3
	2000	7.7	2	57	68	16	20	3.6	6	2.4
Netherlands	1991	31.7	2	23	64	12	21	3.1	2.3	6.9
(NE)	1994	36.4	8	23	68	16	31	2.9	3.2	6.8
Norway	1986	29.6	12	54	64	18	34	3.4	3.6	2
(NO)	1991	26.5	12	53	64	24	36	3.9	3.1	5.9
	1995	26.5	20	53	64	42	39	2.5	3.8	4.9
	2000	26.6	20	52	116	42	36	2.1	1.1	3.2

Table A.2 (Continued)

Country	Year	Percentage of Part-Time Workers	Percentage of Children Age Zero to Two in Public Child Care	Union Density	Parental Leave Weeks	Maternity Leave Weeks	Percentage of Women in Parliament	Service-Sector Growth	Per Capita GDP Growth	Unemployment Rate
Poland (PO)	1995	10.6%	5%	15%	108	16	13%	4.5	7	13.3%
Russian Federation	1992	4.1	17	82	166	20	10	-3.4	-14.5	5.2
(RU)	1995	4.1	15	69	166	20	13	-2.9	-4.1	9.5
	2000	6.5	15	54	166	20	10	0.8	5.4	13.4
Slovenia	1997	8.3	14	41	56	15	15	4	4.6	7.1
(SL)	1999	6.1	13	43	56	15	13	4.8	5.2	7.4
Spain (SP)	1990	4.9	5	09	162	16	15	3.8	3.7	16
Sweden	1992	23.3	32	86	85	64	38	-0.4	-1.7	5.7
(SW)	1995	24.3	33	88	85	64	40	2.8	3.7	9
	2000	23.6	25	86	85	64	43	3.9	4.5	7.1
United Kingdom	1986	19	2	39	18	18	6	4.4	4.2	11.2
(UK)	1991	21.7	2	34	18	18	6	0.3	-1.5	8.3
	1995	24.1	2	33	18	18	10	3.4	2.8	8.6
United States	1969	15.6	2	26	0	0	5	8.8	2.7	3.8
(US)	1974	15.6	2	24	0	0	5	11.1	-0.6	4.9
	1986	18.4	1	16	0	0	5	10.3	3.4	7
	1991	16.9	1	15	0	0	7	8.5	-0.5	6.8
	1994	18.9	5	14	12	0	11	7.1	4.1	6.1
	1997	18.3	5	14	12	0	12	8.2	4.5	4.9
	2000	18.3	4	14	12	0	13	5.2	4.2	4.1

Source: See "Macro-Level Data Sources" section, pp. 180–187.

UNICEF (Personal communication, December 17, 2003, with Anita Svarck-opfa, Project Officer, UNICEF), the United Nations (2003), and Statistis-ches Bundesamt (1993, 1999). Parental leave represents the maximum num-ber of weeks (paid or unpaid) available. To gauge the effects of unionization, we include a measure of the percentage of the workforce that is unionized. The percentage of the workforce that is unionized comes primarily from Golden, Lange, and Wallerstein (2002). Data from other country-years come from Kenworthy (2004). We also include a measure of maternity leave that represents the number of paid maternity leave weeks available. Maternity and parental leave weeks come primarily from Gauthier and Bortnick (2001), with supplemental information from Stropnik (2001, 2003), Kocourkova (2002), United Nations (1991, 1995, 2000), and U.S. Social Security Ad-ministration (1999).

METHODS USED IN CHAPTER 3

The employment analysis conducted in chapter 3 includes sixty-three country-years of data. We model employment outcomes as a function of a number of individual-level covariates. We include information on respondent age, age-squared, educational attainment, marital status, number of children, the presence in the household of a youngest child age three years or younger, the presence in the household of a youngest child age four to six years, and other household income.

Educational attainment is coded into three dummy variables representing low, medium, and high educational attainment. This classification is the rec-ommended approach for "standardizing" educational attainment across countries with divergent credentialing schematics (Sullivan and Smeeding 1997). The classification of each respondent into the category low, medium, or high is based on the respondent's standing relative to other respondents in the same country. In general, the categories roughly approximate less than a secondary education, completion of secondary education, and more than a secondary education. To the extent possible, each category contains 33 per-cent of a country's respondents. In some cases, however, this standard is vio-lated, such as in the case of an Australian survey in which over 50 percent of respondents reported "no qualification" and thus over half of the sample was in the low education category.

Marital status is coded to one if the respondent was married and to zero if the respondent was single, cohabiting, separated, divorced, or widowed. Be-cause of data limitations, we are unable to include a separate category for cohabitation. We have included access to other income, however, to control for cohabiting women's access to other resources.

Number of children is a count of the number of children in the household under the age of eighteen. Because the number of children is measured at the household level, it is possible that some children are not the respondent's own children.

The presence of a youngest child age three years or younger and the presence of a youngest child age four to six years are represented by dummy variables. Compulsory education begins in most countries when children are between four and eight, though in most places children are involved in full-day educational programs by age six. The omitted category is the presence of a youngest child age seven to seventeen years old.

We also include a measure of other household income to gauge women's access to non-employment income. Other household income is calculated as the sum of family income from wages and salaries, farm and nonfarm self-employment, and cash property, minus women's gross wage or salary, divided by 1,000 (Bardasi and Gornick 2001). Income is measured in local currency.

Using the LIS data with national-level indicators, we conduct a multilevel analysis of women's and men's employment. We estimate multilevel models using two sets of regression equations. First, using logistic regression, we model the probability that women or men will be employed in the paid labor force as a function of social and demographic characteristics. Estimating separate equations for each country allows the relationship between employment and social and demographic variables to vary by country.

Second, we treat the coefficients from country-level equations as dependent variables in an OLS regression, including the national characteristics as independent variables. We explore how measures of family policy and labor market arrangements influence social and demographic covariates of employment and involvement in part-time work. We estimate these methods using the variance-known procedure in HLM (Bryk and Raudenbush 1992). This procedure allows us to estimate random effects for the national-level conditions using two-step methodology, while taking account of the covariance structure of the micro-level models. There is potentially an efficiency tradeoff using the two-step process, but because of the restrictive nature of the LIS data, we estimate the model using the v-known procedure.

Table A.3 Employment of Women and Men by Parental Status and Education, LIS Years

Country	Year	Women				Men			
		All	Highly Educated	Young Children Age Zero to Six	Older Children Age Seven to Seventeen	All	Highly Educated	Young Children Age Zero to Six	Older Children Age Seven to Seventeen
Austria	1994	59%	78%	57%	66%	80%	91%	91%	87%
(AT)	1997	60	84	61	67	80	91	93	89
Australia	1985	54	70	43	62	83	92	91	86
(AU)	1989	60	73	47	69	82	91	90	87
	1994	59	77	44	66	81	88	86	85
Belgium	1985	41	61	54	42	74	79	90	82
(BE)	1988	46	68	60	47	74	81	92	81
	1992	49	80	58	55	74	90	93	79
	1997	48	62	62	53	70	72	90	75
Canada	1987	63	75	57	66	81	86	88	85
(CA)	1991	62	73	58	66	72	79	82	76
	1994	63	72	57	68	74	79	83	78
	1997	65	74	61	70	76	81	86	81
Czech Republic	1992	62	73	47	84	74	75	84	80
(CZ)	1996	63	75	37	80	80	88	92	86
Denmark	1987	76	91	81	85	86	94	95	93
(DE)	1992	72	86	76	82	79	90	91	87
Finland	1987	73	78	71	87	80	82	94	90
(FI)	1991	70	75	63	87	77	82	93	88

Table A.3   (Continued)

Country	Year	Women				Men			
		All	Highly Educated	Young Children Age Zero to Six	Older Children Age Seven to Seventeen	All	Highly Educated	Young Children Age Zero to Six	Older Children Age Seven to Seventeen
	1995	59%	74%	50%	74%	64%	80%	84%	75%
	2000	66	84	64	78	72	87	89	81
France (FR)	1989	53	62	52	58	75	73	91	80
	1994	56	60	57	64	73	71	88	80
Germany (GE)	1984	49	68	38	50	78	87	89	82
	1989	54	69	39	57	78	87	92	83
	1994	58	74	40	66	78	86	89	87
	2000	62	73	41	71	77	85	90	84
Hungary (HU)	1991	52	76	33	73	68	84	76	78
	1994	50	80	36	67	64	87	76	68
Italy (IT)	1991	41	58	46	40	73	73	94	76
	1995	41	74	48	44	68	80	88	76
	2000	42	58	47	45	70	75	90	79
Luxembourg (LX)	1985	38	46	33	34	85	89	97	91
	1991	46	57	50	43	87	91	97	96
	1994	48	57	43	46	87	90	100	96
	1997	56	66	51	55	83	90	94	91
	2000	60	68	57	61	84	89	94	93

Country	Year								
Netherlands (NE)	1991	35	60	21	29	75	88	93	83
	1994	55	76	52	56	77	86	94	83
Norway (NO)	1986	62	82	55	68	87	95	94	90
	1991	63	81	60	68	80	88	94	82
	1995	66	80	66	71	81	87	94	82
	2000	68	83	69	74	80	89	93	83
Poland (PO)	1995	45	59	40	59	65	71	79	75
Russian Federation (RU)	1992	62	67	56	82	81	78	89	88
	1995	59	67	50	72	75	79	81	81
	2000	57	69	47	69	69	79	73	75
Slovenia (SL)	1997	55	83	72	68	66	83	82	76
	1999	55	82	71	68	65	81	81	74
Spain (SP)	1990	29	46	28	29	73	72	86	77
Sweden (SW)	1992	80	89	86	90	84	90	93	95
	1995	76	86	81	85	79	84	91	93
	2000	79	85	83	84	83	88	93	93
United Kingdom (UK)	1986	60	74	41	73	88	94	94	92
	1991	63	75	48	71	79	87	85	83
	1995	63	76	48	71	76	85	83	83
United States (US)	1969	48	55	33	60	87	87	92	87
	1974	49	59	35	51	81	87	88	82
	1986	63	74	54	66	82	87	88	84
	1991	71	81	62	76	85	90	90	88
	1994	67	76	58	72	82	87	88	83
	1997	69	77	62	73	82	87	89	83
	2000	75	81	69	78	86	90	92	88

Source: Luxembourg Income Study (LIS 2003).

METHODS USED IN CHAPTER 4

The analyses in chapter 4 replicate those outlined in chapter 3, although the part-time analysis includes forty-six country-years of data from a total of fifteen countries. A number of countries are excluded from the part-time analysis because of missing data on hours worked.

Table A.4A   Percentage of Women Working Full- and Part-Time, LIS Years

Country	Year	Full-Time				Part-Time			
		All	Highly Educated	Young Children Age Zero to Six	Older Children Age Seven to Seventeen	All	Highly Educated	Young Children Age Zero to Six	Older Children Age Seven to Seventeen
Austria (AT)	1994	42%	52%	37%	44%	18%	26%	23%	24%
	1997	41	54	35	40	20	28	28	28
Australia (AU)	1985	35	50	17	36	19	19	26	26
	1989	38	51	19	39	22	22	28	30
	1994	33	49	15	29	20	21	21	30
Belgium (BE)	1985	27	32	33	27	12	26	19	13
	1988	27	39	29	27	14	24	26	14
	1992	32	53	32	34	15	24	25	19
	1997	31	42	37	30	16	21	26	23
Canada (CA)	1987	44	55	36	43	19	20	21	23
	1991	43	52	37	43	19	22	21	23
	1994	43	50	36	44	20	22	22	25
	1997	44	51	39	45	21	22	22	25
Czech Republic (CZ)	1992	—	—	—	—	5	6	5	7
	1996	62	72	33	82	—	—	—	—
Denmark (DE)	1987	—	—	—	—	—	—	—	—
	1992	—	—	—	—	—	—	—	—
Finland (FI)	1987	—	—	—	—	—	—	—	—
	1991	70	78	64	82	8	9	10	9
	1995	—	—	—	—	—	—	—	—
	2000	—	—	—	—	—	—	—	—

Table A.4A   (Continued)

Country	Year	Full-Time				Part-Time			
		All	Highly Educated	Young Children Age Zero to Six	Older Children Age Seven to Seventeen	All	Highly Educated	Young Children Age Zero to Six	Older Children Age Seven to Seventeen
France	1989	—	—	—	—	—	—	—	—
(FR)	1994	39%	44%	40%	42%	16%	15%	17%	19%
Germany	1984	33	46	14	29	18	24	23	23
(GE)	1989	36	47	14	31	19	23	26	28
	1994	38	51	17	36	20	23	22	30
	2000	39	50	13	37	23	22	27	33
Hungary	1991	43	57	24	63	5	15	5	5
(HU)	1994	41	57	31	57	5	19	4	7
Italy	1991	32	42	35	30	9	17	12	10
(IT)	1995	30	33	32	31	12	67	16	14
	2000	31	42	29	32	13	18	19	14
Luxembourg	1985	31	37	21	24	7	8	11	8
(LX)	1991	31	42	28	26	12	14	18	13
	1994	32	41	23	23	15	15	21	22
	1997	37	47	23	29	19	18	28	26
	2000	40	50	31	30	20	18	26	32
Netherlands	1991	22	40	7	12	26	30	30	36
(NE)	1994	24	42	10	12	31	34	43	45

Country	Year								
Norway (NO)	1986	—	—	—	—	—	—	—	—
	1991	—	—	—	—	—	—	—	—
	1995	—	—	—	—	—	—	—	—
	2000	—	—	—	—	—	—	—	—
Poland (PO)	1995	—	—	—	—	—	—	—	—
Russian Federation (RU)	1992	50	51	45	64	9	14	8	11
	1995	40	43	32	50	14	19	12	16
	2000	53	64	49	61	6	8	7	8
Slovenia (SL)	1997	—	—	—	—	—	—	—	—
	1999	—	—	—	—	—	—	—	—
Spain (SP)	1990	—	—	—	—	—	—	—	—
Sweden (SW)	1992	44	58	37	48	25	21	35	30
	1995	36	49	33	39	28	25	33	30
	2000	—	—	—	—	—	—	—	—
United Kingdom (UK)	1986	32	46	11	28	26	24	27	41
	1991	34	47	13	30	24	21	29	35
	1995	32	45	16	25	23	21	24	34
United States (US)	1969	—	—	—	—	—	—	—	—
	1974	33	41	22	32	14	15	12	18
	1986	44	52	34	45	16	18	17	18
	1991	55	63	45	55	19	21	20	23
	1994	55	62	47	55	19	21	21	24
	1997	57	63	50	58	19	20	20	21
	2000	60	65	52	60	17	18	19	20

Source: Luxembourg Income Study (LIS 2003).

Table A.4B   Percentage of Men Working Full- and Part-Time, LIS Years

Country	Year	Full-Time				Part-Time			
		All	Highly Educated	Young Children Age Zero to Six	Older Children Age Seven to Seventeen	All	Highly Educated	Young Children Age Zero to Six	Older Children Age Seven to Seventeen
Austria (AT)	1994	77%	80%	89%	85%	3%	11%	2%	2%
	1997	77	86	90	88	3	5	3	1
Australia (AU)	1985	79	89	90	84	3	4	2	3
	1989	78	87	87	83	4	4	2	3
	1994	64	74	69	66	5	5	3	6
Belgium (BE)	1985	66	61	81	74	4	11	6	4
	1988	62	63	81	66	4	10	6	5
	1992	65	74	81	69	3	7	5	3
	1997	64	62	81	70	4	8	6	3
Canada (CA)	1987	75	79	86	79	7	8	3	6
	1991	65	71	78	70	8	8	5	7
	1994	67	72	80	71	8	8	4	8
	1997	67	72	80	73	8	9	5	9
Czech Republic (CZ)	1992	—	—	—	—	2	2	—	—
	1996	84	89	92	91	2	2	1	2
Denmark (DE)	1987	—	—	—	—	—	—	—	—
	1992	—	—	—	—	—	—	—	—
Finland	1987	—	—	—	—	—	—	—	—

(FI)	1991	79	85	92	89	4	4	3	3
	1995	—	—	—	—	—	—	—	—
	2000	—	—	—	—	—	—	—	—
France (FR)	1989	—	—	—	—	—	—	—	—
	1994	62	59	78	66	4	5	3	4
Germany (GE)	1984	76	80	85	82	4	7	4	4
	1989	78	83	93	83	3	5	1	3
	1994	76	80	85	82	3	7	3	4
	2000	78	76	93	81	5	5	4	2
Hungary (HU)	1991	73	72	85	66	1	5	1	2
	1994	71	72	87	55	2	7	2	1
Italy (IT)	1991	56	67	65	73	4	5	4	4
	1995	51	61	61	72	5	28	6	5
	2000	69	70	91	76	5	6	5	5
Luxembourg (LX)	1985	83	87	95	89	17	3	2	2
	1991	79	86	92	92	2	2	2	2
	1994	81	86	96	90	2	3	1	1
	1997	81	86	93	89	2	14	2	2
	2000	82	87	93	91	2	2	0	2
Netherlands (NE)	1991	71	79	90	79	7	11	4	2
	1994	70	78	89	76	8	8	5	9
Norway (NO)	1986	—	—	—	—	—	—	—	7
	1991	—	—	—	—	—	—	—	—
	1995	—	—	—	—	—	—	—	—
	2000	—	—	—	—	—	—	—	—

Table A.4B (Continued)

Country	Year	Full-Time				Part-Time			
		All	Highly Educated	Young Children Age Zero to Six	Older Children Age Seven to Seventeen	All	Highly Educated	Young Children Age Zero to Six	Older Children Age Seven to Seventeen
Poland (PO)	1995	—	—	—	—	—	—	—	—
Russian Federation	1992	66%	62%	72%	71%	6%	9%	5%	6%
(RU)	1995	57	59	61	62	9	11	8	9
	2000	66	73	69	72	2	4	3	2
Slovenia	1997	—	—	—	—	—	—	—	—
(SL)	1999	—	—	—	—	—	—	—	—
Spain (SP)	1990	—	—	—	—	—	—	—	—
Sweden	1992	67	75	81	82	5	5	4	2
(SW)	1995	52	61	74	69	13	11	9	5
	2000	—	—	—	—	—	—	—	—
United Kingdom	1986	70	77	72	72	4	5	3	4
(UK)	1991	63	72	67	66	3	4	2	3
	1995	55	66	60	61	3	3	2	4
United States	1969	—	—	—	—	—	—	—	—
(US)	1974	70	76	79	70	8	8	7	9
	1986	70	76	79	72	8	8	6	9
	1991	80	84	88	81	9	9	5	10
	1994	80	85	88	82	9	8	5	9
	1997	80	84	88	81	9	9	5	9
	2000	80	84	90	81	8	8	4	9

Source: Luxembourg Income Study (LIS 2003).

METHODS USED IN CHAPTER 5

The occupation analysis includes forty-five country-years of data from a total of eighteen countries. A number of countries are excluded because of missing data on occupation. We model occupational location as a function of a number of individual-level covariates. We include information on respondent age, educational attainment, marital status, number of children, the presence in the household of a youngest child age three years or younger, and the presence in the household of a youngest child age four to six years.

Using the LIS data with national-level indicators, we conduct a multilevel analysis of women's and men's involvement in different occupational categories. We follow the procedures outlined in "Methods Used in Chapter 3."

Table A.5A   Occupational Location of Women by Parental Status and Education, LIS Years

		Professional				Managerial			
Country	Year	All	Highly Educated	Young Children Age Zero to Six	Older Children Age Seven to Seventeen	All	Highly Educated	Young Children Age Zero to Six	Older Children Age Seven to Seventeen
Austria	1994	26%	82%	24%	28%	4%	5%	6%	4%
(AT)	1997	28	73	28	25	4	5	3	2
Australia	1985	18	42	21	11	6	6	4	7
(AU)	1989	19	40	23	16	7	6	5	8
	1994	22	62	27	21	6	5	8	6
Belgium	1985	—	—	—	—	—	—	—	—
(BE)	1988	—	—	—	—	—	—	—	—
	1992	—	—	—	—	—	—	—	—
	1997	34	63	36	37	1	1	2	2
Canada	1987	19	36	19	19	10	13	8	7
(CA)	1991	20	33	20	21	11	14	10	9
	1994	22	32	21	22	13	15	12	11
	1997	23	32	24	22	14	16	13	14
Czech Republic	1992	29	61	31	28	2	3	1	2
(CZ)	1996	28	56	28	29	2	4	2	3
Denmark	1987	35	83	42	39	5	1	3	6
(DE)	1992	26	82	32	28	2	3	1	2
Finland	1987	31	48	36	30	2	3	1	2
(FI)	1991	34	48	40	34	2	4	3	3
	1995	37	54	40	39	2	5	2	2
	2000	34	65	42	37	4	7	4	4
France	1989	20	52	19	21	10	21	8	8
(FR)	1994	19	43	19	19	10	18	9	9
Germany	1984	19	64	26	17	1	1	0	0
(GE)	1989	19	61	26	17	1	5	1	1
	1994	25	60	36	24	2	3	2	2
	2000	30	61	31	31	3	5	1	2
Hungary	1991	23	67	25	23	2	8	1	2
(HU)	1994	27	75	27	27	5	13	3	4
Italy	1991	—	—	—	—	—	—	—	—
(IT)	1995	—	—	—	—	—	—	—	—
	2000	—	—	—	—	—	—	—	—

	Clerical, Sales, and Service				Production		
All	Highly Educated	Young Children Age Zero to Six	Older Children Age Seven to Seventeen	All	Highly Educated	Young Children Age Zero to Six	Older Children Age Seven to Seventeen
55%	12%	56%	52%	7%	1%	6%	6%
54	21	52	53	6	1	7	7
54	45	55	55	22	7	20	27
54	46	55	54	19	8	16	22
54	28	50	52	18	5	15	21
—	—	—	—	—	—	—	—
—	—	—	—	—	—	—	—
—	—	—	—	—	—	—	—
59	35	57	55	6	1	5	6
59	47	61	61	9	4	10	11
58	48	59	57	9	4	8	11
55	47	56	56	9	4	9	9
52	45	50	53	9	5	11	9
41	31	43	42	23	4	20	24
46	36	45	47	20	3	22	19
49	15	45	45	9	1	9	8
61	13	57	61	9	1	9	9
49	44	47	47	11	3	9	12
49	44	45	48	9	2	6	10
47	38	46	44	8	1	6	8
49	25	43	47	8	2	8	7
50	23	54	49	15	2	15	16
52	34	54	53	16	3	16	17
63	27	57	67	14	6	17	14
64	29	60	61	14	5	11	21
63	31	53	63	10	6	9	10
56	30	55	55	9	4	11	10
51	21	42	52	21	3	27	20
47	10	41	48	20	2	26	20
—	—	—	—	—	—	—	—
—	—	—	—	—	—	—	—
—	—	—	—	—	—	—	—

Table A.5A   (Continued)

Country	Year	Professional				Managerial			
		All	Highly Educated	Young Children Age Zero to Six	Older Children Age Seven to Seventeen	All	Highly Educated	Young Children Age Zero to Six	Older Children Age Seven to Seventeen
Luxembourg	1985	15%	27%	19%	12%	0%	1%	0%	1%
(LX)	1991	—	—	—	—	—	—	—	—
	1994	—	—	—	—	—	—	—	—
	1997	31	44	31	21	3	3	1	3
	2000	36	50	37	22	5	6	3	4
Netherlands	1991	26	68	36	22	2	3	2	2
(NE)	1994	29	64	38	27	2	4	1	2
Norway	1986	—	—	—	—	—	—	—	—
(NO)	1991	—	—	—	—	—	—	—	—
	1995	—	—	—	—	—	—	—	—
	2000	—	—	—	—	—	—	—	—
Poland (PO)	1995	—	—	—	—	—	—	—	—
Russian Federation	1992	40	78	36	42	2	3	2	2
(RU)	1995	36	68	37	33	2	5	1	3
	2000	35	52	34	33	4	5	2	4
Slovenia	1997	29	77	29	29	5	13	3	4
(SL)	1999	30	77	33	27	5	14	3	4
Spain (SP)	1990	16	43	18	12	0	0	0	16
Sweden	1992	37		40	44	2	0	2	2
(SW)	1995	42	80	44	47	3	4	2	3
	2000	—	—	—	—	—	—	—	—
United Kingdom	1986	—	—	—	—	—	—	—	—
(UK)	1991	18	35	19	17	5	7	3	4
	1995	—	—	—	—	—	—	—	—
United States	1969	—	—	—	—	—	—	—	—
(US)	1974	—	—	—	—	—	—	—	—
	1986	19	36	18	18	9	12	7	7
	1991	22	37	21	21	6	9	5	6
	1994	24	37	24	23	7	10	6	6
	1997	25	38	23	24	8	11	7	7
	2000	26	39	24	24	9	12	8	8

	Clerical, Sales, and Service				Production		
All	Highly Educated	Young Children Age Zero to Six	Older Children Age Seven to Seventeen	All	Highly Educated	Young Children Age Zero to Six	Older Children Age Seven to Seventeen
78%	67%	73%	80%	5%	3%	5%	5%
—	—	—	—	—	—	—	—
—	—	—	—	—	—	—	—
61	48	66	71	3	3	1	3
54	40	59	71	3	3	1	2
64	29	55	68	6	0	4	7
62	30	54	63	5	0	4	6
—	—	—	—	—	—	—	—
—	—	—	—	—	—	—	—
—	—	—	—	—	—	—	—
—	—	—	—	—	—	—	—
—	—	—	—	—	—	—	—
34	13	34	34	20	5	23	19
42	23	42	42	16	4	16	18
45	36	50	35	14	6	11	15
41	9	39	41	19	0	23	20
40	8	38	41	20	0	21	22
60	50	58	63	16	5	17	16
53	0	49	48	7	0	9	5
47	14	45	44	7	1	8	5
—	—	—	—	—	—	—	—
—	—	—	—	—	—	—	—
68	55	68	70	9	3	10	9
—	—	—	—	—	—	—	—
—	—	—	—	—	—	—	—
—	—	—	—	—	—	—	—
61	48	61	62	11	3	12	12
60	50	61	61	10	4	11	11
57	48	58	59	10	4	11	11
56	47	57	58	10	4	12	10
55	45	57	57	9	4	10	10

Source: Luxembourg Income Study (LIS 2003).

Table A.5B   Occupational Location of Men, by Parental Status and Educatio LIS Years

		Professional				Managerial			
			Highly	Young Children Age Zero	Older Children Age Seven to		Highly	Young Children Age Zero	Olde Child Age Seven
Country	Year	All	Educated	to Six	Seventeen	All	Educated	to Six	Sevent
Austria	1994	26%	68%	26%	24%	11%	22%	10%	12%
(AT)	1997	25	63	26	21	12	27	13	11
Australia	1985	18	58	20	16	14	18	15	16
(AU)	1989	19	51	22	19	14	18	15	16
	1994	20	54	21	21	14	16	17	16
Belgium	1985	—	—	—	—	—	—	—	—
(BE)	1988	—	—	—	—	—	—	—	—
	1992	—	—	—	—	—	—	—	—
	1997	22	50	23	22	4	6	6	4
Canada	1987	13	27	14	12	14	22	17	14
(CA)	1991	14	23	14	13	13	18	14	13
	1994	14	22	15	12	14	19	15	14
	1997	16	24	16	14	13	17	14	13
Czech Republic	1992	23	54	22	23	5	12	5	5
(CZ)	1996	23	53	22	23	6	13	6	7
Denmark	1987	18	64	21	18	4	4	3	5
(DE)	1992	22	66	28	26	8	13	7	9
Finland	1987	18	44	19	18	5	11	5	7
(FI)	1991	20	46	22	22	6	12	6	9
	1995	20	51	22	19	6	16	6	9
	2000	28	62	25	28	10	23	14	14
France	1989	18	42	16	18	17	43	16	18
(FR)	1994	17	35	17	18	18	40	19	19
Germany	1984	21	69	25	18	5	9	7	5
(GE)	1989	22	64	22	23	6	11	7	3
	1994	24	61	26	24	5	8	7	5
	2000	26	58	28	23	5	9	5	5
Hungary	1991	8	41	5	10	6	31	3	9
(HU)	1994	14	53	8	12	8	28	7	10
Italy	1991	—	—	—	—	—	—	—	—
(IT)	1995	—	—	—	—	—	—	—	—
	2000	—	—	—	—	—	—	—	—

Clerical, Sales, and Service				Production			
All	Highly Educated	Young Children Age Zero to Six	Older Children Age Seven to Seventeen	All	Highly Educated	Young Children Age Zero to Six	Older Children Age Seven to Seventeen
20%	5%	21%	18%	34%	3%	34%	37%
19	5	17	20	36	2	37	40
16	14	13	15	52	11	51	52
16	15	13	15	51	16	50	50
16	14	11	15	51	16	50	48
—	—	—	—	—	—	—	—
—	—	—	—	—	—	—	—
42	39	37	39	32	5	33	35
25	23	21	25	42	25	43	43
27	24	22	25	41	32	44	44
26	23	21	25	41	33	44	43
26	24	22	25	40	32	42	42
11	13	12	10	57	20	57	58
14	15	14	13	55	17	55	53
28	20	27	26	43	10	42	42
22	14	22	20	42	6	39	39
20	27	21	19	44	13	44	44
21	26	21	18	43	13	42	42
23	24	22	21	41	7	40	40
12	7	12	9	44	6	43	42
96	11	7	49	8	52	50	
10	8	10	9	49	14	49	49
25	12	20	22	46	8	45	50
24	13	19	23	45	11	48	48
25	18	22	22	45	12	44	47
25	20	21	20	42	12	44	49
20	24	19	19	59	3	64	54
21	13	22	19	53	6	58	55
—	—	—	—	—	—	—	—
—	—	—	—	—	—	—	—
—	—	—	—	—	—	—	—

Table A.5B   (Continued)

Country	Year	Professional All	Professional Highly Educated	Professional Young Children Age Zero to Six	Professional Older Children Age Seven to Seventeen	Managerial All	Managerial Highly Educated	Managerial Young Children Age Zero to Six	Managerial Older Children Age Seven to Seventeen
Luxembourg	1985	12%	22%	14%	11%	1%	1%	1%	2%
(LX)	1991	—	—	—	—	—	—	—	—
	1994	—	—	—	—	—	—	—	—
	1997	34	44	30	31	14	15	12	18
	2000	35	47	32	31	13	14	12	14
Netherlands	1991	25	69	28	23	6	10	6	8
(NE)	1994	26	65	29	25	7	13	8	9
Norway	1986	—	—	—	—	—	—	—	—
(NO)	1991	—	—	—	—	—	—	—	—
	1995	—	—	—	—	—	—	—	—
2000		—	—	—	—	—	—	—	—
Poland (PO)	1995	—	—	—	—	—	—	—	—
Russian									
Federation	1992	16	54	14	19	4	11	4	6
(RU)	1995	13	40	12	11	5	14	4	6
	2000	14	32	12	12	7	15	4	8
Slovenia	1997	21	63	17	21	9	24	10	9
(SL)	1999	21	64	20	21	9	26	9	10
Spain (SP)	1990	9	33	10	7	1	3	1	1
Sweden	1992	27	65	27	33	3	7	3	5
(SW)	1995	28	67	30	33	3	7	3	5
	2000	—	—	—	—	—	—	—	—
United Kingdom	1986	—	—	—	—	—	—	—	—
(UK)	1991	20	39	20	18	11	20	13	12
	1995	—	—	—	—	—	—	—	—
United States	1969	—	—	—	—	—	—	—	—
(US)	1974	—	—	—	—	—	—	—	—
	1986	15	30	15	14	12	20	12	12
	1991	17	30	16	16	9	14	9	10
	1994	18	30	17	17	10	15	10	12
	1997	18	30	17	16	10	15	10	12
	2000	19	31	18	16	11	16	11	13

	Clerical, Sales, and Service				Production		
All	Highly Educated	Young Children Age Zero to Six	Older Children Age Seven to Seventeen	All	Highly Educated	Young Children Age Zero to Six	Older Children Age Seven to Seventeen
28%	24%	24%	29%	54%	49%	54%	55%
—	—	—	—	—	—	—	—
—	—	—	—	—	—	—	—
15	13	13	11	35	25	43	38
17	14	13	16	32	22	42	38
31	16	27	30	34	5	35	34
30	16	27	26	30	3	30	34
—	—	—	—	—	—	—	—
—	—	—	—	—	—	—	—
—	—	—	—	—	—	—	—
—	—	—	—	—	—	—	—
—	—	—	—	—	—	—	—
89	9	6	68	24	69	67	
14	23	18	11	65	22	64	67
15	17	17	13	61	34	62	64
18	6	16	19	44	5	49	45
16	6	17	15	46	4	44	47
29	34	30	28	49	28	51	52
22	18	22	20	43	9	43	37
22	18	21	22	42	7	42	36
—	—	—	—	—	—	—	—
—	—	—	—	—	—	—	—
23	25	20	22	43	15	45	45
—	—	—	—	—	—	—	—
—	—	—	—	—	—	—	—
—	—	—	—	—	—	—	—
26	29	24	25	42	20	45	44
29	31	26	28	41	22	45	42
28	30	26	27	40	23	43	41
29	30	26	27	40	23	43	41
28	29	25	26	39	23	42	41

Source: Luxembourg Income Study (LIS 2003).

METHODS USED IN CHAPTER 6

The wage analysis includes twenty-nine country-years of data from a total of twelve countries. A number of countries are excluded because of missing data on wages. We model wages as a function of a number of individual-level co-

Table A.6   Women's Wages Relative to Men's, by Parental Status and Education, Mid-1990s

		All Adults			Highly Educated		
Country	Year	All (1)	Workers (2)	Difference (2–1)	All (1)	Workers (2)	Difference (2–1)
Austria	1994	60%	89%	29%	91%	102%	11%
(AT)	1997	62	90	28	86	97	11
Australia	1985	57	88	31	63	83	20
(AU)	1989	66	89	23	69	85	16
	1994	—	—	—	—	—	—
Belgium	1985	—	—	—	—	—	—
(BE)	1988	—	—	—	—	—	—
	1992	—	—	—	—	—	—
	1997	67	93	26	91	93	1
Canada	1987	66	83	18	77	86	9
(CA)	1991	74	84	9	82	86	4
	1994	74	85	12	81	87	6
	1997	—	—	—	—	—	—
Czech Republic	1992	—	—	—	—	—	—
(CZ)	1996	—	—	—	—	—	—
Denmark	1987	—	—	—	—	—	—
(DE)	1992	—	—	—	—	—	—
Finland	1987	—	—	—	—	—	—
(FI)	1991	87	85	–2	88	85	–3
	1995	—	—	—	—	—	—
	2000	—	—	—	—	—	—
France	1989	—	—	—	—	—	—
(FR)	1994	76	93	17	87	94	7
Germany	1984	54	84	29	75	96	21
(GE)	1989	58	83	26	71	91	19
	1994	67	87	20	72	84	12
	2000	73	87	14	81	90	9

variates. We include information on respondent age, age-squared, educational attainment, marital status, number of children, the presence in the household of a youngest child age three years or younger, the presence in the household of a youngest child age four to six years, and other household income.

Young Children Age Zero to Six			Older Children Age Seven to Seventeen		
All (1)	Workers (2)	Difference (2–1)	All (1)	Workers (2)	Difference (2–1)
11%	36%	52%	62%	89%	27%
47	87	40	59	89	31
35	88	54	59	82	23
42	90	48	68	85	17
—	—	—	—	—	—
—	—	—	—	—	—
—	—	—	—	—	—
—	—	—	—	—	—
71	97	27	69	93	24
48	81	33	62	81	19
55	81	25	72	79	7
55	82	27	72	80	8
—	—	—	—	—	—
—	—	—	—	—	—
—	—	—	—	—	—
—	—	—	—	—	—
—	—	—	—	—	—
74	86	12	86	80	–7
—	—	—	—	—	—
—	—	—	—	—	—
—	—	—	—	—	—
66	94	28	77	90	12
32	83	52	50	78	28
31	81	50	55	80	25
33	83	50	65	84	19
34	83	49	73	81	8

Table A.6   (Continued)

Country	Year	All Adults			Highly Educated		
		All (1)	Workers (2)	Difference (2–1)	All (1)	Workers (2)	Difference (2–1)
Hungary	1991	—	—	—	—	—	—
(HU)	1994	—	—	—	—	—	—
Italy	1991	39%	98%	59%	86%	96%	10%
(IT)	1995	63	96	33	112	100	–12
	2000	65	97	32	87	97	9
Luxembourg	1985	—	—	—	—	—	—
(LX)	1991	—	—	—	—	—	—
	1994	—	—	—	—	—	—
	1997	—	—	—	—	—	—
	2000	—	—	—	—	—	—
Netherlands	1991	48	83	35	67	85	18
(NE)	1994	60	87	27	78	90	11
Norway	1986	—	—	—	—	—	—
(NO)	1991	—	—	—	—	—	—
	1995	—	—	—	—	—	—
	2000	—	—	—	—	—	—
Poland (PO)	1995	—	—	—	—	—	—
Russian							
Federation	1992	—	—	—	—	—	—
(RU)	1995	—	—	—	—	—	—
	2000	—	—	—	—	—	—
Slovenia	1997	—	—	—	—	—	—
(SL)	1999	—	—	—	—	—	—
Spain (SP)	1990	—	—	—	—	—	—
Sweden	1992	86	87	1	89	89	0
(SW)	1995	86	86	0	89	84	–4
	2000	—	—	—	—	—	—
United Kingdom	1986	—	—	—	—	—	—
(UK)	1991	72	82	10	76	84	7
	1995	79	85	6	85	87	2
United States	1969	—	—	—	—	—	—
(US)	1974	45	74	30	54	79	25
	1986	63	79	16	72	81	9
	1991	72	83	11	81	86	5
	1994	75	85	10	82	87	5
	1997	77	86	9	83	87	5
	2000	79	87	8	84	88	4

	Young Children Age Zero to Six			Older Children Age Seven to Seventeen		
All (1)	Workers (2)	Difference (2–1)	All (1)	Workers (2)	Difference (2–1)
—	—	—	—	—	—
—	—	—	—	—	—
54%	101%	47%	50%	97%	48%
54	96	42	59	93	34
58	97	39	61	96	35
—	—	—	—	—	—
—	—	—	—	—	—
—	—	—	—	—	—
—	—	—	—	—	—
27	84	57	38	77	39
47	93	47	50	78	28
—	—	—	—	—	—
—	—	—	—	—	—
—	—	—	—	—	—
—	—	—	—	—	—
—	—	—	—	—	—
—	—	—	—	—	—
—	—	—	—	—	—
—	—	—	—	—	—
—	—	—	—	—	—
—	—	—	—	—	—
—	—	—	—	—	—
70	81	11	81	84	3
63	81	18	76	82	6
—	—	—	—	—	—
—	—	—	—	—	—
48	82	34	74	78	4
54	85	31	73	80	7
—	—	—	—	—	—
25	71	46	45	71	26
45	77	32	61	74	13
57	79	22	70	77	7
61	83	21	72	79	7
64	82	18	74	81	7
64	82	18	78	83	5

Source: Luxembourg Income Study (LIS 2003).

METHODS USED IN CHAPTER 7

In the analysis of Germany, we combine data from 1994 and 2000 to increase our sample size. We omit nationals from other European and English-speaking countries ($n = 114$), the Middle East ($n = 12$), Africa or the Caribbean ($n = 9$), Asia ($n = 28$), and Central and South America ($n = 10$). In the United States, we use pooled data from 1995, 1996, and 1997. We omit Native Americans and Asians and Pacific Islanders.

REFERENCES

Autor, David, Lawrence Katz, and Melissa Kearney. 2004. "Trends in U.S. Wage Inequality: A Re-Assessment of the Revisionists." NBER working paper no. 11627.
Cambridge, Mass.: National Bureau of Economic Research.

Bardasi, Joan, and Janet Gornick. 2001. "Women and Part-Time Employment:
Workers' 'Choices' and Wage Penalties in Five Industrialized Countries." Working
paper 223. Luxembourg: Luxembourg Income Study.

Becker, Gary. 1981. *A Treatise on the Family*. Cambridge, Mass.: Harvard University
Press.

Bentivogli, Chiara, and Patrizio Pagano. 1999. "Regional Disparities and Labor Mobility: The Euro-11 Versus the USA." *Labour* 13(3): 737–60.

Bernhardt, Annette, Martina Morris, and Mark Handcock. 1995. "Women's Gains
or Men's Losses? A Closer Look at the Shrinking Gender Gap in Earnings." *American Journal of Sociology* 101(2): 302–28.

Bernhardt, Annette, Martina Morris, Mark Handcock, and Marc Scott. 2001. *Divergent Paths: Economic Mobility in the New American Labor Market*. New York:
Russell Sage Foundation.

Bielby, William, and James Baron. 1986. "Men and Women at Work: Sex Segregation and Statistical Discrimination." *American Journal of Sociology* 91(4): 759–99.

Blair-Loy, Mary. 2003. *Competing Devotions*. Cambridge, Mass.: Harvard University
Press.

Blau, Francine, and Andrea Beller. 1992. "Black-White Earnings over the 1970s and
1980s: Gender Differences in Trends." *Review of Economics and Statistics* 74(2):
276–86.

Blau, Francine, Mary Brinton, and David Grusky. 2006. "The Declining Significance of Gender?" In *The Declining Significance of Gender?* edited by Francine Blau, Mary Brinton, and David Grusky. New York: Russell Sage Foundation.

Blau, Francine, and Marianne Ferber. 1992. *The Economics of Women, Men, and Work*, 2nd ed. Englewood Cliffs, N.J.: Prentice-Hall.

Blau, Francine, and Lawrence Kahn. 1996. "Wage Structure and Gender Earnings Differentials: An International Comparison." *Economica* 63(250): S29–62.

———. 2002. *At Home and Abroad: U.S. Labor Market Performance in International Perspective*. New York: Russell Sage Foundation.

Blossfeld, Hans-Peter. 1997. "Women's Part-Time Employment and the Family Cycle: A Cross-National Comparison." In *Between Equalization and Marginalization: Women Working Part-Time in Europe and the United States*, edited by Hans-Peter Blossfeld and Catherine Hakim. Oxford: Oxford University Press.

Blossfeld, Hans-Peter, and Catherine Hakim. 1997. "Introduction: A Comparative Perspective on Part-Time Work." In *Between Equalization and Marginalization: Women Working Part-Time in Europe and the United States*, edited by Hans-Peter Blossfeld and Catherine Hakim. Oxford: Oxford University Press.

Boeri, Tito, Daniela Del Boca, and Christopher Pissarides, eds. 2005. *Women at Work: An Economic Perspective*. Oxford: Oxford University Press.

Bradley, Karen. 2000. "The Incorporation of Women into Higher Education: Paradoxical Outcomes?" *Sociology of Education* 73(1): 1–18.

Brainerd, Elizabeth. 2000. "Women in Transition: Changes in Gender Wage Differentials in Eastern Europe and the Former Soviet Union." *Industrial and Labor Relations Review* 54(1): 138–62.

Breen, Richard, and Cecilia García-Peñalosa. 2002. "Bayesian Learning and Gender Segregation." *Journal of Labor Economics* 20(4): 899–922.

Bridges, William. 2003. "Rethinking Gender Segregation and Gender Inequality: Measures and Meanings." *Demography* 40(3): 543–68.

Brown, Charles. 1984. "Black-White Earnings Ratios Since the Civil Rights Act of 1964: The Importance of Labor Market Dropouts." *Quarterly Journal of Economics* 99(1): 31–44.

Browne, Irene, and Joya Misra. 2003. "The Intersection of Race and Gender in the Labor Market." *Annual Review of Sociology* 29: 487–513.

Bryk, Anthony, and Stephen Raudenbush. 1992. *Hierarchical Linear Models: Applications and Data Analysis Methods*. Newbury Park, Calif.: Sage Publications.

Buddelmeyer, Hielke, Gilles Mourre, and Melanie Ward. 2008. "Why Do Europeans Work Part-Time? A Cross-Country Panel Analysis." Working paper 872. Frankfurt, Germany: European Central Bank.

Budig, Michelle, and Paula England. 2001. "The Wage Penalty for Motherhood." *American Sociological Review* 66(2): 204–25.

Card, David, Thomas Lemieux, and Craig Riddell. 2003. "Unionization and Wage Inequality: A Comparative Study of the U.S, the U.K., and Canada." NBER working paper no. 9473. Cambridge, Mass.: National Bureau of Economic Research.

Chang, Mariko. 2000. "The Evolution of Sex Segregation Regimes." *American Journal of Sociology* 15(6): 1658–1701.

Charles, Maria. 1992. "Cross-National Variation in Occupational Sex Segregation." *American Sociological Review* 57(4): 483–502.

Charles, Maria, and David Grusky. 2004. *Occupational Ghettos: The Worldwide Segregation of Women and Men*. Palo Alto, Calif.: Stanford University Press.

Christopher, Karen, Paula England, Timothy Smeeding, and Katherin Ross Phillips. 2002. "The Gender Gap in Poverty in Modern Nations: Single Motherhood, the Market, and the State." *Sociological Perspectives* 45(3): 219–42.

Clawson, Dan, and Mary Ann Clawson. 1999. "What Happened to the U.S. Labor Movement? Union Decline and Renewal." *Annual Review of Sociology* 25: 95–119.

Cohen, Philip, and Suzanne Bianchi. 1999. "Marriage, Children, and Women's Employment: What Do We Know?" *Monthly Labor Review* 122: 22–31.

Corcoran, Mary, Colleen Heflin, and Belinda Reyes. 1999. "The Economic Progress of Mexican and Puerto Rican Women." In *Latinas and African American Women at Work: Race, Gender, and Economic Inequality*, edited by Irene Browne. New York: Russell Sage Foundation.

Correll, Shelley, Stephen Benard, and In Paik. 2007. "Getting a Job: Is There a Motherhood Penalty?" *American Journal of Sociology* 112(5): 1297–1338.

Crain, Marion. 1994. "Gender and Union Organizing." *Industrial and Labor Relations Review* 47(2): 227–48.

Crompton, Rosemary, and Fiona Harris. 1997. "Women's Employment and Gender Attitudes: A Comparative Analysis of Britain, Norway, and the Czech Republic." *Acta Sociologica* 40(2): 183–202.

Darity, William, and Patrick Mason. 1998. "Evidence on Discrimination in Employment: Codes of Color, Codes of Gender." *Journal of Economic Perspectives* 12(2): 63–90.

Del Boca, Daniela, and Marilena Locatelli. 2007. "Motherhood and Participation." In *Social Policies, Labor Markets, and Motherhood: A Comparative Analysis of European Countries*, edited by Daniela Del Boca and Cecile Wetzels. New York: Cambridge University Press.

Del Boca, Daniela, Silvia Pasqua, Chiara Pronzato, and Cecile Wetzels. 2007. "An Empirical Analysis of the Effects of Social Policies on Fertility, Labor Market Participation, and Hourly Wages of European Women." In *Social Policies, Labor Markets, and Motherhood: A Comparative Analysis of European Countries*, edited by Daniela Del Boca and Cecile Wetzels. New York: Cambridge University Press.

Dinner, Deborah. 2004. "Transforming Family and State: Women's Vision for Universal Child Care, 1966–1971." Interdisciplinary Law and Humanities Junior Scholar Workshop Paper (September 4). Available at: http://ssrn.com/abstract =582001 (accessed April 28, 2009).

Ebbinghaus, Bernhard, and Jelle Visser. 1999. "When Institutions Matter: Union Growth and Decline in Western Europe, 1950–1995." *European Sociological Review* 15(2): 135–58.

Elison, Sonja Klueck. 1997. "Policy Innovation in a Cold Climate: The Family and Medical Leave Act of 1993." *Journal of Family Issues* 18(1): 30–54.

England, Paula. 2005. "Gender Inequality in Labor Markets: The Role of Motherhood and Segregation." *Social Politics* 12(2): 264–88.

Esping-Andersen, Gøsta. 1990. *The Three Worlds of Welfare Capitalism*. Princeton, N.J.: Princeton University Press.

———. 1999. *Social Foundations of Postindustrial Economies*. Oxford: Oxford University Press.

Europa. 2006. "Part-Time Working." Brussels: European Commission. Available at: http://europa.eu/legislation_summaries/employment_and_social_policy/employ ment_rights_and_work_organisation/c10416_en.htm (accessed February 15, 2008).

Euwals, Rob, Jaco Dagevous, Merove Gijsberts, and Hans Roodenburg. 2007. "Immigration, Integration, and the Labor Market: Turkish Immigrants in Germany and the Netherlands." Discussion paper 2677. Bonn: Institute for the Study of Labor (IZA).

Fagan, Colette, and Jacqueline O'Reilly. 1998. "Conceptualizing Part-Time Work: The Value of an Integrated Comparative Perspective." In *Part-Time Prospects: An International Comparison of Part-Time Work in Europe, North America, and the Pacific Rim*, edited by Jacqueline O'Reilly and Colette Fagan. London: Routledge.

Farber, Henry. 1999. "Alternative and Part-Time Employment Arrangements as a Response to Job Loss." *Journal of Labor Economics* 17(S4): S142–69.

Filer, Randall. 1985. "The Role of Personality and Tastes in Determining Occupational Structure." *Industrial Labor Relations Review* 39(3): 412–24.

Freeman, Richard B. 1973. "Changes in the Labor Market for Black Americans, 1948–1972." *Brookings Papers on Economic Activity* 1973(1): 67–131.

Gauthier, Anne. 1993. *Family Policies in OECD Countries*. Oxford: Clarendon Press.

———. 1996. *The State and the Family: A Comparative Analysis of Family Policies in Industrialized Countries*. Oxford: Clarendon Press.

Gauthier, Anne, and Anita Bortnik. 2001. *Comparative Maternity, Parental, and Child Care Database*, version 2 (December 2003). Calgary, Alberta: University of Calgary, Families, Youths, and Public Policies Comparative Research Project. Available at: http://www.soci.ucalgary.ca/fypp/family policy databases.htm (accessed March 15, 2008).

Gerstel, Naomi, and Katherine McGonagle. 1999. "Job Leaves and the Limits of the Family and Medical Leave Act." *Work and Occupations* 26(4): 510–34.

Golden, Miriam, Peter Lange, and Michael Wallerstein. 2002. "Union Centralization Among Advanced Industrial Societies: An Empirical Study" (version of July 28, 2004). Data set available at: http://www.shelley.polisci.ucla.edu/data (accessed March 15, 2008).

Goldin, Claudia. 1990. *Understanding the Gender Gap: An Economic History of American Women*. New York: Oxford University Press.

———. 2006. "The Rising (and Then Declining) Significance of Gender." In *The Declining Significance of Gender?* edited by Francine Blau, Mary Brinton, and David Grusky. New York: Russell Sage Foundation.

Goldin, Claudia, and Cecilia Rouse. 2000. "Orchestrating Impartiality: The Impact of 'Blind' Auditions on Female Musicians." *American Economic Review* 90(4): 715–41.

Goldscheider, Frances. 2000. "Men, Children, and the Future of the Family in the Third Millennium." *Futures* 32(6): 525–38.

Goldscheider, Frances, and Linda Waite. 1991. *New Families, No Families? The Transformation of the American Home*. Berkeley: University of California Press.

Gornick, Janet. 1999. "Gender Equality in the Labor Market." In *Gender and Welfare State Regimes*, edited by Diane Sainsbury. Oxford: Oxford University Press.

Gornick, Janet, and Jerry Jacobs. 1998. "Gender, the Welfare State, and Public Employment: A Comparative Study of Seven Industrialized Countries." *American Sociological Review* 63(5): 688–710.

Gornick, Janet, and Marcia K. Meyers. 2003. *Families That Work: Policies for Reconciling Parenthood and Employment*. New York: Russell Sage Foundation.

Gornick, Janet, Marcia K. Meyers, and Katherin E. Ross. 1997. "Supporting the Employment of Mothers: Policy Variation Across Fourteen Welfare States." *Journal of European Social Policy* 7(1): 45–70.

———. 1998. "Public Policies and the Employment of Mothers: A Cross-National Study." *Social Science Quarterly* 79(1): 35–54.

Grodsky, Eric, and Devah Pager. 2001. "The Structure of Disadvantage: Individual and Occupational Determinants of the Black-White Wage Gap." *American Sociological Review* 66(4): 542–67.

Grusky, David B., and Maria Charles. 1998. "The Past, Present, and Future of Sex Segregation Methodology." *Demography* 35(4): 497–504.

Gustafsson, Siv. 1992. "Separate Taxation and Married Women's Labor Supply: A Comparison of Germany and Sweden." *Journal of Population Economics* 5(1): 61–85.

Hakim, Catherine. 1996. *Key Issues in Women's Work*. London: Athlone Press.

———. 1997. "A Sociological Perspective on Part-Time Work." In *Between Equalization and Marginalization: Women Working Part-Time in Europe and the United States*, edited by Hans-Peter Blossfeld and Catherine Hakim. Oxford: Oxford University Press.

———. 2000. *Work-Lifestyle Choices in the Twenty-First Century: Preference Theory*. Oxford: Oxford University Press.

Hansen, Marianne. 1997. "The Scandinavian Welfare State Model: The Impact of the Public Sector on Segregation and Gender Equality." *Work, Employment, and Society* 11(1): 83–99.

Harmonised European Time Use Survey. 2005–2007. Online database version 2.0. Created by Statistics Finland and Statistics Sweden [reference date October 1, 2007]. Available at: http://www.testh2.scb.se/tus/tus (accessed June 24, 2008).

Heilman, Madeline. 1995. "Sex Stereotypes and Their Effects in the Workplace." *Journal of Social Behavior and Personality* 10(6): 3–26.

Hochschild, Arlie. 1997. *The Time Bind: When Work Becomes Home and Home Becomes Work*. New York: Henry Holt.

Hook, Jennifer L. 2006. "Care in Context: Men's Unpaid Work in Twenty Countries, 1965–2003." *American Sociological Review* 71(4): 639–60.

———. 2010. "Gender Inequality in the Welfare State: Task Segregation in Housework, 1965–2003." *American Journal of Sociology* 115(5).

Huber, Evelyn, and John Stephens. 2000. "Partisan Governance, Women's Employment, and the Social Democratic Service State." *American Sociological Review* 65(3): 323–42.

Hunt, Jennifer. 2002. "The Transition in East Germany: When Is a Ten-Point Fall in the Gender Wage Gap Bad News?" *Journal of Labor Economics* 20(1): 148–69.

Inglehart, Ronald, and Pippa Norris. 2003. *Rising Tide: Gender Equality and Cultural Change Around the World*. Cambridge: Cambridge University Press.

International Labor Office (ILO). 1986. *Statistical Sources and Methods*, vol. 3, *Eco-*

nomically Active Populations, Employment, Unemployment, and Hours of Work. Geneva: ILO.

Iversen, Torben, and Frances Rosenbluth. 2006. "The Political Economy of Gender: Explaining Cross-National Variation in the Gender Division of Labor and the Gender Voting Gap." *American Journal of Political Science* 50(1): 1–19.

Jacobs, Jerry. 1993. "Theoretical and Measurement Issues in the Study of Sex Segregation in the Workplace." *European Sociological Review* 9(3): 325–30.

———. 1999. "The Sex Segregation of Occupations: Prospects for the Twenty-First Century." In *Handbook of Gender and Work*, edited by Gary Powell. Thousand Oaks, Calif.: Sage Publications.

Jacobs, Jerry, and Kathleen Gerson. 2004. *The Time Divide: Work, Family, and Gender Inequality.* Cambridge, Mass.: Harvard University Press.

Jacobs, Jerry, and Suet Lim. 1995. "Trends in Occupational and Industrial Sex Segregation in Fifty-Six Countries." In *Gender Inequality at Work*, edited by Jerry Jacobs. Thousand Oaks, Calif.: Sage Publications.

Jacobs, Jerry, and Ronnie Steinberg. 1990. "Compensating Differentials and the Male-Female Wage Gap: Evidence from the New York State Comparable Worth Study." *Social Forces* 69(2): 439–68.

Katz, Lawrence and David Autor. 1999. "Changes in the Wage Structure and Earnings Inequality." In *Handbook of Labor Economics*, vol. 3A, edited by Orley Ashenfelter and David Card. Amsterdam, The Netherlands: North Holland.

Katz, Lawrence, and Kevin Murphy. 1992. "Changes in Relative Wages 1963–1989: Supply and Demand Factors." *Quarterly Journal of Economics* 107(1): 35–78.

Kenworthy, Lane. 2004. *Egalitarian Capitalism: Jobs, Income, and Growth in Affluent Countries.* New York: Russell Sage Foundation.

———. 2009. "Who Should Care for Under-Threes?" In *Gender Equality: Transforming Family Divisions of Labor*, edited by Janet Gornick et al. New York: Verso.

Kocourkova, Jirina. 2002. "Leave Arrangements and Child Care Services in Central Europe: Policies and Practices Before and After Transition." *Community, Work, and Family* 5(3): 301–18.

Korpi, Walter. 2000. "Faces of Inequality: Gender, Class, and Patterns of Inequalities in Different Types of Welfare States." *Social Politics* 7(2): 127–91.

Lewis, Jane, and Ilona Ostner. 1995. "Gender and the Evolution of European Social Policy." In *European Social Policy: Between Fragmentation and Integration*, edited by Stephan Leibfried and Paul Pierson. Washington, D.C.: Brookings Institution Press.

Liebig, Thomas. 2007. "The Labor Market Integration of Immigrants in Germany." OECD Social, Employment, and Migration Working Papers 47. Paris: OECD.

Lundberg, Shelly, and Elaina Rose. 2002. "The Effects of Sons and Daughters on Men's Labor Supply and Wages." *Review of Economics and Statistics* 84: 251–68.

Luxembourg Income Study (LIS). Database. 2003. Available at: http://www.lispro ject.org/techdoc.htm (accessed April 15, 2008).

Mandel, Hadas. 2008. "Configurations of Inequality: Understanding Cross-National Differences in Gender Economic Inequality." Paper presented to the annual meeting of the American Sociological Association. Boston (August 1–4).

Mandel, Hadas, and Moshe Semyonov. 2005. "Family Policies, Wage Structures, and Gender Gaps: Sources of Earnings Inequality in Twenty Countries." *American Sociological Review* 70(6): 949–67.

———. 2006. "A Welfare State Paradox: State Interventions and Women's Employment Opportunities in Twenty-Two Countries." *American Journal of Sociology* 111(6): 1910–49.

Marks, Michelle. 1997. "Party Politics and Family Policy: The Case of the Family and Medical Leave Act." *Journal of Family Issues* 18(1): 55–70.

McCall, Leslie. 2000. "Explaining Levels of Within-Group Wage Inequality in U.S. Labor Markets." *Demography* 37(4): 415–30.

———. 2005. "Managing the Complexity of Intersectionality." *Signs: Journal of Women in Culture and Society* 30(3): 1771–1800.

Melkas, Helinä, and Richard Anker. 1997. "Occupational Segregation by Sex in Nordic Countries: An Empirical Investigation." *International Labour Review* 136(3): 341–63.

Meulders, Daniele, and Sile O'Dorchai. 2007. "The Position of Mothers in a Comparative Welfare State Perspective." In *Social Policies, Labor Markets, and Motherhood: A Comparative Analysis of European Countries*, edited by Daniela Del Boca and Cecile Wetzels. New York: Cambridge University Press.

Meyers, Marcia, and Janet Gornick. 2000. "Early Childhood Education and Care: Cross-National Variation in Service Organization and Financing." Paper presented to the "Consultative Meeting on International Developments in Early Childhood Education and Care" (May).

Michel, Sonya. 1999. *Children's Interests/Mothers' Rights: The Shaping of America's Child Care Policy*. New Haven, Conn.: Yale University Press.

Mincer, Jacob. 1958. "Investment in Human Capital and Personal Income Distribution." *Journal of Political Economy* 66(4): 281–302.

———. 1962. "Labor Force Participation of Married Women: A Study of Labor Supply." In *Aspects of Labor Economics*. Princeton, N.J.: Princeton University Press.

Mincer, Jacob, and Solomon Polachek. 1974. "Family Investments in Human Capital: Earnings of Women." *Journal of Political Economy* 82(2): S76–108.

Misra, Joya. 1999. "Latinas and African American Women in the Labor Market: Implications for Policy." In *Latinas and African American Women at Work: Race, Gender, and Economic Inequality*, edited by Irene Browne. New York: Russell Sage Foundation.

Moen, Phyllis. 2003. "Introduction." In *It's About Time: Couples and Careers*, edited by Phyllis Moen. Ithaca, N.Y.: Cornell University Press.

Montgomery, Mark. 1988. "On the Determinants of Employer Demand for Part-Time Workers." *Review of Economics and Statistics* 70(1): 112–17.

Morgan, Kimberly. 2006. *Working Mothers and the Welfare State: Religion and the Politics of Work-Family Policies in Western Europe and the United States*. Stanford, Calif.: Stanford University Press.

Morgan, Kimberly, and Katherin Zippel. 2003. "Paid to Care: The Origins and Effects of Care Leave Policies in Western Europe." *Social Politics* 10(1): 49–85.

O'Connor, Julia. 1993. "Gender, Class, and Citizenship in the Comparative Analysis of Welfare State Regimes: Theoretical and Methodological Issues." *British Journal of Sociology* 44(3): 501–18.

O'Connor, Julia, Ann Shola Orloff, and Sheila Shaver. 1999. *States, Markets, and Families*. New York: Cambridge University Press.

Ondrich, Jan, Katharina Spiess, and Qing Yang. 1996. "Barefoot and in a German Kitchen: Federal Parental Leave and Benefit Policy and the Return to Work After Childbirth in Germany." *Journal of Population Economics* 9(3): 247–66.

Oppenheimer, Valerie. 1970. *The Female Labor Force in the United States*. Westport, Conn.: Greenwood Press.

———. 1994. "Women's Rising Employment and the Future of the Family in Industrial Societies." *Population and Development Review* 20(2): 293–342.

O'Reilly, Jacqueline, and Silke Bothfeld. 2002. "What Happens After Working Part-Time? Integration, Maintenance, or Exclusionary Transitions in Britain and Western Germany." *Cambridge Journal of Economics* 26(4): 409–39.

Organization for Economic Cooperation and Development (OECD). 2001. *Starting Early and Strong: Early Childhood Education and Care*. Paris: OECD Publications.

———. 2002. *Labor Force Statistics 1981–2001*. Paris: OECD Publications.

———. 2004. *Education at a Glance*. Available at: http://www.oecd.org/dataoecd/32/26/33710913.xls (accessed April 1, 2006).

Orloff, Anne. 1993. "Gender and the Social Rights of Citizenship." *American Sociological Review* 58(3): 303–28.

Padavic, Irene, and Barbara Reskin. 2002. *Women and Men at Work*, 2d ed. Thousand Oaks, Calif.: Pine Forge Press.

Pettit, Becky, and Stephanie Ewert. Forthcoming. "Employment Gains and Wage

Declines: The Erosion of Black Women's Relative Wages Since 1980." *Demography*.

Pettit, Becky, and Jennifer Hook. 2005. "The Structure of Women's Employment in Comparative Perspective." *Social Forces* 84(2): 779–801.

Pfau-Effinger, Birgit. 1998. "Culture or Structure as Explanations for Differences in Part-Time Work in Germany, Finland, and the Netherlands." In *Part-Time Prospects: An International Comparison of Part-Time Work in Europe, North America, and the Pacific Rim*, edited by Jacqueline O'Reilly and Colette Fagan. London: Routledge.

———. 2004. *Development of Culture, Welfare States, and Women's Employment in Europe*. Burlington, Vt.: Ashgate.

Reskin, Barbara. 1993. "Sex Segregation in the Workplace." *Annual Review of Sociology* 19: 241–70.

Roos, Patricia, and Barbara Reskin. 1992. "Occupational Desegregation in the 1970s: Integration and Economic Equity." *Sociological Perspectives* 35(1): 69–91.

Rosenfeld, Rachel, and Arne Kalleberg. 1990. "A Cross-National Comparison of the Gender Gap in Income." *American Journal of Sociology* 96(1): 69–106.

Ruhm, Christopher. 1998. "The Economic Consequences of Parental Leave Mandates: Lessons from Europe." *Quarterly Journal of Economics* 113(1): 285–317.

Sainsbury, Diane. 1996. *Gender, Equality, and Welfare States*. Cambridge: Cambridge University Press.

Sawyers, Traci, and David Meyer. 1999. "Missed Opportunities: Social Movement Abeyance and Public Policy." *Social Problems* 46(2): 187–206.

Saxonberg, Steven, and Dorota Szelewa. 2007. "The Continuing Legacy of the Communist Legacy? The Development of Family Policies in Poland and the Czech Republic." *Social Politics* 14(3): 351–79.

Semyonov, Moshe, and Frank Jones. 1999. "Dimensions of Gender Occupational Differentiation in Segregation and Inequality: A Cross-National Analysis." *Social Indicators Research* 46(2): 225–47.

Simonton, Deborah. 1998. *A History of European Women's Work: 1700 to the Present*. New York: Routledge.

Sorensen, Annemette, and Sara McLanahan. 1987. "Married Women's Economic Dependency: 1950–1980." *American Journal of Sociology* 92(3): 659–87.

Spiess, Katharina, and Katharina Wrohlich. 2008. "The Parental Leave Benefit Reform in Germany: Costs and Labor Market Outcomes of Moving Towards the Nordic Model." *Population Research and Policy Review* 27(5): 575–91.

Statistisches Bundesamt Deutschland (Federal Statistical Office of Germany). 1993. *Statistisches Jahrbuch* (Statistical Yearbook). Wiesbaden: Statistisches Bundesamt.

———. 1999. *Statistisches Jahrbuch* (Statistical Yearbook). Wiesbaden: Statistisches Bundesamt.

Stier, Haya, Noah Lewin-Epstein, and Michael Braun. 2001. "Welfare, Family, and Women's Employment Along the Life Course." *American Journal of Sociology* 106(6): 1731–60.

Stropnik, Nada. 2001. "Preferences in Slovenia Versus Reality in Europe: The Case of Parental Leave and Child Benefit." Paper presented to the European Population Conference. Helsinki. (June 7–9).

———. 2003. "Impact of Transition on Family Policies." Paper presented to the European Population Conference, Warsaw (August 26–30). Reprinted in *Population of Central and Eastern Europe: Challenges and Opportunities*, edited by Irena Kotowska and Janina Jozwiak. Warsaw: Statistical Publishing Establishment.

Stryker, Robin, Scott Eliason, and Eric Tranby. 2007. "The Welfare State, Family Policies, and Women's Labor Market Participation." In *Method and Substance in Macrocomparative Analysis*, edited by Lane Kenworthy and Alexander Hicks. London: Palgrave Macmillan.

Sullivan, Dennis, and Timothy Smeeding. 1997. "Educational Attainment and Earnings Inequality in Eight Nations." Working paper 164. Luxembourg: Luxembourg Income Study.

Tietze, Wolfgang, and Debby Cryer. 1999. "Current Trends in European Early Child Care and Education." *Annals of the American Academy of Political and Social Science* 563(1): 175–93.

Treiman, Donald, and Patricia Roos. 1983. "Sex and Earnings in Industrial Society: A Nine-Nation Comparison." *American Journal of Sociology* 89(3): 612–50.

Trzcinski, Eileen. 2006. "Integration of Immigrant Mothers in Germany: Policy Issues and Empirical Outcomes." *Population Research Policy Review* 25(5–6): 489–512.

United Nations. 1991. *The World's Women: Trends and Statistics, 1991*. New York: The United Nations.

———. 1995. *The World's Women: Trends and Statistics, 1995*. New York: United Nations.

———. 2000. *The World's Women: Trends and Statistics, 2000*. New York: United Nations.

———. 2003. *Population by Five-Year Age Group and Sex*. New York: Population Division of the Department of Economic and Social Affairs of the United Nations Secretariat, World Population Prospects: The 2002 Revision and World Urbanization Prospects; The 2001 Revision, available at http://esa.un.org/unpp (accessed December 17, 2003).

U.S. Social Security Administration. 1999. *Social Security Programs Throughout the World, 1999.* Washington: U.S. Social Security Administration.

van der Lippe, Tanja, and Liset van Dijk. 2001. "Women's Employment in a Comparative Perspective." In *Women's Employment in a Comparative Perspective*, edited by Tanja van der Lippe and Liset van Dijk. New York: Walter de Gruyter.

Waldfogel, Jane. 1997. "The Effect of Children on Women's Wages." *American Sociological Review* 62(2): 209–17.

Western, Bruce. 1997. *Between Class and Market: Postwar Unionization in the Capitalist Democracies.* Princeton, N.J.: Princeton University Press.

Wetzels, Cecile. 2007. "Motherhood and Wages." In *Social Policies, Labor Markets, and Motherhood: A Comparative Analysis of European Countries*, edited by Daniela Del Boca and Cecile Wetzels. New York: Cambridge University Press.

Wilpert, Czarina Huerta. 1990. "Immigrant Women in the Federal Republic of Germany." Paper 12 in Institute for Social Science Research, *California Immigrants in World Perspective: The Conference Papers*, vol. 5, http://repositories.cdlib.org/issr/volume5/12.

World Bank. 2002. *2001 World Development Indicators* (CD-ROM). Washington, D.C.: International Bank for Reconstruction and Development.

Xie, Yu, and Kimberlee Shauman. 2003. *Women in Science: Career Processes and Outcomes.* Cambridge, Mass.: Harvard University Press.

INDEX

Boldface numbers refer to figures and tables.